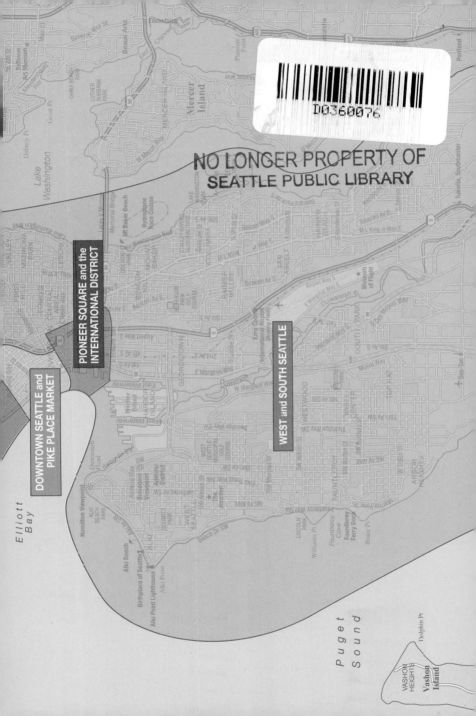

DOWNTOWN SEATTLE and PIKE PLACE MARKET

PIONEER SQUARE and the INTERNATIONAL DISTRICT

WEST and SOUTH SEATTLE

Elliott Bay

Puget Sound

INSIGHT ⊙ GUIDES

SEATTLE
CITY GUIDE

◉ Walking Eye App

YOUR FREE DESTINATION CONTENT AND EBOOK AVAILABLE THROUGH THE WALKING EYE APP

Your guide now includes a free eBook and destination content for your chosen destination, all for the same great price as before. Simply download the Walking Eye App from the App Store or Google Play to access your free eBook and destination content.

HOW THE WALKING EYE APP WORKS

Through the Walking Eye App, you can purchase a range of eBooks and destination content. However, when you buy this book, you can download the corresponding eBook and destination content for free. Just see below in the grey panels where to find your free content and then scan the QR code at the bottom of this page.

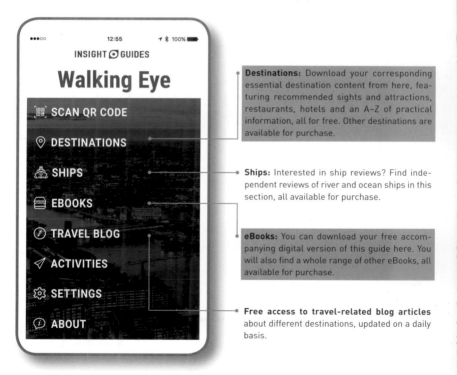

Destinations: Download your corresponding essential destination content from here, featuring recommended sights and attractions, restaurants, hotels and an A–Z of practical information, all for free. Other destinations are available for purchase.

Ships: Interested in ship reviews? Find independent reviews of river and ocean ships in this section, all available for purchase.

eBooks: You can download your free accompanying digital version of this guide here. You will also find a whole range of other eBooks, all available for purchase.

Free access to travel-related blog articles about different destinations, updated on a daily basis.

HOW THE DESTINATION CONTENT WORKS

Each destination includes a short introduction, an A–Z of practical information and recommended points of interest, split into 4 different categories:

- Highlights
- Accommodation
- Eating out
- What to do

You can view the location of every point of interest and save it by adding it to your Favourites. In the 'Around Me' section you can view all the points of interest within 5km.

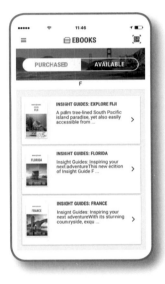

HOW THE EBOOKS WORK

The eBooks are provided in EPUB file format. Please note that you will need an eBook reader installed on your device to open the file. Many devices come with this as standard, but you may still need to install one manually from Google Play.

The eBook content is identical to the content in the printed guide.

HOW TO DOWNLOAD THE WALKING EYE APP

1. Download the Walking Eye App from the App Store or Google Play.
2. Open the app and select the scanning function from the main menu.
3. Scan the QR code on this page – you will then be asked a security question to verify ownership of the book.
4. Once this has been verified, you will see your eBook and destination content in the purchased ebook and destination sections, where you will be able to download them.

Other destination apps and eBooks are available for purchase separately or are free with the purchase of the Insight Guide book.

Contents

Travel Tips

TRANSPORTATION

A – Z

FURTHER READING

Maps

THE BEST OF SEATTLE: TOP ATTRACTIONS

At a glance, the Seattle attractions you can't afford to miss, from the longest-running farmers' market in the nation to cutting-edge architecture, captivating museums, and the chance to see some of that prized salmon.

◁ **Hiram M. Chittenden Locks**. In a remarkable feat of engineering, boats (and salmon) travel along the Ship Canal between freshwater Lake Washington, Lake Union, and the saltwater Puget Sound via the Hiram M. Chittenden Locks. See page 144.

△ **Pike Place Market.** A farmers' market extraordinaire, with flying fish, the freshest produce, and flowers galore, all sold by local vendors, with street entertainers and tantalizing ethnic food also on offer. See page 104.

▷ **Space Needle.** Since its debut for the World's Fair in 1962, the Space Needle has been an iconic symbol of Seattle, immortalized in such films as *It Happened at the World's Fair*, starring Elvis Presley. See page 113.

▷ **Pioneer Square.** Home of the original Skid Road and underground city, Pioneer Square is the best neighborhood for gallery-hopping, and retains the flavor of the oldest part of the city. See page 85.

◁ **Seattle Central Library.** With steel-and-glass walls jutting out at unexpected angles over the sidewalk and into the sky, the Seattle Central Library, designed by Dutch architect Rem Koolhaas, has garnered much critical acclaim. See page 101.

△ **Museum of Flight.** Aviation-pioneer Bill Boeing propelled Seattle onto the world's radar, and the fascinating Museum of Flight chronicles the industry's history with a whopping 43 airplanes. See page 181.

△ **Woodland Park Zoo.** The Woodland Park Zoo isn't just for families: anyone who loves seeing animals, including penguins and lions, and lush scenery in the middle of the city will enjoy exploring its grounds. See page 141.

△ **The Seattle Art Museum.** This institution attracts major traveling exhibitions in addition to its large permanent collection spanning ancient Islamic art, Italian Renaissance paintings, Northwest tribal art, and contemporary art. See page 103.

▷ **Museum of Pop Culture (MoPOP).** Occupying Frank Gehry's polychromatic, amorphous structure at the Seattle Center is MoPOP, an interactive popular-culture museum with exhibits on rock 'n' roll artists, iconic film franchises, and even gaming. See page 120.

◁ **Olympic Sculpture Park.** With views of Puget Sound and the Olympic Mountains, the Olympic Sculpture Park is a fantastic reclamation of post-industrial land that serves as the setting for major outdoor art installations. See page 110.

THE BEST OF SEATTLE: EDITOR'S CHOICE

Setting priorities, saving money, unique attractions... here, at a glance, are our recommendations, plus some tips and tricks even Seattleites won't always know.

Viewing the city from the deck of the Space Needle.

BEST FESTIVALS AND EVENTS

Bumbershoot. This annual Labor Day weekend festival includes top-name concerts, a small film festival, comedy, author readings, lectures, crafts, and more. See page 231.

Skrillex performance at Bumbershoot.

Fremont Solstice Parade. Held on the closest Saturday to the Summer Solstice. Naked bicyclists, political satire, street theater, and more. See page 230.

Bite of Seattle. Local restaurants and food companies offer tastes of their goods, while famous chefs demonstrate secrets of the kitchen. See page 231.

Northwest Folklife Festival. Memorial Day brings out a hippie vibe every year at the Seattle Center; music acts, food merchants, colorful wares, and happy dancing abound. See page 230.

BEST MUSEUMS

Henry Art Gallery. A modern art center at the University of Washington, with innovative exhibitions and lectures. See page 137.

Burke Museum. Celebrating both the natural world and the cultures of the Pacific Rim. See page 137.

Pacific Science Center. Home to a planetarium, laser-dome theater, and educational exhibits for kids and adults. See page 118.

Frye Art Museum. See a collection of 19th- to 20th-century representational art and hear engaging lectures tied in with the exhibitions. See page 95.

Pacific Science Center.

Gas Works Park.

BEST VIEWS

Space Needle. Get a 360-degree bird's-eye view of the entire region from the top of the Space Needle. See page 113.

Ray's Boathouse. Watch the boats headed from Puget Sound toward the Hiram M. Chittenden Locks from the deck here. See page 142.

Kerry View Point Park. Enjoy picture-perfect views of the snowcapped, 14,410ft (4,392-meter) Mount Rainier from this park on Queen Anne Hill on a clear day. See page 131.

West Seattle. The Downtown view from Alki Beach. See page 149.

Washington State Ferry. Watch the receding city from the deck of a ferry as it pulls away from the terminal. See page 107.

Smith Tower. Take in Puget Sound and the Port of Seattle from the observation deck of the historic Smith Tower in Pioneer Square. See page 91.

BEST PARKS AND TRAILS

Green Lake. Circled by a paved trail for walking, jogging, or skating that draws a steady stream of people and dogs. See page 140.

Seward Park. On Lake Washington, this park has wilderness, a waterfront, a swimming area, and a long, paved trail. See page 153.

Burke-Gilman Trail. This former railroad line allows cyclists or joggers to go for miles, largely free from traffic. See page 135.

Alki. The city's best sandy beaches are in Alki in West Seattle, where barbecues, volleyball, and sunbathing are all part of the scene. See page 149.

Volunteer Park. Home to the Seattle Asian Art Museum as well as a lovely glass conservatory for plants. See page 124.

Discovery Park. Enormous Discovery Park on Magnolia bluff has beaches, sand dunes, forest trails, sea cliffs, and a lighthouse. See page 132.

Gas Works Park. Rusting parts of the old gas plant are part of the picture, along with kite-flyers on the hill. See page 138.

BEST FOR FAMILIES

Seattle Center. Home to the Pacific Science Center, IMAX Theater, Children's Museum, Chihuly Garden and Glass, and International Fountain, the Seattle Center will keep the whole family happy. See page 113.

Waterfront Activities Center. Here a canoe to observe the wildlife on Union Bay or paddle through the Washington Park Arboretum, pulling ashore for a picnic. See page 137.

Seattle Aquarium. See, touch, and marvel at sea mammals and scaly underwater creatures of the deep at the waterfront aquarium. See page 109.

Woodland Park Zoo. Watch nearly 300 species of animal in this lovely park, which includes an African savannah where animals roam freely. See page 141.

Underwater Dome at the Seattle Aquarium.

Fresh fish, creatively presented.

The Seattle Great Wheel on the city's waterfront.

BEST COFFEE SHOPS

Caffé Vita. In the center of the Capitol Hill scene, Caffé Vita is a hip hangout serving its own beautifully roasted coffee. Don't miss their delicious pressed pita sandwiches. www.caffe vita.com.

Voxx Coffee. A lovely coffee shop with a conscience. Fair-trade organic Stumptown coffee is served in a stylish, modern building in the quirky Eastlake neighborhood. voxxcoffee.com.

Victrola. Free weekly 'cuppings' and 'pour-overs' (different brewing methods) are among the pleasures here, where they take their coffee seriously. Thought-provoking art exhibitions make the walls interesting. www.victrolacoffee.com.

Starbucks. For a taste of Seattle's caffeine history, stop by the small, original Star-bucks at Pike Place Market for a brew – where the international empire began. See page 106.

BEST RESTAURANTS

Café Juanita. On the Eastside, it is well worth the trek for Chef Holly Smith's Northern Italian food. www.cafe juanita.com.

Cascina Spinasse. Arguably Capitol Hill's best Italian eatery – warm, welcoming, and delicious. If it's full, try next-door Artusi. www. spinasse.com.

Poppy. Run by former Herbfarm executive chef Jerry Traunfeld, Poppy presents a selection of small, perfectly seasoned dishes on a platter. www.poppyseattle.com.

Boat Street Kitchen. Near the Olympic Sculpture Park, this delightful place serves tasty French food using local ingredients. www. boatstreetkitchen.com.

Matt's in the Market. In Pike Place Market, this restaurant uses fresh ingredients in its sophisticated North-west cuisine. www.matts inthemarket.com.

A barista in local behemoth, Starbucks.

BEST TOURS

Bill Speidel's Underground Tour. A fascinating inspection of the shops and rooms that were left abandoned when Seattle caught fire in 1889. See page 87.

Argosy Cruises. Choose to take a tour of the Seattle waterfront or Lake Washington; either way, the city is at its best when seen from the water. www.argosycruises.com.

Seattle Wine Tours. Let someone else do the driving as you enjoy tasting wines from several outstanding Washington vineyards. www.seattlewinetours.com.

Market Ghost Tours. Hear the ghostly legends of Pike Place Market that haunt the arcades and alleys. Be afraid; be very afraid. See page 107.

Safeco Field Tours. Take me out to the ballgame and visit one of the finest baseball stadiums in America, home to the Mariners, with panoramic views of the Seattle skyline. See page 92.

BEST EXCURSIONS

Hoh. Visit the extraordinary Hoh temperate rain forest on the Olympic Peninsula, with its enormous, lush, moss-strewn trees looking like a primeval forest. See page 206.

Victoria, BC. Ride the *Victoria Clipper* to old-English Victoria, with its double-decker buses, illuminated harborside buildings, and grand Empress Hotel. See page 212.

Mount Rainier. Journey here for excellent hiking, alpine flowers and wildlife, and fresh air. See page 217.

San Juan Islands. Travel by passenger ferry or a seaplane and enjoy the laid-back existence far from the city. See page 210.

Mount St Helens. Explore the lava tubes at Mount St Helens, and see how life has returned after the devastating eruption of 1980. See page 218.

Port Townsend. Stroll the charming streets of Victorian Port Townsend, home to many galleries, bookshops, and boutiques displaying local arts and crafts. See page 201.

Bainbridge Island. Take a 35-minute ferry ride to visit pretty towns, beautifully maintained gardens, and a winery. See page 195.

In Mount Rainier National Park.

MONEY-SAVING TIPS

If you're planning to visit most or all of the city's main attractions, purchase a Seattle CityPass. This book of tickets will get you into the Woodland Park Zoo or the Museum of Flight, MoPOP, Space Needle, Seattle Aquarium, and Argosy Cruises for a fraction of the price of individual tickets. Go to www.citypass.com/seattle.

Dine Around Seattle is a great way to save money while sampling the fare at many of Seattle's best restaurants. The promotion offers diners prix-fixe three-course lunches ($18) or dinners ($22, 33 or 44), Sunday through Thursday. Prices do not include drinks, tax, or tips. Go to www.dinearoundseattle.org to find out details.

For traveling around Downtown, forget the cabs and hop on a Metro bus. You can also jump on the Monorail (www.seattlemonorail.com) between Downtown and Seattle Center.

Seattle Downtown highway traffic at sunset.

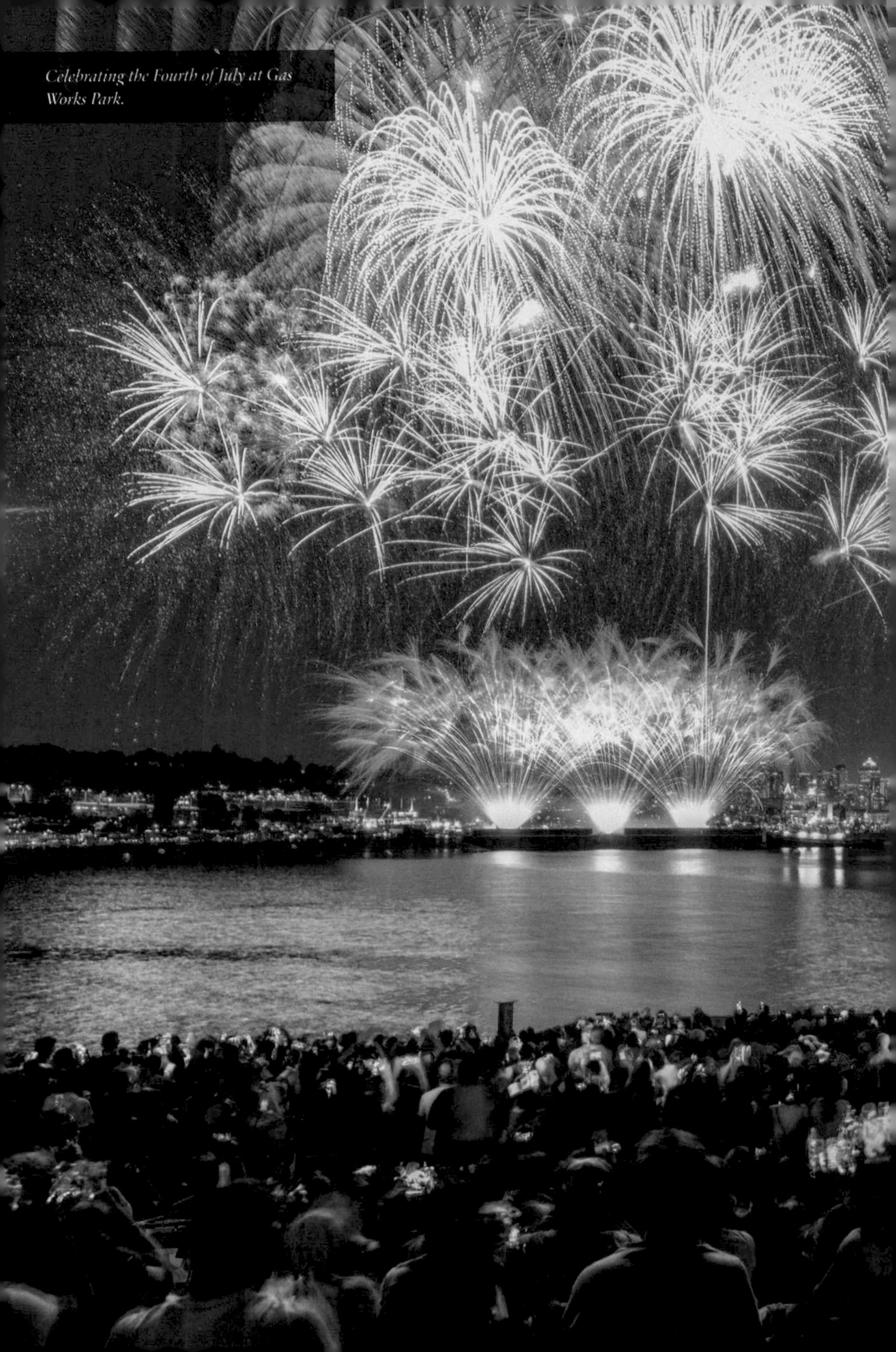

Celebrating the Fourth of July at Gas Works Park.

THE EMERALD CITY

Set against one of the most spectacular city backdrops in North America, Seattle has always been a city that moves with the times and is full of surprises.

Throughout its short history, from the sawmills of the pioneers to its position today at the vanguard of software, biomedical research, and philanthropy, Seattle has always been a forward-looking city with an unyielding entrepreneurial spirit that has resulted in some phenomenal success stories.

It is grounded in a multicultural, progressive, well-educated society. For a city its size (with more than 680,000 people), the arts are very well represented. You can see an exhibition at one of the fine art museums in the morning, stroll through a sculpture park in the afternoon, and rock out to a local gig at dozens of spots around the city any night of the year.

But what sets this city apart is its striking setting, between two snowcapped mountain ranges and bordered by Puget Sound and Lake Washington. It's a verdant city of

Buskers at Pike Place Market.

steep hills and sparkling waters, with beautiful views all around. If you look up, it's not uncommon to see bald eagles flying overhead. With nature on its doorstep, it's hardly surprising that an outdoor lifestyle prevails. Boating, skiing, and hiking are just some of the pleasures that await active visitors.

The dining scene, too, draws on nature's abundance. Some stars of the restaurant scene focus on freshly caught wild fish and seafood, seasonal produce, and excellent Washington State wines or innovative local microbrews. Ethnic foods of all varieties can be found in restaurants throughout the city, from casual to gourmet.

Seattle is a city that keeps evolving. From the boom and bust of the Klondike Gold Rush years, to the grunge explosion that rocked the music world in the 1990s, to the city filing a lawsuit against the Trump administration in 2017, you never know what's next on the horizon. After all, the city that launched an aerospace leader and the world's most recognizable coffee shop may yet have a few surprises up its sleeve.

A coffee-shop sign in this city of coffee lovers.

SEATTLE AND SEATTLEITES

Seattleites are cool – in every sense of the word. Climate and geography are said to affect behavior, and this is definitely the case in the Emerald City.

Nestled in the far northwest corner of the United States, with Canada just a couple of hours to the north, Seattle acquired its Emerald City moniker thanks to the abundance of evergreen forests in its vicinity. South Seattle is the most ethnically diverse part of town, but neighborhoods across town are home to people from around the world, particularly Latin America, Asia, and Africa.

The place and the people

Seattleites approach life with an enviable blend of New York-style sophistication and West Coast nonchalance and know how to enjoy their city. Despite a strong work ethic, there's also a lot of hanging out in the ubiquitous coffee shops and getting outdoors at any opportunity, be it kayaking on Lake Union or cycling the Burke-Gilman Trail. The region has a mild climate, with most of its infamous rain falling from October to April.

The 'flying fish' at Pike Place Market.

A cup of coffee is one of the standard pieces of equipment for Seattleites to carry around with them. With hundreds of local coffee shops beckoning, it becomes a habit quickly.

Seattleites' political views tend to be overwhelmingly liberal. The past eight Seattle mayors have been Democrats and in 2012 the state voted in favor of legalizing gay marriage and marijuana for recreational use – indeed, the city's current mayor, Ed Murray, is openly gay and has been married to his long-term

partner Michael Shiosaki since 2013. The minimum wage was raised to $15 an hour in 2015, which businesses will introduce gradually. And in contrast to the night of Barack Obama's re-election victory, when the city erupted in a shower of spontaneous street parties and fireworks, Donald Trump's 2016 ascension to the presidency was generally met by Seattleites with a mixture of disbelief and despair. Citizens and activists often get involved on a wide range of issues with passionate debate, from the replacement of the damaged Alaskan Way Viaduct along the waterfront to demonstrating against the Keystone XL pipeline.

Enjoying the view from Marshall Park.

The high (tech) life

It was the region's abundant natural resources that attracted the settlers and led to the earliest industries of logging and fishing. Not many bar-

> *Polite driving reaches an extreme here, resulting in confusion over who's going next at four-way stops as each driver yields to the other. On the freeways, though, it's more rough and tumble.*

rel-chested loggers are clomping around Seattle these days, but outside the city, especially toward the mountains, there are still large swathes of forest that continue to be logged and managed. Commercial fishermen, however, can still be spotted unloading their catch at Fishermen's Terminal in Magnolia. More and more, though, Seattle's economy is based on technology.

Up until the 1990s, being an 'engineer' in Seattle meant being someone who worked at Boeing. The aviation company's wings still cast a giant shadow across the region, where Boeing employs tens of thousands, but the job title nowadays is more often preceded by 'software' and means he or she works for Microsoft, Amazon, Adobe, Expedia, Nintendo, or one of dozens of other local internet and tech companies.

Charitable foundations

Seattle has a lot of wealth, but not a lot of bling. You won't catch Microsoft co-founders Bill Gates and Paul Allen or Amazon's Jeff Bezos riding around in stretch Bentley limos, flashing gold chains – or even wearing neckties most of the time. Seattle has no shortage of dotcom millionaires who live very well indeed, but their mansions tend to be nestled discreetly and anonymously behind a curtain of fir trees.

Many of those who are doing well are also doing good. The Bill & Melinda Gates Foundation, for example, is focused on global issues such as poverty, gender inequality, AIDS, and polio. Charity auctions have no trouble raising generous sums to help organizations such as the Fred Hutchinson Cancer Research Center, which trains physicians from around the world in bone-marrow and stem-cell transplants, and Seattle Children's Hospital, which leads the field in research on birth defects and gene therapy.

Hey, growth happens

The Space Needle remains a proud – if retro – landmark, but Seattleites have grown up a lot since *It Happened at the World's Fair* with Elvis Presley more than 40 years ago. For example, the locals don't get all giddy now when Hollywood celebrities touch down at Boeing Field. After Elvis (1962), the Beatles (1964), starring roles in *Sleepless in Seattle* (1993), and the TV series *Frasier* (1993–2004) and *Grey's Anatomy* (2005–present), celebs aren't a big deal anymore.

Finding a true, born-in-Seattle native is quite a challenge, however. It has gotten to the point where some now say that 20 years' residency qualifies a person to be an honorary native. Alongside well-established Chinese, Japanese, Vietnamese, Indian, and Latino communities, people are moving in from *every* state and from Russia, Europe, and the Pacific Islands.

Local characters.

The colorful MoPOP Building.

The Space Needle as seen from Kerry Park.

Ferry travel is common around Seattle.

Seattleites aren't in denial about the city's daily struggle with population growth, tangled traffic, and crime, but with so many people moving here, they must be getting something right. After all, Seattle was ranked the second best US city to live in by the *Business Insider* in 2016, right behind Denver (Colorado).

Coffee on the go Downtown.

Sustainable growth

Managing the city's projected growth over the coming decades is something the city planners are taking seriously. Mass transit is being expanded, roads and bridges are being replaced or brought up to earthquake code, and higher-density mixed-use commercial and residential development is occurring on a large scale in areas like South Lake Union to ensure that Seattle remains a vibrant, accessible, quality place to live.

SEATTLEITES

According to former local columnist and councilwoman Jean Godden, Seattleites never carry umbrellas, never shine their shoes, and never turn on windshield wipers unless it's absolutely pouring. Godden also wrote that Seattleites seldom visit the Space Needle unless accompanied by visitors, seldom hail taxis, can describe 42 shades of gray, and think that a perfect day is 68 degrees F (20 degrees C), partly sunny, with a light breeze from the north. Seattleites also buy more sunglasses than residents of any other city in the United States, perhaps because they never expect to use them – only 50 days' sun on average each year – and so invariably have left them at home.

Seattlespeak

Place names in the Puget Sound area can try the most ardent of linguists, but don't worry; many have struggled before you.

Mukilteo. Sequim. Humptulips. Enumclaw. Influenced especially by local Native American names, cartographers have made the state of Washington a minefield of barely pronounceable monikers. Skookumchuck? Puyallup? Pysht? The days when men spoke 'with forked tongues' may be gone, but they've been surviving in Seattle in the era of the twisted tongue. It's these interesting names that help to preserve the history of this region and remind today's population of the area's rich heritage.

The most colorful place names have been taken from Chinook jargon a mishmash of Native dialects that white settlers used to communicate with the previous stewards. Alki, for instance, which is a beach and an area of West Seattle, means 'by and by.' La Push, referring to a town at the mouth of the Quillayute River ('river with no head'), is at least geographically correct: it means, simply, 'mouth.' The language is still in use.

Other names are simply garbled versions of Native words. Snohomish, which refers to a city, a river, and a county north of Seattle, does not exist in any known Native language, according to linguists. Its suffix, however – *ish*, which translates as 'people' – is everywhere on local road maps. Sammamish means 'the hunting people.' Skykomish translates as 'the inland people.' Stillaguamish, Duwamish... these words come from different Native dialects, but they both mean 'people living on the river.'

Many names for water

So prominently did rivers and other bodies of water figure in the language of Northwest Indians that if someone were to ask you what a peculiar-sounding Washington name means, you could say 'water' and stand a chance of being right. Lucile McDonald, a prolific Washington historian, wrote that 'Skookumchuck, Entiat, Cle Elum, and Skamania all have to do with strong, swift, or rapid water. Walla Walla and Wal ula mean small, rapid river; Washougal is rushing water; Tumwater, a waterfall; Wenatchee, a river issuing from a canyon; Selah, still water; Pilchuck, red water; Newaukum, gently flowing water; Paha, big water. Yakima is lake water. Sol Duc is magic water. Chelan is deep water.' Which is exactly what outsiders find themselves in when trying to pronounce these names. Locals sometimes see these mispronounceable monikers as their revenge against the accents in other parts of the US.

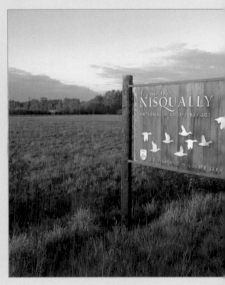

Nisqually: an example of a distinctive local name.

The Northwest's language differences are subtle. In New England, men who used to risk their lives cutting down forests were called 'lumberjacks.' In the Northwest, they're known as 'loggers.' Call somebody on a horse in eastern Washington a 'cowpoke' and you're liable to earn a mean stare at best, a poke in the nose at worst. They prefer the name 'cowboy,' or just 'rancher,' pardner.

DECISIVE DATES

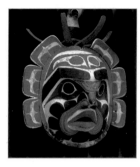

A tribal mask of Goomokwey, master of the deep.

20,000 BC
Small bands of Ice Age hunters cross the Bering Land Bridge from Asia.

7000–1000 BC
Tribes of the Puget Sound region become dependent on fishing.

1592
Spanish ships visit the region.

1790
Chief Sealth – also known as Chief Seattle – is born in the Puget Sound area.

1792
English navigator Captain George Vancouver lands near present-day Everett, north of Seattle. His expedition explores Puget Sound, named for Peter Puget, a lieutenant on Vancouver's crew.

1820s
The Hudson's Bay Company expands its operations in the Pacific Northwest, based in Fort Vancouver, at the mouth of the Columbia River.

1833
The Hudson's Bay Company establishes Fort Nisqually in present-day Tacoma.

1851
David Denny and a group of settlers arrive at Alki Point, in what is now West Seattle. They name their settlement Alki-New York for Denny's home city.

1852
Disappointed by Alki Point's severe weather and poor port potential, Denny and his crew shift north to Elliott Bay, near present-day Seattle.

1853
The relocated settlement is laid out and named for Chief Sealth (Seattle) – the leader of the Duwamish, Suquamish, and other Puget Sound tribes – and a friend of the settlers.

1854
A hastily drawn-up treaty with the local tribes provides for the newcomers to 'buy' Indian land.

1855
Chief Seattle signs the Port Elliott treaty, giving away Indian land and establishing a reservation.

1856
Some Indians rebel against the treaty, but the rebellion is quickly quenched by the US Army.

Wood engraving depiction of the construction of the first Transcontinental Telegraph.

Heart of the Klondike, as written by Scott Marble.

1861
The University of Washington is established.

1864
The transcontinental telegraph connects Seattle with the rest of the United States.

1866
Chief Seattle dies at the Port Madison Reservation, Washington.

1882
Flamed by the economic depression, animosity against Chinese immigrants increases.

1883
The city of Tacoma is incorporated.

1886
Racial violence breaks out against Chinese residents. Five men are shot and Chinese stores and homes are destroyed. Two hundred Chinese are forced onto a San Francisco-bound ship.

1889
A handyman pours water onto a flaming pot of glue in a paint store. The resulting explosion and fire destroys the entire 60-block downtown area of Seattle.

1890
The population of Seattle reaches 50,000; the city erects a monument to Chief Seattle.

1893
The Great Northern Railway arrives, making Seattle a major rail terminus.

1897
The SS *Portland* sails into the city, carrying hundreds of thousands of dollars' worth of gold from the Yukon's Klondike. Seattle's mayor resigns and heads north for the gold.

Late 1890s
Japanese laborers begin arriving.

1900
In Tacoma, Midwesterner Frederick Weyerhaeuser buys 900,000 acres (360,000 hectares) of timberland from Northern Pacific Railroad.

Early 1900s
Downtown hills are razed; the earth is used for harbor landfill. Ten surrounding cities are annexed by Seattle.

1909
The Alaska-Yukon-Pacific Exposition is held.

1910
The city's population reaches 250,000.

1914
The Panama Canal opens, increasing Seattle's importance as a Pacific port.

1916
The Lake Washington Ship Canal opens. William Boeing, a prosperous lumberman, incorporates the Pacific Aero Products Company.

1917
Pacific Aero Products Company is renamed the Boeing Airplane Company.

1919
The country's first and longest general strike is held in Seattle; however, it becomes a tactical error as some of its supporters are targeted as Communists.

1928
Boeing becomes part of the United Aircraft & Transport

Corporation, a merger of several aircraft manufacturers and airlines.

1934
Antitrust rules force United Aircraft & Transport to break up. Boeing emerges, as does United Airlines and United Aircraft.

1935
The B-17 *Flying Fortress* is first flown.

1941
The US entry into World War II invigorates Seattle's importance, both in shipbuilding and in aircraft manufacturing.

1942
7,000 Japanese-Americans are moved from Seattle to Idaho internment camps. Jimi Hendrix is born in Seattle.

1950
An economic recession is squelched by the Korean War; Seattle builds B-47 bombers.

1958
The Boeing 707 commercial passenger jet is introduced for regular service.

1962
The Seattle World's Fair introduces the city – and the Space Needle – to the world.

1965
Seattle's population exceeds half a million.

1969
Boeing lays off 60 percent of its employees. The city's

Mount St Helens erupting in 1980.

economy heads into a tailspin.

1970
The Boeing 747 is put into service, with twice the carrying capacity of any previous passenger jet.

1971
The first branch of Starbucks coffee shops opens.

1979
Seattle's SuperSonics win the National Basketball Association (NBA) championship.

1980
Mount St Helens explodes south of Seattle.

1982
The so-called Green River Killer begins a 49-person murder spree.

1992
Seattle becomes a music center as grunge music –

Nirvana, Pearl Jam – sweeps the world.

1993
Forbes magazine rates Microsoft chairman Bill Gates as the richest man in the world.

1998
Adobe moves into an office park under the Fremont Bridge.

1999
Safeco Field replaces the Kingdome to host Major League baseball; Canada and the US sign a salmon-fishing treaty. Protesters shut down the World Trade Organization conference; an antitrust trial involving Microsoft begins.

2001
The tech boom collapses and many people leave town. An earthquake measuring 6.8 on the Richter scale hits the area.

Bill Gates in 2017.

Boeing moves its corporate headquarters to Chicago and many jobs are lost.

2002
Seahawks Stadium (now CenturyLink Field) opens for the NFL season. The US District Court conditionally approves a Microsoft antitrust settlement.

2003
Seattle-based Amazon. com turns its first profit after several years of trading.

2004
With women's national basketball, the city wins its first national sports title since 1979.

2005
Voters pass the strictest smoking ban in the US.

2006
Starbucks CEO Howard Schultz sells the Seattle SuperSonics to a group of Oklahoma City businessmen; the Seahawks play their first Super Bowl;

Seattle breaks a 73-year-old record for the most rain in a month.

2007
The Olympic Sculpture Park opens.

2008
Bill Gates steps down as Microsoft CEO to concentrate on the Bill & Melinda Gates Foundation. Washington Mutual collapses.

2009
Sound Transit light rail link begins service between Downtown and SeaTac Airport. Boeing's long-awaited 787 Dreamliner makes its first test flight.

2010
Amazon begins moving into its enormous new campus in Seattle's South Lake Union neighborhood.

2012
Washington State voters approve same-sex marriage and the legalization of marijuana.

2013
Construction of the Alaskan Way Viaduct replacement tunnel begins, to be completed by 2019.

2014
Democrat Ed Murray becomes mayor; Seattle Seahawks football team wins Super Bowl.

2016
Light rail extended to Capitol Hill and Husky Stadium; First Hill tram line opens.

2017
Seattle files a lawsuit against President Trump and his administration over their threat to hold back federal grant money from 'sanctuary cities'.

'Henry Hemp', a proponent for legalizing marijuana, at a rally on Seattle's waterfront in 2012.

Native village, Alert Bay.

THE MAKING OF SEATTLE

The natural beauty of the Pacific Northwest, rich with fish, fruit, produce, and lumber, nourished the nation for centuries. Then it gave us the aerospace and software industries.

The impression that visitors receive of Seattle today – a self-confident, prosperous, and eminently livable city – belies the eccentricity and gritty character that mark its earlier history.

First inhabitants

The Puget Sound area, with its mild climate, abundant with fish, wildlife, and crops, was inhabited by peaceful tribes like the Salish and Duwamish. Fishing and hunting only their own lands, with seashells for currency, they bought dressed deer and elk skins from easterly inland tribes.

The first Europeans to see this area landed under the command of an Englishman, Captain George Vancouver, near what is now Everett, north of Seattle, in 1792. The Hudson's Bay Company was based to the south in Fort Vancouver on the Columbia River, along the present-day border between

Chief Sealth, for whom the city is named.

> Dressed in a breechcloth and faded blue blanket, the 6ft (1.8-meter) -tall Chief Sealth, with steel-gray hair hanging to his shoulders, caused quite a stir among the early settlers of Seattle.

Washington and Oregon. A ragtag group of social outcasts was engaged to bring in the pelts of sea otters and beavers and deal with the indigenous peoples. For three decades, the distant landlords of the Hudson's Bay Company dominated the Northwest, but

the mid-19th century gold strike in northern California and the opening of new trails to the West pushed out the corporate bureaucrats and fur traders.

Pristine regions of the Pacific Coast were carved up by zealous city builders and entrepreneurs, and there were already a handful of settlers in Puget Sound when David Denny and his party reached the sandy spit of Alki Point – south of present-day downtown Seattle – in September 1851, which they named Alki-New York (*alki* means 'by-and-by' in Chinook, and New York was Denny's home town).

Flattery and fraud

A dismal winter revealed that Alki-New York was an unsuitable site for a cabin, let alone a city. Denny realized that a deep-water harbor would be needed, so he borrowed a clothesline, tied horseshoes to it, and took a dugout canoe along the coastline, plumbing the depths until he found deep water in Elliott Bay. The site for present-day Seattle had been chosen.

Denny, Carson Boren, and William Bell staked out claims on the waterfront and were soon joined by Dr David Swinson Maynard. Medical doctor, merchant, lumberman, blacksmith, entrepreneur, and all-around visionary, Maynard – like thousands of pioneer settlers – had come by the Oregon Trail, a 2,000-mile (3,200km) trek, fraught with dangers of death and disease, from the Mississippi River through the Rocky Mountains to the mouth of the Columbia River.

The first store

Maynard hired local tribesmen to build near the Sag, as they called the land by the water, and within a few days his new store was selling 'a general assortment of dry goods, groceries,

Lumberjack family, Cascade Mountains c.1899.

Dr David Swinson Maynard established the first store in 1853 and promoted the city enthusiastically.

hardware, etc., suitable for the wants of immigrants just arriving.'

In Olympia, Maynard had befriended a local *tyee* (chief) named Sealth (pronounced *see-alth* and sometimes *see-attle*), leader of the tribe at the mouth of the Duwamish River, where it entered Elliott Bay. Europeans in the region considered him among the most important *tyee* in the territory, and Maynard's suggestion to name the new city Seattle – in honor of his noble friend – became reality, replacing the native name Duwamps.

Maynard employed Native Americans to cut a stand of fir behind the store into shakes, square logs, and cordwood, while others caught salmon and made rough barrels. When the ship *Franklin Adams* docked in October, the entrepreneur had 1,000 barrels of brined salmon, 30 cords of wood, 12,000ft (3,700 meters) of squared timbers, 8,000ft (2,400 meters) of piling, and 10,000 shingles ready for shipping.

The salmon spoiled, which ruined most of his profits, but 'Doc' Maynard's enthusiasm wasn't dimmed. What was good for Seattle was good for Maynard, so when Henry Yesler arrived scouting the Sound to locate a steam-driven

Sawmills dominated the streets of early Seattle.

sawmill, Maynard and Boren both contributed land at the water frontage.

Sawmills and strained relations

The rugged residents built a log cookhouse and started on 'Skid Road,' a log slide for the timber to slip down the hill to the sawmill. When Yesler returned from San Francisco and set up his equipment, Seattle took a large step forward 'Huzza for Seattle!' said the paper in Olympia. 'The mill will prove as good as a gold mine to Mr Yesler, besides tending greatly to improve the fine town site of Seattle and the fertile country around it, by attracting thither the farmer, the laborer, and the capitalist. On with improvement'

Seattle became the government seat for King County, and Doc Maynard's little store became the site not only of the post office but even the Seattle Exchange.

Though the local tribes had at first welcomed the outsiders – and their tools, blankets, liquor, guns, and medicines – they soon rued new diseases; a religion that called Indian ways wicked (for reasons less than clear); and most perniciously, the notion of private property. By the time Doc Maynard helped broker a deal to buy

their land, they were in a weak bargaining position. In 1854, a proposal, the Port Elliott treaty, was put to the local tribes by a drunken Governor Stevens in Chinook Creole, a bastard tongue used by fur traders, more suited to rough commerce than diplomacy.

The US government offered the Native American tribes $150,000, paid over 20 years in goods, and a reservation, for 3,000 sq miles

EARLY PIONEERS

City building was a booming enterprise in 19th-century America. A determined developer laid claim to a location with promise, devised a town plan, then enticed settlers and investors, using any means at his disposal – from bribery and exaggeration to flattery and fraud. Thus began the towns of Steilacoom, Olympia, Whatcom, Port Townsend. Tacoma and, most successfully, Seattle. Men heavily outnumbered women to start with, and prostitution became part of the landscape. Eventually more women were brought to the area to boost morale and become future brides, but it must have taken a hardy spirit to accept the less-than-genteel conditions in those early days.

The Great Fire of 1889 allowed the city fathers to rebuild a safer, better metropolis.

(8,000 sq km) of land. Chief Seattle answered on behalf of all the Indians in his language, Duwamish. Recalling the speech over three decades later, Dr Henry Smith was taken 'with the magnificent bearing, kindness, and paternal benignity' of Chief Seattle.

'The Big Chief at Washington sends us word that he wishes to buy our lands but is willing to allow us enough to live comfortably,' goes Smith's version of Chief Seattle's speech. 'His people are many. They are like the grass that covers vast prairies. My people are few. They resemble the scattering trees of a storm-swept plain. Every part of this soil is sacred in the estimation of my people. Every hillside, every valley, every plain and grove has been hallowed by some sad or happy event in days long vanished, and when the last Red Man shall have perished and the memory of my tribe shall have become a myth among the White Men, these shores will swarm with the invisible dead of my tribe.'

The next year the treaty was signed and most Native Americans moved to reservations across Puget Sound. In 1856, though, some rebelled. There were few casualties on either side, and the

US Army easily defeated the small group. Leschi was a rebel Native American leader, caught by the perfidy of a nephew, tried and convicted of murdering an officer during the war, and hanged. The so-called Indian War was over and the whites had won, but many issues, like territorial fishing rights, remain disputed to this day. Leschi became a regional hero, with a neighborhood, a park, and a statue dedicated to his memory.

Seattle became an industrious village. While Yesler's sawmill prospered, sending lumber to San Francisco and transferring sawdust to fill the swampy lowland, not everybody benefited to the same degree. Angeline, the daughter of Chief Seattle, worked as domestic help. 'A good worker,' said Sophie Frye Bass, niece of founder David Denny, 'but when she had a fit of temper she would leave, even though she left a tub full of clothes soaking.'

Racial problems

The mid-1880s were difficult times in Seattle. The city was hard hit by an economic depression afflicting the entire country. Out-of-work fishermen, lumber workers, and miners competed for jobs – not only with unemployed city clerks and carpenters, but also with the many Chinese laborers discharged after the completion of the railroads. The Chinese workers became a scapegoat for the area's problems. The hardworking Asian immigrants were resented by many unemployed Seattleites. The Knights of Labor, a white fraternal organization, wanted them ejected from the Northwest by force. In 1885, about 30 Chinese were driven out of nearby Newcastle. In early 1886 Seattle exploded in racial violence. Five men were shot, Chinese stores and homes were demolished, and 200 Chinese were forced aboard a San Francisco-bound steamer. By March, when federal troops restored order, the Chinese community of about 500 had been eliminated.

By 1890, Seattle's population had more than quadrupled in a decade to 50,000. Three years later, the surge was over, but the city had become a very different place. Seattle was developing a sense of place, a personality, and an identity.

The Great Fire and Skid Row

Nothing demonstrates Seattle's 'can-do' attitude better than the city's reaction to John Back's blunder on June 6, 1889. Back, a handyman, threw a bucket of water on a flaming pot of glue in the middle of a paint store. The building exploded into flames, and 12 hours later the entire commercial district – 60 city blocks – was consumed.

Before the 'Great Fire,' the commercial section of Seattle had become a pestilential morass. The downtown area was built on mudflats, and sewers backed up when the tide came in. Chuckholes and pools of mud would open up at intersections, swallowing a schoolboy, horses, and even carriages. Typhoid and tuberculosis were rampant.

The fire allowed the overhaul of the municipal systems, and the city was rebuilt. Civic improvement began three days after the blaze, while the embers were still warm. Three years later, a new Seattle of brick and stone stood ready to lead the Pacific Northwest. New, higher roadways now reached the second stories of the buildings; people crossed the street by ladders. But the sidewalks and the ground levels 12ft (4 meters) below needed to remain accessible. This two-tier city is now the subject of a rambling, entertaining 'Underground Seattle' tour (see page 87).

Anti-Chinese riot led by the Knights of Labor, 1886.

Miners pose on a Downtown street; the Yukon Gold Rush of 1897 made local merchants wealthy.

New wharves, railroad depots, freight sheds, coal bunkers, and warehouses lined the mile-long waterfront strip. The sawmills moved out of town, leaving behind the name of Skid Road (now called Yesler Way). In later years, as this part of town became the haunt of homeless men and women, 'Skid Row' became a term used in other US cities to describe poor and urban neighborhoods of broken dreams.

For much of the 1890s, Seattle was in decline. Skid Road was becoming dangerous and derelict, and business slumped – until the arrival from Alaska of the SS *Portland* in July of 1897. Headlines screamed across the country the next day that the *Portland* docked bearing 'A Ton of Gold Aboard.' Seattle's then-mayor, W.D. Wood, heard news of the Yukon gold strike while visiting San Francisco, wired his resignation, and headed straight for gold country.

Yukon Gold Rush

The mania swept the Western world, as men from Sydney to Switzerland uprooted their lives and headed to the frozen fields of the Yukon, far to the north. Many of these treasure seekers needed to pass through Seattle.

Miners panning for gold in the Klondike, 1897.

> By the beginning of the 20th century, Seattle had become a center for traffic in white slaves. Women were in great demand, many coaxed onto ships bound for the Northwest with promises of the good life.

Tens of thousands of prospectors and unprepared fortune hunters hit the city, wanting supplies for their northbound adventure. Schwabacher's Outfitters rose to the top of the provisioning industry, and supplies for the trek north were stacked on the boardwalk 10ft (3 meters) high. By the spring after the SS *Portland*'s arrival, Seattle merchants raked in some $25 million, against the previous year's revenues of $300,000. Hotels and restaurants were over-booked and Seattle banks filled with Yukon gold. Schools taught mining and classes were even given in dogsled driving. This, in a city that rarely saw a snowflake.

The transient Gold-Rush population craved entertainment. John Considine, patriarch of the famous acting family, opened up the People's Theater and brought in famed exotic dancer

1866 cartoon mocking Asa Mercer's importation of marriageable women to Seattle.

Little Egypt, who, clad in diaphanous harem clothes, gave a lesson in international culture – the muscle dance, the Turkish dance, and the Damascus dance – for appreciative crowds almost every night of the year. Box-houses – so-called for the private alcoves at the sides of the theater – were a feature of Seattle's nightlife.

Prostitution was a natural product of the mostly male lumber town. The demographic discrepancy between men and women led Asa Mercer, a carpenter on the newly built Territorial University (and its first president), to secure a $300 fee from lonely Northwest bachelors with the promise of marriageable young maidens from the East Coast. He aimed to bring 500 women, but returned to Seattle a year later with just 100. But Mercer managed to placate his male clients, married one of his imports, and moved inland.

The Klondike Gold Rush also confirmed Seattle as the Northwest's trade center, surpassing the older city of Portland to the south. The boom raised Seattle's population to 80,000 by 1900; with three railroad lines and a road over the Cascade Mountains, numbers rose to a quarter of a million by 1910. Swedes populated the then-separate sawmill city of Ballard (now part of North Seattle). Laborers from Japan came in large numbers in the late 1890s,

foreshadowing Seattle's later role as a shipping link to Asia and the Pacific.

The downtown area was regraded to reduce the inclines of the hills. Areas like Capitol Hill became neighborhoods of the utmost propriety. The high-class bordellos and cheaper 'crib-houses' were closed, and John Considine moved from his first box-house theater on Skid Road into a vaudeville-theater chain that soon extended across the United States. Alexander Pantages, who began as a bartender in a Dawson saloon and also ran a box-house theater, rivaled Considine's chain.

The birth of Boeing

Seattle dominated the Alaskan shipping routes of the West Coast, and when the Panama Canal opened in 1914 and World War I brought increased demand for navy vessels, Seattle saw its future in shipbuilding and the sea. In 1910, at a makeshift airport south of Los Angeles, one wealthy Seattleite set his sights higher. The scion of a wealthy Minnesota iron-and-timber family with his own fortune from local timber, William Boeing attended the first US international flying meet.

Gold-diggers leaving for Klondike.

Seattle shantytown, 1933.

Boeing's initial interest in flying may have been on a par with his purchase of the Heath shipyards just in order to finish a yacht, but over Lake Washington, while testing a Curtiss-type hydroplane he built with friend and fellow Yale graduate George Conrad Westervelt, he found a profession and a mission. In 1916, the company was incorporated in Seattle.

In the early 1930s, the economic body blow that followed the Great Depression hit Seattle harder than most cities. Skid Road saw an ever-growing population of the haggard and the hungry. A meal cost only 20 cents, but few on Skid Road could afford it. Still, there was order among the destitute.

The city's so-called Hooverville (Depression-era shantytowns were named after then-President Hoover), built on the tide flats in an abandoned shipyard, was among the largest temporary communities in the US. It had its own self-appointed vigilante committee to enforce a sanitation code. The Unemployed Citizens' League reached a peak membership of 50,000 in 1931, and formed a separate community – called the Republic of the Penniless – with a system of work and barter to feed and house its members. Those lucky enough to hold jobs were members of a network held in lock step with the powerful Teamsters union.

> Bertha Knight Landes was elected mayor in 1926. She was the first female elected executive in a major American city, and the only woman to date who has held the position of Seattle's mayor.

When non-union beer from the East Coast appeared in the Seattle area, teamsters refused to move it from warehouses. Local breweries benefited, helping to establish the strong Seattle tradition of regional breweries.

Big bombers and the Jet Age

World War II brought Seattle's next great economic boom. Although based partly on ship-building, this time the recovery was centered predominantly on one industry – aircraft – and one company – Boeing. Borne on the wings of Boeing's mass-produced B-17 *Flying Fortress* and

B-29 *Super Fortress* bombers, the 1940 greater metropolitan population of about 450,000 continued to grow. But the economic benefits didn't extend to everyone; the war and Japan's bombing of Pearl Harbor brought misery to the local Japanese population.

When President Franklin D. Roosevelt signed Executive Order 9066 in February 1942, 110,000 Japanese were summarily removed from their jobs and homes and interned in camps along the West Coast, Wyoming, and Idaho. In Seattle, 7,000 Japanese lost everything they owned and spent the next three years in an Idaho camp.

Yet, like the Chinese before them, many Japanese returned to Seattle after the end of the war, even though their property was taken and despite the racism they encountered almost daily.

In the 1950s Seattle's economy also benefited from the Korean War, with growing demand for B-47 and B-52 bombers. The civilian 707 launched Seattle's confident entry into the Jet Age.

Nothing symbolized this better than the landmark of the skyline, the Space Needle, built for the 1962 World's Fair in Seattle. The Century 21 Exposition, as the fair was named, left a lasting legacy of futuristic structures for the people of Seattle, not just with the Needle but with the entire Seattle Center, including the Pacific Science Center, the International Fountain, indoor and outdoor concert venues, and the Monorail that connects Seattle Center with Downtown.

By 1965, the population had grown to more than half a million. Despite the massive lay-offs at Boeing in the late 1960s, Seattle continued to be a draw for newcomers. Attempts were made to raze older sections of the city, but the growing population was fostering an interest in preservation and renovating what remained of old Seattle. Civic visionaries saw to it that Pioneer Square was designated a National Historic District, preserving its unique architectural character. One notable hero of preservation was the architect Victor Steinbrueck, who led a citizens' campaign to save the Pike Place Market from the wrecking ball of developers. In 1971 the first branch of Starbucks opened in the market, selling dark-roasted whole-bean coffee.

It was also during this decade that the first major festival of music and arts took root.

A Boeing 707, the USA's first successful commercial jet, flies over Mount Rainier in 1954.

The World's Fair of 1962 was responsible for Seattle's most prominent landmark, the Space Needle.

Later to be known as Bumbershoot, it has since become the city's largest and most popular festival, held every Labor Day weekend. In 1978, the Seattle Art Museum (SAM) mounted the hugely successful King Tut exhibition, which attracted 1.3 million visitors and gave SAM the impetus to think bigger, including plans to move from Volunteer Park in Capitol Hill to Downtown. The 72,000-seat Kingdome was built as a venue for Seahawks football, major rock concerts, and trade shows for boats, RVs, and much more.

The region's economy was continuing to diversify. By 1979, the young Microsoft company moved from Albuquerque to the Eastside city of Bellevue, Washington, returning to the area where its founders, Bill Gates and Paul Allen, were raised. Now the Puget Sound area was home to logging, spearheaded by the Weyerhaeuser Corporation headquartered in the southern suburb of Federal Way, aerospace engineering, and the fledgling high-tech industry.

Fire Mountain explodes

On May 18, 1980, nature took a stab at containing the growth of Seattle and the Pacific Northwest itself when Mount St Helens, south of Seattle, lived up to its Native American name of Fire Mountain. After 200 years of being virtually dormant, 9,677ft (2,950-meter) Mount St Helens erupted, sending much of the mountain's summit 60,000ft (18,000 meters) into the air.

The eruption came after warnings from scientists and attempts to evacuate the area, but the flow of molten rock and clouds of ash still resulted in as many as 60 deaths. Damage was estimated at $1 billion. Within three days, the ash cloud had crossed North America; within two weeks, it had traveled right around the globe. Mount St Helens itself became 1,300ft (400 meters) shorter than it had been before the blast. Ash fell throughout the Northwest in heavy amounts, hindering transportation, industry, and – in the short term – agriculture. Ultimately, the ash injected nutrients into the soil, as it has throughout the formation of the earth's lands.

Other factors were also contributing to the changing landscape. In 1986, Microsoft went public, and the ensuing rise of the stock price created thousands of millionaires. In 1981 Starbucks hired Howard Schultz, who led a group to purchase it in 1987. It would go on to become one of the world's best-known brands, selling coffee across the globe.

In a bid to attract more business to the city, the Washington State Convention Center opened its doors in downtown Seattle, creating a large

Seattle's annual Bumbershoot arts and music festival.

Crushed car and flattened bare trees in the aftermath of Mount St Helens' 1980 eruption.

central venue for conferences and conventions. A subsequent expansion doubled the meeting-space capacity, and hotel space in the city center also continued to grow.

Logging and protests

During the 1990s Seattle grew less economically dependent on logging and on aerospace, becoming a high-tech mecca for companies such as Amazon and Nintendo of America. Even after the dotcom bubble burst, these companies stayed strong.

In 1994, Pioneer Square-based Aldus Software, maker of popular programs such as Page-Maker and founded by Paul Brainerd, merged with Adobe Systems and set up shop in the Seattle neighborhood of Fremont.

Jeff Bezos launched his online bookstore, Amazon, in 1995, and soon added software, CDs, movies, and video games. The company, headquartered at the time in a former hospital on Beacon Hill, survived the 'dot bomb,' but remarkably didn't turn its first annual profit for another eight years.

Starbucks continued to go from strength to strength, too. The first Starbucks outside North America opened in Tokyo in 1996, and

> In 1990 Seattle hosted the Goodwill Games, with 2,300 participants from 54 countries. The event was held in reaction to the political troubles and boycotts over the 1980s Olympic Games.

today the company sells coffee in more than 70 countries.

The explosive growth in high-tech industries produced scores of young millionaires, as well as changes in the landscape. Local boy Bill Gates became the richest man in the world in 1993 (see page 44). Paul Allen, who had stepped out of day-to-day operations at Microsoft a decade earlier, spent huge amounts of money in civic projects around the Puget Sound area. He purchased and began preservation work on Union Station, a century-old Seattle landmark. He bought the Seattle Seahawks football franchise, securing the team's future in the city, and constructed a world-class stadium and exhibition center on the site of the old Seattle Kingdome, adjacent to Safeco Field, the state-of-the-art baseball stadium that opened in 1999. He also founded the EMP Museum (now the Museum

Seattle Art Museum.

of Popular Culture, or MoPOP), a dynamic interactive music museum designed in high style by architect Frank Gehry (see pages 120).

These are only some of many ambitious projects the city launched in the 1990s. Both the Seattle Art Museum and Benaroya Hall, home of the Seattle Symphony with a 2,500-seat concert hall and highly enviable acoustics, helped to revitalize Downtown.

But it wasn't just in the upper echelons that the arts were thriving. A local sound that had been gaining momentum since the late 1980s, grunge now burst onto the world music scene, with bands including Nirvana, Pearl Jam, Soundgarden, Alice in Chains, and Mudhoney, and record label Sub Pop creating the phenomenon that was nicknamed 'the Seattle sound'. This brought a new cachet to the city, and scores of young people and musicians headed to Seattle.

Protests and anti-globalization

Another pivotal event that focused the world's attention on Seattle was the World Trade Organization protest-turned-riot. In 1999 the WTO held its ministerial meeting at the Washington State Convention Center. A broad range of activists, made up of environmentalists, human-rights activists, trade unionists, and pro-democracy campaigners came to protest against what they perceived to be abuses by the WTO's trade practices. Although the city, Seattle police, and WTO organizers expected the protests, nobody was prepared for what followed, dubbed the Battle in Seattle. Clashes between police and protesters turned violent, tear gas was sprayed into the crowd, property was damaged, protestors were injured, arrests were made, and Mayor Paul Schell declared a state of emergency and ordered a curfew. The National Guard and the Washington State Patrol were called in to restore order. The mishandling of the situation ultimately led to the resignation of the chief of police.

In another contentious arena, the tension between environmentalists and the logging industry had been growing. In the 1990s, environmentalists had some cause for optimism. Activists began to see some success in halting the clear-cutting of ancient forests. The US Forest Service was becoming more environmentally sensitive and more responsive to public desires. Pressure groups forced the government of nearby British Columbia to cancel logging rights and to protect some magnificent, centuries-old, first-growth, temperate rain forests, principally on southwest Vancouver Island. Last-minute decisions made by outgoing president Bill Clinton in 1999 included a moratorium on new forest road construction on nearly 60 million acres (24.3 million hectares) of national forests – used as access roads for timber companies – as well as a program to close many such roads and to restore them to a natural state.

But America under President George W. Bush saw a roll back on environmental protections. The Bush administration revised Clinton's plans, causing outrage among environmentalists and relief among lumber companies. A report presented by US Forest Service chief Dale Bosworth in 2002 criticized specifically the Northwest Forest Plan – implemented by the Clinton administration – to balance timber harvests and wildlife preservation in the region.

21st-century Seattle

A magnitude-6.8 earthquake struck the Seattle area in February 2001, and caused property damage throughout the region, including to the Capitol building in Olympia. The epicenter of the quake was about 10 miles (16km) northeast of Olympia, and 32.5 miles (52km) underground. Unlike many regions on the continent, the Pacific Northwest coastal area has constant reminders of its geological history and origins.

That year Seattle suffered another seismic shock; this time when Boeing moved its corporate headquarters to Chicago, cutting 20,000 jobs in the process. The regional economy had become less dependent on Boeing over time, but the company still has a sizeable presence in the area.

50 SHADES OF SEATTLE

Cuffs, paddles, and ropes, oh my! With her best-selling trilogy, *50 Shades of Grey* writer E.L. James drew attention away from the small town of Forks on the Olympic Peninsula (made famous by the *Twilight* series) and put it squarely on Seattle, where her three lusty S&M-themed books take place. In the story, Christian Grey's condominium (home to his 'Red Room of Pain') is in the Escala – an actual building in downtown Seattle. Several local hotels (including the Edgewater and Hotel Max) offer 50 Shades of Grey-themed packages.

Seattle's latter-day phenomenal success has been at some cost, however. It has a dubious distinction as one of the nation's worst cities for traffic. The Interstate-5 corridor is particularly crowded. The Alaskan Way viaduct, a 1950s concrete double-decker roadway running along the waterfront and past Pioneer Square, was damaged in the earthquake, and after heated debate is being replaced by an expensive tunnel, expected to open in 2019.

Neighborhoods have changed. House prices have risen. But then so have fantastic new buildings. Recent years have seen a building boom sweep the downtown area, where more than 60 buildings were under construction at the end of 2016. Insignia Towers, Amazon Tower II, Madison Centre, and the Mark are just a few out of 16 skyscrapers already or about to be completed in downtown Seattle.

The Washington State Ferries terminal, the Seattle Art Museum, and the Seattle Aquarium have been expanded or remodeled. The aquarium's upgrades were part of the wider, extensive seven-year regeneration program along the waterfront of Elliott Bay from Pioneer Square

Anti-WTO protestors hit the streets in 1999.

Bill Gates and Microsoft

One of the world's wealthiest men, the co-founder of Microsoft is now focused on advancing global health and education.

William H. Gates III, the son of a successful Seattle attorney, was born on October 28, 1955. Prodigious in math and science, he gained programming experience at the city's prestigious Lakeside School. At the age of 19, taking time out from Harvard, he founded Microsoft with an old friend, Paul Allen. Microsoft's phenomenal success is rooted in a 1981 coup to supply operating

Bill Gates, founder of Microsoft.

systems for IBM's new line of personal desktop computers. They licensed a system known as QDOS (Quick and Dirty Operating System), adapted it to produce PC-DOS, and effectively created a stranglehold on the nascent PC market. In 1986, Gates sold some of his stock at $21 a share; in 1999, he sold nearly 10 million shares at $86 a share. In its heyday, Gates' worth increased by an average of $1 million a second.

Much is made of Gates' and Allen's wealth, but scores of employees also made millions through stock options. In the 1990s, the neighborhoods around Microsoft's headquarters in Redmond were (and still are) lush with dotcom success stories.

Microsoft's power base is still the Windows operating system, but as the internet gained momentum in the mid-1990s, Gates steered the company's focus toward the net. Fearing alternative browsers could relieve users' dependence on Windows, Microsoft began the 'browser war' by creating Explorer. It allied with NBC to create the cable-TV and online news service MSNBC and bought up web businesses.

Microsoft today

IBM and Microsoft parted ways long ago, but Microsoft has gone from strength to strength. The operating system that powers more than 90 percent of the world's PCs makes Microsoft formidable. The company took a big and lucrative step into the games-console market with the Xbox, and is tilting at Apple's iPhone market its Windows Mobile series and the surface hybrid tablets aimed at young people. In 2016, Microsoft bought the professional social-network service LinkedIn for more than $26 billion in a bid to further diversify its business model.

Such staggering success has not gone unopposed. Microsoft attracted massive antitrust suits from both the US Government and the European Union, and there have been open-source movements in South America, and the development of open-source operating systems like Linux. But as a company that is still wealthier than all but half-a-dozen countries in the world, Microsoft is unlikely to be in any danger.

In 2008 Gates stepped down from running the company full-time, handing the reins over to Steve Ballmer (who was succeeded by current CEO Satya Nadella in 2014) in order to administer the charitable Bill & Melinda Gates Foundation, which he established with his wife. Its impressive Visitor Center, across the street from Seattle Center, opened to the public in 2012. Bill and Melinda have been awarded several prestigious accolades for their charity work, including the Presidential Medal of Freedom by Barack Obama in 2016, and the Legion of Honour in Paris in 2017.

In 2014, Bill Gates stepped down as chairman of Microsoft to take up the hands-on role of technology advisor to Nadella.

The Seattle skyline at night from the Space Needle.

to Belltown (the Waterfront Seattle Program). With program completion expected in 2020, the project is rebuilding the seawall and adding parks, paths, and enhanced access routes. It has already expanded historic Pike Place Market to give it a new 'MarketFront', which opened in June 2017. Better transportation links are underway too, with light rail and streetcars both expanding their services and the cyclepath network being constantly extended.

Sports, too, have become big business. Starbucks CEO Schultz endeared himself to Seattleites by leading a group to buy the city's basketball team, the SuperSonics, in 2001, but incurred their wrath by selling the franchise – including its women's team, the Seattle Storm – in 2006. The Sonics were bought by a group of Oklahoma businessmen, and left town, while a local group of businesswomen bought the Storm, securing its future in Seattle. The Seattle Seahawks, owned by Microsoft co-founder Paul Allen, fought their way to the Super Bowl in 2006, but lost to the Pittsburgh Steelers. Glory eventually came in 2014, when they overwhelmed the Denver Broncos to win their first NFL championship title. Meanwhile, the Sounders FC, the city's wildly popular soccer team, has a loyal fan base.

During the elections of 2012, Washington voters not only helped to award Barack Obama another term in the White House, they also approved same-sex marriage and the legalization of marijuana. Four years later in 2016, Seattle voters – of whom 87 percent voted for Hilary Clinton to just 8 percent who voted for Donald Trump – were left in dismay as Trump was elected president.

The city's current, openly gay mayor, Ed Murray, is considered to be one of the most liberal in the US. In 2015 he introduced a $15 minimum-wage package, later adopted by San Francisco and Los Angeles; in 2017, paid parental leave was extended; also in 2017, Seattle filed a lawsuit against Donald Trump and his administration over threats to withhold federal grant money from 'sanctuary cities' – those that refuse to comply with immigration agents' requests to detain illegal immigrants. Although initially announcing plans to seek a second term in the 2017 mayoral election, Murray subsequently withdrew amidst four men claiming he sexually abused them as teenagers – the mayor vehemently denies all claims.

Today, ongoing challenges face local government, including homelessness, public transportation and road infrastructure, and balancing large-scale projected growth with environmental impacts in order to keep Seattle the highly liveable, resilient, and beautiful city that it is.

The exterior design of the Seattle Central Public Library.

The Seattle waterfront as viewed from a harbor cruise.

LIVING WITH WATER

Seattle is so close to the water it's an integral part of the city's environment, and Seattleites take full advantage of it.

The water is more than a feature of the Northwestern landscape. The voluptuous shores and salt tides of Puget Sound, and the deep currents of the Columbia, Salmon, and Snake rivers have carved the living environment. They are an integral part of it. The proverbial edge of the world is a Pacific coastline where the rain forests and rocky peninsulas are entwined with the sea.

It's water that keeps Washington green (a popular slogan on highway signs), and which also supports such a healthy fish, bird, and sea-mammal population. It also provides plenty of opportunities for recreation; it's estimated that one in every six Seattleites owns a boat – whether it's a rowboat, a sailboat, a yacht, or a kayak. With saltwater Puget Sound and a handful of in-city freshwater lakes, plus an 8-mile (13km) ship canal linking the Sound to Lake Washington via another lake – Lake Union – Seattle has more than enough places to cruise, paddle, and sail.

For visitors who come to Seattle without a boat in tow, one of the easiest ways to get out onto the water is on a Washington State Ferry. Some of the most dramatic views of the Seattle skyline are from the ferries, particularly at sunset and at night. There are more ferries, carrying more passengers and vehicles, in Washington State than anywhere else in the US. Every year, 22 ferries transport more than 23 million passengers. Popular routes link Seattle's Coleman Dock with Bremerton on the Olympic Peninsula, and downtown Seattle to Bainbridge Island. A passenger-only ferry takes commuters to Vashon Island. These are only a few of the

Sailboats on Lake Union.

many water routes that link Seattle to the rest of the Pacific Northwest.

Surrounded by water, people here don't expect to impose rhythm and tempo on nature in the way that southern Californians do or asphalt does across a Southwestern desert. This distinction – that Northwesterners are more changed by environment than it is by them – is crucial to understanding the local character.

Stories about the water

The early Native Americans were known not as warriors but as fishermen. Although there were disputes over territory, there was also a

Writing in the rain

Seattle's infamous rain has long been immortalized in print, but how much is truth and how much is fiction, intended to keep the city's fair climate a secret?

The *Seattle Times* in 1953 announced: 'This January, Wettest Ever, Getting Wetter,' proclaiming a 40-year-old record for January 27 broken that day. In June 1985, column-

Rain is possible year-round in Seattle.

ist Don Hannula asked, 'Rainless Seattle: Will We Become Another Tucson?' 'Drop In the Bucket: That Splatter Didn't Matter,' was a later headline in the *Seattle Times*. In a city with only 50 totally clear days per year, it is the lack of rain that provided the most stories. 'How long, O Lord, how long?' bemoaned columnist John Hinterberger in a year that clocked up only about half of the

city's usual annual downpour. 'What is giving us all this troublesome, lovely weather?'

Rainless summers can be troublesome indeed for Seattle, and that particular year lowered the Cedar River, where 300,000 salmon spawn, and slowed the turbines that supply much of the city's power to half speed. The Fisheries Department worried, 'There isn't enough water to cover all the gravel [in the river]'.

An erroneous reputation

Seattle's reputation as the rainiest city in America began to dry up. According to *The Best and Worst of Everything* by Les Krantz, Seattle doesn't even make it into the top-10 list of US cities. The wettest ones – including Hilo, Hawaii; Pensacola, Florida; and New Orleans, Louisiana – actually get at least 10 inches (25cm) more rain each year than the Emerald City does. Just as things were calming down, though, on November 30, 2006, the *Seattle Post-Intelligencer* reported, 'It's Never Been This Wet', announcing that a 73-year-old record for the rainiest month had been broken (previous record: 15.33ins/38.9cm in 1933).

Records to one side, what seems to make the difference here is the rain's ubiquity, a sheer, steady saturation slanting from what a 1902 columnist called 'the humid vats of heaven.' It rains so frequently yet so unobtrusively in Seattle that few people wear coats and fewer admit to owning umbrellas. A *Seattle Weekly* writer said, 'Drizzle and gray become the badge of pride for those who stay, and the curse that drives others away.'

Walter Rue, author of *Weather of the Pacific Coast*, said, 'If the sun doesn't shine we don't consider the day lost. People here don't complain about a little rain'.

The late *Seattle Times* man Emmett Watson advocated The Lesser Seattle Movement, a disinformation program to promote the wet weather and discourage would-be Seattleites. Columnist Jean Godden helped his cause with '38 Things To Do In the Rain.' High on the list was 'Write letters to all your friends, and tell them how horrible the weather is. Tell them this isn't even a nice place to visit...'

Looking out over Elliott Bay.

diversity and abundance of food that was different from other tribes' struggles over scarce resources. With all this plenitude, traditions of Northwestern art flourished, and with it the richness of tribal storytelling.

Unlike the white men who came to settle here, tribesmen felt that the land could not be owned. Even now, Puget Sound property rights ebb and flow according to the tides, not by the boundaries set by legal land ownership. If ownership of Northwest land can be influenced by movements of the tides, how much more deeply might we be affected by the water's relationship with us?

In keeping with the landscape's watery changes, Native stories are full of legends in which animals change easily into people and back again. The Salmon People are an underwater tribe who also spend a season on land; the whales and seals can metamorphose into humans as easily as the ever-present mist; and clouds change into different shapes. Many Northwest coast tribes tell of merpeople – part human, part fish – who mediate between the worlds to keep a watery balance.

Many tribal mythologies have their roots in the water, the floods, and the seas creating what we now know as, 'the people'. A Skagit creation story describes this beginning as happening when one of the most respected Native American gods, known as Changer, decided to 'make all the rivers flow only one way', and that 'there should be bends in the rivers so that there would be eddies where the fish could stop and rest. It was decided that beasts should be placed in the forests. Human beings would have to keep out of their way'.

Stewardship of the water

In the Northwest it is human beings who are urged to take a step back. People here tend to pride themselves, perhaps a little arrogantly, on living within nature's laws, on listening to the environment. It is here in the Northwest where the last nurturing old-growth forests stand in the lower 48 states – a topic of sharp, ongoing economic and social debate.

Oil spills have blackened the beaches, and species of salmon are endangered. Gray whales

Clouds descend over the Seattle skyline.

are found on their migrating courses belly-up from pollution in Puget Sound. There have been major closures of shellfish beds throughout the region because of toxic contaminations from industrial waste.

There is a growing movement among Pacific Northwest corporations to return some of their profits to protect the wilderness.

SEATTLE'S SOUND

Puget Sound, known by the native tribes as Whulge, was explored in 1792 by Captain George Vancouver. He named the sound for Peter Puget, a lieutenant in his expedition who probed the main channel. The southern terminus of the Inside Passage to Alaska, Puget Sound is a deep inlet stretching south for 100 miles (160km) from Whidbey Island (north of which are the straits of Georgia and Juan de Fuca). Hood Canal, which defines the Olympic Peninsula, is an extension of the Sound. Rivers that enter the Sound include the Skagit, Snohomish, and Duwamish. Puget Sound has several deepwater harbors, among them Seattle, Tacoma, Everett, and Port Townsend.

Recreational Equipment Inc. (REI) and Eddie Bauer are two such businesses that believe in investing in local environmental resources. Boeing and the corporation's employees contribute to numerous charities, some of them environmental. Environmental groups are active in clean-up efforts and pressuring government and corporations to do their part in reducing pollution and cleaning up contamination.

Just as Northwesterners claim closeness with their natural world, so too, they claim to be close to their history. The non-Native history here is less than 200 years compared with thousands of years of Skagit, Suquamish, Muckleshoot, Okanogan, and other tribes' presence. Some of the myths favored by Native Americans calmly predict that 'the human beings will not live on this earth forever.'

This prediction is an agreement between Raven, Mink, Coyote, and what the Skagits call 'Old Creator', concluding that human beings 'will stay only for a short time. Then the body will go back to the earth and the spirit back to the spirit world.'

Paddleboarding on Lake Union.

It's a surreal sight to see the occasional mist move in, obscuring the Space Needle and the higher skyscrapers, so that the structures appear to float in and out of the clouds.

mountains, feeding the rivers that irrigate Eastern Washington's orchards, and providing a home for the salmon. These rivers also supply hydroelectric power to the region via dams, and create some of the most sensational natural scenery in the world. From the temperate Hoh rain forest to the rushing rapids of the Wenatchee and Skykomish rivers, to the fertile Skagit valley, rain feeds the beauty and bounty of this region.

What's more, it is believed to be one of the few things that keep outsiders from migrating here en masse. Rain is a Northwest native, and perhaps is all that shelters locals from the massive population and industrial exploitations seen in other parts of the country.

Human worries and foibles appear to carry less weight in this region surrounded by water. It is typically Northwestern that this 'gone-fishing-while-the-world-falls-apart' attitude prevails. It's not that Northwesterners aren't involved; it's just that nature can be an antidote to such strong doses of conflict. Being surrounded by huge bodies of water, towering evergreen trees, and giant snow-capped mountains gives a different perspective to man's place in the natural world.

Where would we be without rain?

Port Angeles poet Tess Gallagher explains it this way: 'It is a faithful rain. You feel it has some allegiance to the trees and the people... It brings an ongoing thoughtfulness to their faces, a meditativeness that causes them to fall silent for long periods, to stand at their windows looking at nothing in particular. The people walk in the rain as within some spirit they wish not to offend with resistance.'

Water is intrinsic to the Pacific Northwest, with abundant rainfall in the western part of Washington State, falling as snow in the

A kayaker on Lake Union.

TRIBES OF THE NORTHWEST

There are more than 25,000 Native Americans in the Greater Seattle area; indeed, this region's history is inextricably tied to the local tribes that inhabited the land long before white explorers arrived in the 1700s.

Tlingit woman in traditional dress.

Evidence of the original band of Seattleites, the Duwamish, can be hard to find, but the city does have numerous resources for learning about Native American art and culture. The tribes that are the best documented are those of Southeast Alaska and British Columbia.

The Burke Museum of Natural History and Culture (see page 137), on Seattle's University of Washington campus, has one of the country's largest collections of Northwest coastal native art and artifacts. These include totem poles, model canoes, baskets, tools, and a house front. It's a very interesting place to visit.

The Seattle Art Museum (see page 103) also has a valuable First Nations collection, with many fine pieces created by members of the Tlingit, Haida, and Makah tribes.

The Daybreak Star Cultural Center (see page 132), in Seattle's Discovery Park, coordinates events and services for the city's native population. The center also has a collection of contemporary tribal art, and a small gallery where traveling shows are staged.

Members of the Nez Perce tribe at Colville Indian Reservation dressed to perform a dance, c.1910. Traditional clothing is still worn by the Nez Perce at pow wows and other ceremonial events.

A wooden bowl from the Haida tribe.

A Tlingit dream catcher.

A 19th-century line engraving depicting a Native American being captured by four colonists to serve as a slave in the 17th century. There were Native American slaves in every colony, many of whom were forced to endure dismal conditions.

CHIEF JOSEPH OF THE NEZ PERCE

Chief Joseph of the Nez Perce, who said, 'If the white man wants to live in peace with the Indian, he can live in peace. Treat all men alike. Give them a chance to live and grow.'

One of the most dramatic stories in Northwest Native American history is that of Chief Joseph, shown here in a photograph by Edward S. Curtis. He was a chief of the Nez Perce (Nimiipuu).

In 1877, the US government enacted a new treaty with the Nez Perce, stripping the tribe of valuable lands. Violence erupted. Several chiefs, including Chief Joseph, refused to sign the treaty and a band that Joseph led fled on horseback and on foot toward Canada. The natives held off the US cavalry for 1,500 miles (2,400km), surviving more than 20 battles along the way.

The Nez Perce eventually surrendered in northern Montana near the Canadian border, where Chief Joseph delivered his historic speech, with the conclusion, 'I will fight no more forever'.

Exiled to Oklahoma until 1885, Chief Joseph finally returned to the Pacific Northwest and lived on Washington State's Colville Reservation until his death in 1904.

Elaborately carved cedar totem pole at the Burke Museum of Natural History and Culture, which has an enviable collection of Native American art and artifacts.

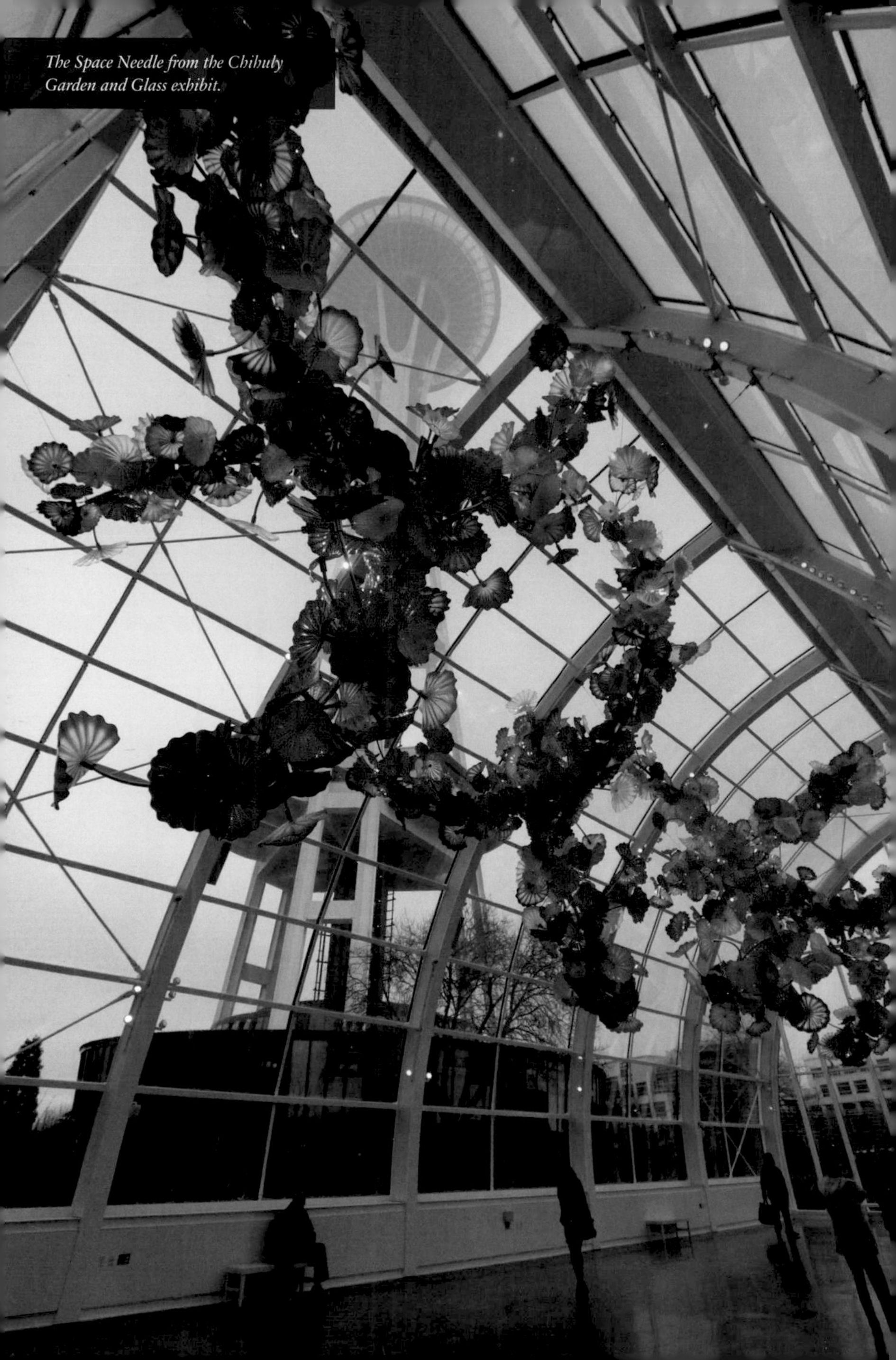

The Space Needle from the Chihuly Garden and Glass exhibit.

MUSIC, CULTURE, AND THE ARTS

Go to an event and the audience will be dressed in anything from couture to rags. This anything-goes mix of chic and casual is a reflection of the Northwest's cultural style.

From grunge band Nirvana to expatriate author Alice B. Toklas, Seattle's arts and culture scene is as varied as its inhabitants. At once discerning and laid-back, Seattleites love both high- and lowbrow entertainment any night of the week. Small clubs throughout the city host live music; local playwrights showcase their talents to packed houses in fringe theaters; and neighborhood galleries lure jeans-clad crowds to view local, national, and international art. Seattle is a place where Armani and Old Navy mingle – sometimes in the same outfit – and its arts and culture scene reflects this.

Live music

Long known as the birthplace of grunge rock (à la Kurt Cobain and Eddie Vedder), Seattle has a lively music scene beyond bass guitars and gritty vocals. From the highly regarded Seattle Symphony and Seattle Opera to concert series featuring star-studded line-ups and small ven-

> Grunge might have made Seattle an essential stop on the live-music circuit, but today you are more likely to hear electronica, hip-hop, or indie punk in the clubs that made grunge famous.

ues hosting up-and-coming musicians – from jazz to indie rock – Seattle is a mecca for all musical tastes. Classical music aficionados head to Benaroya Hall, where Ludovic Morlot conducts the Seattle Symphony and a distinguished roster of guest artists perform. Marion Oliver

Whiling away the hours at one of Seattle's many book stores.

McCaw Hall is home to the Seattle Opera, with sold-out performances and its critically acclaimed Wagner's *Ring Cycle* performed every four years.

Beyond these first-class venues for the performing arts, there is an intense and varied music scene of innovative sounds for today's tastes. Those looking for live music find it at a variety of small venues – the Crocodile (www.thecrocodile.com), Tractor Tavern (www.tractortavern.com), Dimitriou's Jazz Alley (www.jazzalley.com), Showbox (www.showboxpresents.com), and Chop Suey (www.chopsuey.com), among others. The most complete gig listings can be found in the city's two free weekly publications, *Seattle Weekly* and *The Stranger*.

In summer, outdoor concerts feature a top-notch list of popular artists – plus opportunities to enjoy live music while picnicking. The Woodland Park Zoo (see page 141) hosts Zoo Tunes, drawing artists such as Ziggy Marley and Melissa Etheridge. And Woodinville's Chateau Ste Michelle winery (see page 168) presents a blend of blues, jazz, and rock, June through September, at its outdoor amphitheater. Concertgoers bring their own dinners, buy a bottle of wine, and dance in the grass to big-draw performers such as James Taylor, Stevie Wonder, and the Beach Boys.

Dance

In the 1970s, a generation of aspiring choreographers moved to Seattle to perform and study with acclaimed modern-dance choreographer Bill Evans. Since then, dance – from classic to interpretive to modern – has found a sturdy foundation on Seattle stages, which have spawned choreographers such as Trisha Brown, Mark Morris, Pat Graney, and Christian Swenson.

The state's largest professional contemporary dance company, Spectrum Dance Theater, has garnered national and international attention. When the company is not touring, it holds most of its performances at the Moore Theatre.

And, recognized as one of the first institutions in the country to premiere experimental modern works by both national and international artists, On the Boards – founded in 1978 – is Seattle's premier contemporary performance organization. It showcases breakthrough performances by local artists in its spring Northwest New Works Festival and 12 Minutes Max, which highlights emerging artists.

Seattle's celebrated ballet company, the Pacific Northwest Ballet, draws the highest per-capita dance attendance in the country. Led by artistic director Peter Boal, the ballet's active repertoire includes classics such as *Swan Lake* and the popular annual performance of *Nutcracker*.

On the screen

Far from the snowy peaks of Sundance or the sun-drenched beaches of Cannes, Seattle hosts the largest, most attended film festival in the United States. Seattle International Film Festival (SIFF), founded in 1976, draws over 150,000 people to see more than 450 films each spring at venues throughout the city. From late May to mid-June, SIFF premieres independent,

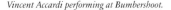

Vincent Accardi performing at Bumbershoot.

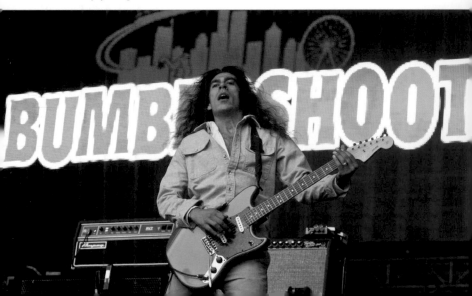

The Pacific Northwest Ballet performing West Side Story.

documentary, and foreign films from many genres. Recent winners of SIFF's Golden Space Needle award for best film include *At the End of the Tunnel* (2017), *Captain Fantastic* (2016), *The Dark Horse* (2015), and *Boyhood* (2014).

SIFF may be the city's largest film festival, but Seattle hosts several others throughout

CELEBRATING SUMMER

Every Labor Day weekend, Bumbershoot (http://bumbershoot.com), one of the nation's largest urban arts festivals, floods the Seattle Center with creative folk. Though music is a primary draw, the nonstop showcase of musicians and rising stars at 30 indoor and outdoor venues is complemented by craft booths, fare from local restaurants, and even an animated short-film festival. Summer sees numerous other festivals, including Seafair, Seattle Pride Fest, Bite of Seattle, Seattle Beerfest, Hempfest and Capitol Hill Block Party. After months of rain, Seattleites take full advantage of the warm months. Nearly every weekend from mid-June through early September sees outdoor festivals, parades, neighborhood events, outdoor concerts, or excuses for eating. Expect large crowds and world-class people-watching – summer festivals bring out the crazier side of the city.

the year. Washington State's largest showcase for Asian American films, the Northwest Asian American Film Festival, is held at Theatre Off Jackson in January. Other local fests include Children's Film Festival Seattle (January–February); the Seattle Jewish Film Festival (March); the Seattle Arab and Iranian Film Festival (March–April); the Langston Hughes African American Film Festival (April–May); Seattle's True Independent Film Festival (June); the Seattle Latino Film Festival (October); and the Twist: Seattle Queer Film Festival (October).

Visual arts

As varied and distinctive as its inhabitants, Seattle's visual arts scene has a lot to offer – from paintings and photography to sculptures and video installations. At the center of it all, the Seattle Art Museum (see page 103) is internationally recognized for its extensive collection of African, Native American, and Asian art, as well as modern art by Pacific Northwest artists. The permanent collection includes 21,000 pieces, and blockbuster exhibits visit the museum on an ongoing basis.

The museum's sister space, the Seattle Asian Art Museum (see page 125; under renovation until 2019), is housed in an Art Deco structure on Capitol Hill and comprises an incomparable collection of Asian art and artifacts, from 4,000-year-old Japanese tomb art to 19th-century Chinese snuff bottles, as well as contemporary pieces. Thanks to its stately assemblage of items, the museum ranks as one of the top collections outside Asia. SAM's Olympic Sculpture Park (see page 110), a 9-acre (3.6-hectare) outdoor sculpture museum on the waterfront, features visiting installations, as well as permanent works by celebrated artists like Louise Bourgeois, Roy McMakin, and Richard Serra. And additionally, the park features one of the city's most celebrated visuals: dynamic views of the Olympic Mountains, Puget Sound, and Seattle's cityscape.

On First Hill is the Frye Art Museum (see page 95), where a modern facade hides a classical interior filled with representational landscape and portrait works as well as 19th-century German paintings from the collection of the museum's founders, Charles and Emma Frye. The Henry Art Gallery (see page 137), on the University of Washington campus, is the Northwest's premier contemporary art space.

Seattle Art Museum.

Millefiori display at Chihuly Garden and Glass.

South of Seattle, in Tacoma, is the Museum of Glass, offering glassblowing demonstrations as well as three galleries of contemporary glass-art exhibitions. The museum is linked to the Tacoma campus of the University of Washington by the Chihuly Bridge of Glass, a 500ft (152-meter) pedestrian overpass filled with glass. Tacoma is the hometown of world-renowned glass artist Dale Chihuly, who co-founded the Pilchuck Glass School in Stanwood, Washington, in 1971. Visitors who would rather not make the trek south can tour many of Chihuly's works at the Chihuly Garden and Glass Museum, which is located in the Seattle Center.

Art collectors and browsers find endless fodder in Seattle's many galleries, some of which are positioned within walking distance of one another in Pioneer Square.

Literature

Year round, in cafés throughout the city, you'll find Seattleites lost in books – lattes in hand. But reading is not just a casual pastime for its literary-inclined residents, it's a *joie de vivre*.

Author events are held – and highly attended – throughout the area, from theater-packed lectures by famous authors to intimate readings at locally owned bookstores and Capitol Hill's celebrated literary center, Richard Hugo House. Writers such as Jonathan Raban (*Arabia: A Journey Through the Labyrinth*), Sherman Alexie (*The Absolutely True Diary of a Part-Time Indian*) and David Guterson (*Snow Falling on Cedars*) have made the city their home, further raising Seattle's reputation as a creative hub.

> Pioneer Square's First Thursday Gallery Walk draws an estimated 6,000–10,000 art lovers in the summer, and 1,000–2,000 in the winter.

Seattle Arts & Lectures hosts an annual poetry series and its annual Literary Lecture Series, which has presented numerous literary giants including Stephen King, Frank McCourt, and Margaret Atwood. The quintessential Northwest bookstore, Elliott Bay Books – independent and family-owned since 1973 – offers a noteworthy line-up of speakers, paying equal attention to local and international writers. The store hosts several author events a month.

Theater

Theater has well-established roots in Seattle. From fringe to top-notch traveling shows, the Seattle stage has a devoted audience. The city has a reputation as the Broadway capital of the West Coast, with many Broadway-bound shows making their debuts in Seattle.

Broadway-style shows can be found at the 5th Avenue Theatre, where *Hairspray*, which went on to win eight Tony Awards, and *The Wedding Singer* premiered for Seattleites before finding glory in New York. The Paramount Theatre, in a beautifully restored historic building, draws large crowds for award-winning shows and traveling companies and performers, as well as top names in music and comedy. Another historic Seattle theater, the Moore Theatre (1907) hosts a rotating line-up of everything from off-Broadway shows to stand-up comics.

Professional performances can also be found in the more intimate settings of smaller theaters. Intiman Theatre, Book-It, and Seattle Shakespeare Company, all at the Seattle Center, specialize respectively in revivals, adaptations of classic literature, and productions of the Bard. But don't expect lowbrow performances at these smaller venues. Intiman Theatre premiered *A Light in the Piazza*, which later garnered numerous Tony Awards in New York and toured the country.

One of America's premier non-profit resident theatres, Seattle Repertory Theatre is an internationally recognized, Tony Award-winning regional theater. The Rep produces high-caliber shows on two different stages, the Bagley Wright Theatre and Leo K. Theatre.

ACT Theatre is among the largest theaters in Seattle and presents innovative contemporary performances. From annual favorites like *A Christmas Carol* to world premieres that have gone on to New York (like *Scent of the Roses* and *In the Penal Colony*), it's no wonder ACT's subscribers continue coming back for more.

While many fringe and alternative theaters have come and gone, others have found a loyal audience in Seattle's discerning and culturally inclined crowd.

Many book stores host readings and other events.

Fresh fish at Pike Place Market.

SALMON AND SIMPLE INGREDIENTS

With one of the oldest produce markets in the country and surrounded by nature that provides everything from fresh fish to fabulous fruits, it's no wonder Seattle's chefs are winning accolades.

olumnist Frank Bruni said of Seattle in *The New York Times* 'To eat in and around Seattle, which I did recently and heartily recommend, isn't merely to eat well. It is to experience something that even many larger, more gastronomically celebrated cities and regions can't offer, not to this degree: a profound and exhilarating sense of place.' Seattleites' connection to their food – from locavore restaurants to residents hosting chickens, bees, and goats in their own backyards – is a byproduct of living in an urban landscape nearly choking with nature. The city's outdoorsy population has sailed through the waters where their fish are netted, played on the beaches where their clams are dug, and hiked through the woods where their mushrooms are foraged. Pacific Northwest cuisine isn't so easily replicated outside the region – with a fresh

Many Seattle restaurateurs try to provide locally sourced, sustainable ingredients, and it's quite common for menus to state the origin of fish, meat, poultry, and even eggs and cheeses.

and local focus and Pacific Rim influences, this fusion food relies primarily on incomparable ingredients handled with care.

Local bounty

Before the 1980s, Seattle's restaurant scene was dominated by upscale chophouses and seafood palaces, family restaurants, and a few Japanese

Creative use of salmon.

and Chinese places. The city also had elegant Scandinavian restaurants such as King Oscar's and the Norselander (which described itself as 'matched only by restaurants in European travel capitals'). The spirit of northern Europe does live on, however, in the Ballard neighborhood, where there are Scandinavian food shops and an annual seafood festival, as well as one of Seattle's best farmers' markets (Sundays). The spirit of upscale chophouses prevails, too, in the form of Canlis, which opened in 1950 and is respected for its excellent service (including valets who remember you by face), beautifully prepared dishes, and

Prized Dungeness crab for sale at Pike Place Market.

wonderful water views – if not necessarily groundbreaking food.

Nowadays, Seattle has no dearth of chefs who know their way around the local bounty. One of the best is Jerry Traunfeld; after a decade of creating legendary dinners at The Herbfarm restaurant in Woodinville, he brought his talents to Capitol Hill's Poppy, a stylish neighborhood restaurant serving local and seasonal cuisine on a platter of small dishes inspired by the *thali*. In the Madison Valley, Thierry Rautureau (the 'Chef in the Hat') prepares French food for a loyal clientele at Loulay Kitchen & Bar; Maria Hines delivers local, organic delights at her three ingredient-focused restaurants; and Downtown, Nathan Uy creates memorable Asian dishes at Wild Ginger. Stuart Lane, of Capitol Hill's Spinasse, delivers sublime nose-to-tail bounty and the best fresh pasta in town, while Ethan Stowell, whose Anchovies & Olives and How to Cook a Wolf serve Italian-inspired seafood and pasta dishes, wows with fresh Northwest ingredients. Jason McClure , of Matt's in the Market, couldn't find much fresher ingredients given the location in Pike Place Market; the menu is inspired by what's fresh and available each day. All this may not add up to a 'local cuisine' – but no one is complaining.

Fish on ice at the market.

A fresh vegetable produce vendor.

Seattle's favorite fish

Seattle and salmon are near-synonyms. In the world's mind, Seattleites probably eat smoked salmon hash for breakfast, a blackened salmon sandwich for lunch, and grilled king salmon for dinner. This would not be a bad way to spend the day, but here's the dirty secret: Washington salmon populations are listed under the Endangered Species Act, and nearly all the salmon consumed in Seattle is from Alaska – or farmed from who knows where, the same stuff available in supermarkets nationwide.

Wild Alaskan salmon is worth the search and the price. (The run lasts from May through late fall, so if you see 'fresh' wild salmon for sale in the dead of winter, it was probably frozen while fresh and now defrosted, or mislabeled.) Five species of salmon are pulled from Pacific waters, but they are rechristened seemingly every season with an array of marketing names. Luckily, the two best species, sockeye and king, are always called sockeye and king. The others (coho, pink, and chum) may be sold under names such as

keta, silver, and 'SilverBrite.' If these are fresh and well-treated, they can be very good, but most of the lesser species end up smoked or in cans.

Like steak, salmon is best medium rare, and better restaurants serve it this way. Don't skip the skin: crispy salmon skin is the most delicious of all fish skin.

More offerings from the sea

Other Northwest fish of note include Columbia River sturgeon, Alaskan halibut, and black cod. The latter is often marinated in *kasu* (a sweet byproduct of sake production) and grilled, a preparation that originated in Seattle and is still rarely found elsewhere.

Oysters are another specialty, with many species farmed locally. Unlike salmon, oyster farming is ecologically benign. Two of the best local varieties are Totten Virginicas, which *The New York Times* called 'the best oysters in the world', and Olympias, a tiny oyster with a distinct cucumber flavor. Try them (preferably in a month with an 'r' in its name) at Emmett

Watson's Oyster Bar in Pike Place Market, or The Walrus and the Carpenter in Ballard.

With so much seafood to go around, it's no surprise that sushi is a major obsession. Downtown, Shiro's is masterminded by a serious artisan, while excellent sushi bars can be found in many neighborhoods, including Nishino in Madison Park and the phenomenal Mashiko in West Seattle, which serves only sustainably harvested fish.

Pike Place Market

Like the 'festival markets' that have sprung up in other cities, Pike Place Market is a tourist haven, and you won't be disappointed if you go there seeking postcards and knickknacks. Unlike other markets, however, Pike Place is over 100 years old and still serves mainly local customers. Saved from the urban-renewal wrecking ball in 1972, it's the oldest continuously operating produce market in America. (Referring to it as 'Pike's Market,' however, is a sure way to make locals groan.)

With a recent expansion as part of the Waterfront Seattle Program and a new 'MarketFront'

Noodles for sale at Uwajimaya.

You will never struggle to find a quick bite in Seattle.

opened in June 2017, Pike Place Market now incorporates an additional Producers' Hall and 30,000 sq ft (2790 sq meters) of open public space, making it bigger and better than ever.

Where to begin? Pike Place Fish, with its fish-throwing traders, is only one of four fishmongers. Sosio's produce is known for local 'Holy Shit Peaches' in season. Delaurenti Specialty Food and Wine has the best (and most expensive) cheese counter and one of the better meat counters in town.

A block away, you can watch the people at Beecher's Cheese make Flagship cheddar and buy their macaroni and cheese (lauded by MSNBC and _The Washington Post_) – frozen or ready to eat. Bavarian Meats offers every German meat you've heard of – and probably 20 you haven't – and the city's best bacon. Corner Produce is the place for the best fresh fruit and vegetables.

No self-catering facilities? No problem. The market has a variety of restaurants (including a number of good French ones such as Café Campagne and Le Pichet), as well as classic casual and takeout options such as Pike Place Chowder and the Market Grill, where you can, in fact, have a blackened salmon sandwich for lunch.

The Douglas effect

The undisputed king salmon of Seattle dining continues to be Tom Douglas. On the scene since 1984, Douglas' rise corresponds with an explosion in Seattle dining in general. His restaurant portfolio currently stands at 13 (including favorites Dahlia Lounge, Etta's, Serious Pie, and Lola), plus a bakery, and the Bravehorse Tavern in the South Lake Union neighborhood.

He's a talented chef whose freewheeling style incorporates frequent Asian touches, plus whatever influences strike his fancy. Most of his restaurants are within a few blocks of each other, on the edge of Downtown and Belltown.

Pacific winds

Probably the most popular dish in Seattle has nothing to do with local ingredients. It's pad Thai, the spicy noodle stir-fry made in every one of Seattle's hundred-plus Thai restaurants. Even more Vietnamese people than Thai live in Seattle, and upscale Vietnamese in particular is flourishing, both in Little Saigon (around 12th and Jackson) and outside it. Try Green Leaf, Tamarind Tree, and Monsoon.

> Washington wine is constantly winning accolades; Syrah and Riesling are among its successful grapes. For more on wine, see page 166.

Seattle's suburbs have sizable Korean populations. In Federal Way, especially, enormous Korean supermarkets sell dozens of varieties of handmade *kimchi*. But you don't need to leave Seattle for this: Uwajimaya, in the International District, sells ingredients from all over Asia, with a special emphasis on Japan and Hawaii. And the store's food court features every east-Asian cuisine you can think of – plus burgers.

While visitors may not leave with an easy definition of a 'typical Seattle meal', chances are everyone will discover – and love – quintessentially Seattle flavors.

Seafood restaurants line Seattle's waterfront.

The bald eagle is the only eagle unique to North America and, thanks to curbs on pesticides, is now a fairly common sight in Seattle.

NATURE IN THE NORTHWEST

Bald eagles nest in Seward Park and harbor seals follow ferries within sight of Downtown. And true wilderness is only a couple of hours' drive away.

Around Seattle and Puget Sound, nature is never far away. The blaze of foods and produce that bedeck the markets attest to Seattle's coexistence with the natural world. Always in view, the snowcaps and tree lines of the great Cascade Mountains and the verdant foliage covering the region are colorful reminders of the blanket of ancient wilderness within which the city snuggles.

The combination of fresh- and saltwater, marshes, and forested hills gives Seattle abundant bird habitats, right in the city center. Double-crested cormorants are seen from fall to spring, perched with their wings outstretched on buoys or on bridge pilings. Glaucous-winged gulls are regularly spotted in fresh- and saltwater settings. Mallards and coots nest all year round in the freshwater lakes punctuating Seattle, along with great blue herons and pied-billed grebes. Migratory waterfowl as diverse as buffleheads, western grebes, and surf scooters are common in winter.

Seattle's bird life

Two native birds – crows and Canada geese – have thrived so well in this urban environment that they have come to be seen as pests. During the day, crows scavenge for food in shrubbery, garbage cans, around park benches, or even in cars with open windows. At night, they return to communal roosts; the largest is on Foster Island in the Washington Park Arboretum, where up to 10,000 birds congregate.

In the early 1960s, Seattle's goose population was down to about 100, and geese were brought from the Columbia River. Unfortunately, they

Geese on Lake Union, near Gasworks Park.

In 2013, a project to replace Seattle's seawall began. Completion was initially expected in mid-2017, but parts of the project will likely be postponed for at least a year. The new design incorporates textured surfaces and shelves, which marine organisms can colonize, sloping beaches, crevices, and vegetated hiding places for fish – creating a more salmon-friendly shoreline and feeding ground for young fish migrating to the sea.

A male wild sea lion keeps a lookout.

were a non-migratory type, and the abundant grassy fields and a predator-free shoreline formed the perfect habitat. The present population is about 5,000 geese. They have crashed into a jet landing in Renton; set off alarms at the Bangor nuclear submarine base north of the city; and forced the closure of beaches on Lake Washington because of fouling. Attempts to hunt them, roust them with dogs, or return them to eastern Washington have had little effect.

The peregrine falcon has made a spectacular comeback after being endangered – they were not introduced but returned to the area naturally. Peregrines dive at speeds of up to 200mph (320kmh) to feed on pigeons, sparrows, and wrens in the urban corridor; there was once

THE SALMON'S ENDLESS CYCLE

One biologist wrote that salmon 'reduce life to its simplest, most heroic terms'. During its life, a local salmon may travel up to 10,000 miles (16,000km), swimming from a small freshwater stream in the Seattle area to Alaska, and eventually back again, to spawn and die. Other salmon start from 2,000 miles (3,200km) inland up the Columbia and Snake rivers.

Five species of salmon – coho (silver), chum (dog), king, sockeye, and pink – inhabit the waters of the Puget Sound region. Salmon range in size from 3lbs (1.4kg) to more than 100lbs (45kg), and in color from mottled grey with tinges of red to brilliant red.

The salmon's life ends where it began, in its birth stream. Before they die, the salmon release eggs and milt (sperm), which settle into the gravelly streambed. After hatching, the young remain nearby for up to two years before migrating to saltwater, returning to where they were born up to seven years later, to complete the cycle. Overfishing, dams, logging (which allows sediments to wash into streams, smothering the eggs), and suburban sprawl have all driven down the population.

Many of the Puget Sound species are now listed under the Endangered Species Act, preserving the hope that their numbers will rise again.

even a pair of peregrine falcons nesting on the 56th floor of a Downtown office building.

Nesting pairs of bald eagles can be spotted at Seattle's Seward, Discovery, and Green Lake parks. They live in the parks year-round, feeding on fish and waterfowl from the nearby waters, successfully raising their young in this urban environment.

The bald eagle population grows in winter with the arrival of northern migrants. Several hundred eagles descend on the Skagit River valley along Highway 2, about two hours north of Seattle, for the nearly perfect combination of flora and fauna. The river teems with spawned-out and dying salmon, and Douglas firs along the riverbanks offer ideal perches.

Less popular species

'Once seen, never forgotten' could describe the state's only marine bivalve honored in song. The clam's most laudable attribute is also celebrated by the motto of Evergreen State College in Olympia, *Omni Extaris*, which translates as 'let it all hang out'. This is the geoduck (pronounced 'gooey-duck'). Unlike most clams, the

> *Outdoor tables at waterfront restaurants regularly attract flocks of seagulls, cawing and clamoring for scraps. Residents have a love-hate relationship with these marine scavengers.*

geoduck is not contained within its shell. The gray, tubular, wrinkled neck can grow to 3ft (1 meter) in length. Geoducks spend most of their lives buried in the sand, static save for the contraction and extension of their necks.

Described by one ecologist as 'a cruelly destructive pest, if there ever was one', slugs seem to be almost universally detested. Slugs are champion herbivores, using a tongue-like organ, the radula, to rasp plants into edible nuggets. Their vegetable consumption is the root of their unpopularity with gardeners. The Northwest area has 23 species of native slugs, of which the best known is the banana slug; these yellow-green forest dwellers grow to 12 inches (30cm) in length. Like all slugs, they are hermaphroditic, having both male and female organs.

Marine mammals

The most commonly sighted marine mammals are harbor seals, year-round residents of Puget Sound and coastal Washington. The mottled adults can reach more than 6ft (2 meters) in length. In summer, mothers are seen tending young pups. Like most marine mammals, harbor seals are wary of human contact. When surprised by walkers along the beach, they scramble en masse into the water.

Often confused with seals, the Northwest's two sea lion species are distinguished by their ears. California and Steller sea lions both have small, rolled-up earflaps; harbor seals don't. Other differences are apparent underwater. Sea lions employ their broad, flat front flippers to propel themselves, often with show-off acrobatics. Harbor seals scull conservatively with their hind flippers.

Male sea lions grow to more than 6ft (2 meters) long and can weigh 600lbs (270kg). Females are smaller, and usually weigh around 200lbs (90kg). Steller sea lions migrate from

American bittern.

A whale-watching boat tour from Victoria.

A starfish in Puget Sound.

breeding grounds in California and British Columbia and are easily recognized by size alone. Bull males approach 10ft (3 meters) in length and can weigh 2,000lbs (900kg).

Killer whales – or orcas – are a primary consumer of salmon, and their common name is from the hunting ability that makes them the top marine predator. They are efficient hunters and form cooperative groups to kill larger prey, such as gray or baleen whales. Nearly 100 individuals in several pods – extended family units – spend late spring to early autumn in waters around the San Juan Islands. Orcas are the largest of the dolphin family and grow to 25ft (7.5 meters) in length, weighing up to 6 tons (5,500kg). Females typically live for 50 years, while a male's lifespan averages around 25 years. Orcas have a highly evolved social structure and communicate with a repertoire of whoops, whistles, and chirps. Each pod has its own dialect.

Look for the orca's back fin, 5–6ft (1.5–1.8 meters) tall, slicing through the water. The distinctive black-and-white creatures may also be seen breaching the water. The Whale Museum, at Friday Harbor in the San Juans (see page 210), offers whale-watching tours throughout the summer. Gray whales, minke whales, and harbor and Dall's porpoises also make excursions into the waters of Puget Sound.

The harbor porpoise, seen around Puget Sound and the San Juan Islands, is the smallest oceanic cetacean. Unlike the bottlenose dolphin, harbor porpoises are not gregarious. Dall's porpoises can swim at up to 30 knots in front of ships' bows. Pacific white-sided dolphins travel in schools of more than 50 members and turn somersaults up to 20ft (6 meters) in the air.

Gray whales are seen along the ocean coast on their 12,000-mile (19,000km) annual migration. Once endangered with just a few hundred remaining, protection has increased their numbers to 20,000 or more. Distinguishing it from other whales are the 10–14 'knuckles' along the ridge of its 40–50ft (12–15-meter) back.

Douglas firs and flowers

Douglas firs were key in the economic development of Seattle and the Puget Sound area. Within a month of the city's founding, the first boatload of Douglas fir trees was booked for exportation to San Francisco, and they are still the most important timber in the Northwest. Unfortunately, the high value has led to extensive clear-cutting throughout the region.

Only a handful of monumental Douglas firs remain standing in Seattle – in Seward, Carkeek, and Schmitz parks. These reserves pale in comparison to the Northwest's old-growth forests, mostly in the national parks, with some remnants in national forests, and on state lands. Alongside the western red cedar and western hemlock, the fir was the primary conifer of the old-growth ecosystem. Cedars have always been the most important tree for the native peoples, who cut the wood for canoes and houses, and used the bark in clothing.

The common name of the firs honors David Douglas, a Scottish botanist who took the first seeds back to Britain. Douglas introduced more than 200 plants to Britain, describing his namesake tree as 'one of the most striking and truly graceful in Nature'.

Neighborhood namesake

Three neighborhoods in Seattle – Laurelhurst, Magnolia, and Madrona – were all named after one of the area's most beautiful native trees, the madrona, which comes from the same family as the laurel. Captain George Davidson, of the US Coast Survey, named Magnolia in 1856, thinking he saw magnolias on the bluffs. A better botanist would have recognized the distinctive red-barked madrona trees, which produce white flowers in the spring and orange fruit in late summer.

Rhododendrons are a common relative of the madrona. In the Cascade foothills, they favor the shady understory of Douglas firs and western hemlocks. Native varieties produce spectacular pink blooms in spring and, along with azaleas, add color to yards, parks, and gardens around Puget Sound. The western rhododendron became the Washington state flower in 1892.

The Northwest has a reputation for edible, juicy berries of all kinds, including several varieties of huckleberry, blueberries, strawberries, blackberries, squashberries, snowberries, salmonberries, thimbleberries, dewberries, cranberries, and elderberries. But berry-loving hikers might have to compete for their fruit with bears, who may live on little else during late summer, when the berries are at their ripest.

Evergreen tree by Puget Sound.

The dramatic interior of the Seattle Public Library.

Posters plaster a wall in Pike Place.

Snowshoers in front of mammoth Mount Rainier.

INTRODUCTION

A detailed guide to Seattle and its surroundings, with the principal sights numbered and clearly cross-referenced to the maps.

The city's distinct neighborhoods beckon exploration. Pioneer Square has been beautifully preserved as a National Historic District. Brick-and-stone buildings, cobblestone plazas, and preserved gallery spaces transport you back in time. The International District (ID) is a bustling community of Asian restaurants, stores, and businesses. Streetlamps are decorated with dragons, and Asian architectural touches are evident on many buildings. Downtown has many features typical of American cities – towering skyscrapers abuzz with commerce, upscale shopping and dining, splendid theaters – but also the one-of-a-kind Pike Place Market. Follow the Space Needle to the Seattle Center, which was created for the 1962 World's Fair and continues to be a favorite recreational and civic gathering place. But spreading out

View from Kerry Park.

from the central core are many other diverse neighborhoods, such as Capitol Hill, Ballard, the University District, and West Seattle, where visitors can get away from the crowds and soak up the local atmosphere over a cup of coffee.

Chihuly Garden and Glass display.

Seattle lies at the center of a large metropolitan area of nearly 3.8 million residents, stretching along Interstate 5 from Everett in the north to the state capital Olympia in the south, and from the bucolic Puget Sound islands of Vashon and Bainbridge in the west to the eastside conurbation of Bellevue, Kirkland, and Redmond on the eastern shores of Lake Washington. Surrounded by snowcapped mountains and sparkling waters, the Greater Seattle Area offers plenty of museums and galleries, wine-tasting adventures, antiques shopping, picturesque historic centers, and many more attractions that visitors can explore in easy day trips.

For nature-lovers, there are abundant opportunities to explore the beautiful islands of Puget Sound, a temperate rain forest on the Olympic Peninsula to the west, and volcanoes in the Cascade Mountains to the east.

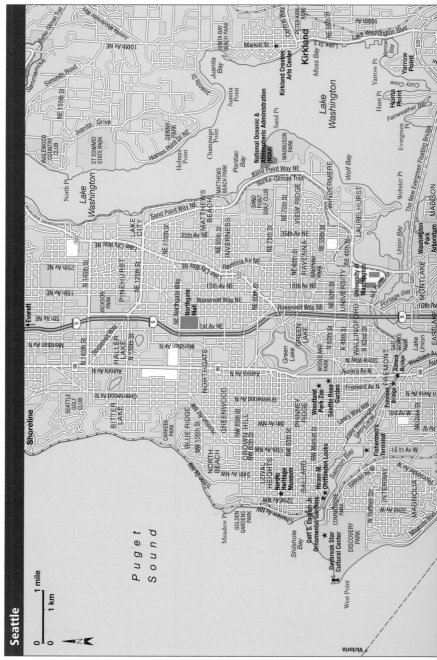

Seattle

0   1 mile

0   1 km

N

Puget Sound

West Point

Shilshole Bay

Meadow Pt

GOLDEN GARDENS PARK

Daybreak Star Cultural Center

Carl S. English Jr. Ornamental Gardens

COMMODORE PARK

DISCOVERY PARK

Nordic Heritage Museum

Hiram M. Chittenden Locks

Fishermen's Terminal

Salmon Bay

INTERBAY

MAGNOLIA

Magnolia Blvd

W Armour St

W Emerson St

W Dravus St

Smith Cove

3rd Av W

15 th Av W

Gilman Av W

LOYAL HEIGHTS

NORTH BEACH

BLUE RIDGE

CROWN HILL

BALLARD

CARKEEK PARK

NW 105th St

NW 85th St

NW 80th St

NW 65th St

NW Market St

NW 45th St

Shoreline

Shilshole Av NW

Seaview Av NW

32nd Av NW

24th Av NW

15th Av NW

8th Av NW

Holman Rd NW

Victoria

Lake Washington

North Pt

ST EDWARD STATE PARK

Holmes Point Dr NE

Holmes Point

DENNY PARK

INGLEWOOD COUNTRY CLUB

Juanita Drive

Juanita Dr

Juanita Point

Juanita Bay

JUANITA BAY BEACH PARK

Market St

Kirkland Creative Arts Center

Kirkland

Central Way

PETER KIRK PARK

Central Way

108th Av NE

Lake Washington Blvd

520

NE 68th St

NE 85th St

Moss Bay

Sand Pt

Lake Washington

WINDERMERE

LAURELHURST

Webster Pt

Yarrow Bay

Yarrow Pt

Yarrow Point

Hunt Pt

Cozy Cove

Hunts Point

Fairweather Bay

Evergreen Pt

Fairweather Bay

The New Evergreen Floating Bridge

520

Union Bay

Washington Park Arboretum

MADISON

MONTLAKE

Portage Bay

Portage Pt

Lake Union

NE 45th St

University of Washington

UNIVERSITY

5

10th Av E

Eastlake Av E

Westlake Av N

N 45th St

Stone Way N

WALLINGFORD

Aurora Av N

FREMONT

Aurora Bridge

Fremont Bridge

GAS WORKS PARK

N 42nd St

Fremont Av N

Westlake Av N

McGraw St

W McGraw St

Queen Anne Av N

1st Av N

99

National Oceanic & Atmospheric Administration (NOAA)

Sand Point Way NE

MAGNUSON PARK

Pontiac Bay

Champaign Point

Juanita Bay

Sand Point

MATTHEWS BEACH PARK

MATTHEWS BEACH

SAND POINT GOLF CLUB

Burke-Gilman Trail

VIEW RIDGE

INVERNESS

35th Av NE

35th Av NE

NE 70th St

NE 75th St

NE 65th St

NE 60th St

NE 55th St

NE 50th St

RAVENNA PARK

RAVENNA

5th Av NE

15th Av NE

Roosevelt Way NE

Ravenna Av NE

LAKE CITY

Lake City Way NE

NE 115th St

NE 125th St

NE 145th St

NE 155th St

PINEHURST

JACKSON PARK

NORTHGATE

Northgate Mall

NE Northgate Way

1st Av NE

5th Av NE

Roosevelt Way NE

15th Av NE

25th Av NE

Lake City Way NE

GREEN LAKE

Green Lake

WOODLAND PARK

Woodland Park Zoo

Seattle Rose Garden

Leary Way NW

PHINNEY RIDGE

GREENWOOD

Greenwood Av N

N 85th St

N 65th St

N 46th St

Phinney Av N

Fremont Av N

Aurora Av N

99

522

Burke-Gilman Trail

Sand Point Way NE

HALLER LAKE

BITTER LAKE

SEATTLE GOLF CLUB

N 145th St

N 130th St

Aurora Av N

Greenwood Av N

Meridian Av N

Roosevelt Way N

Linden Av N

5

Meridian Av N

Aurora Av N

N Northgate Way

5

5th Av NE

15th Av NE

25th Av NE

Everett

Sammamish

Burke-Gilman Trail

Juanita-Woodinville Way

100th Av NE

Simonds Road

Sammamish Road

NE 155th St

522

Historic Pioneer Square.

where Seattle begins

PIONEER
SQUARE

PIONEER SQUARE AND THE INTERNATIONAL DISTRICT

The oldest part of Seattle has a distinctive architectural style and fascinating history, tall totem poles, and some fine museums and galleries.

Modern Seattle was established in 1852 when Arthur and David Denny, along with other pioneers, moved up from Alki Point, on which they had first landed only a few months earlier. They named their home after a Native American – Chief Sealth (or Seattle) – of the Duwamish and Suquamish tribes, who was among the settlement's first visitors.

The businessmen who came later were less respectful to the locals. A group representing the Seattle Chamber of Commerce visited Alaska's Fort Tongass in 1899 and stole a tribal totem pole while the men of the village were out on a fishing expedition. For nearly 40 years this totem stood at 1st Avenue and Yesler Way until it was set on fire by an arsonist. Shamelessly, the city asked for a replacement. An unsubstantiated but amusing story follows: when the tribe said it would cost $5,000, the city sent a check. The reply came back: thanks for finally paying for the first one – and the second one will cost another $5,000. The city duly paid up.

PIONEER SQUARE ❶

The 60ft (18-meter) replacement totem pole today stands on a brick

plaza where 1st, James, and Yesler intersect in front of the Pioneer Building. This plaza is commonly known as **Pioneer Square**, although the name actually refers to the entire 20-square-block neighborhood, which is now a designated historical park. The official name of this popular triangular park is Pioneer Park Place.

As well as being low-rise and walkable, Pioneer Square is a great place for gallery-hopping. In a few funky old bars and restaurants, music can

Main Attractions
Pioneer Square
Waterfall Garden Park
Klondike Gold Rush
    National Historical Park
Smith Tower and
    Observatory
Wing Luke Museum of the
    Asian Pacific American
    Experience
Uwajimaya
Frye Art Museum

Map
Page 86

The Pioneer Square pergola.

*Pioneer Square's pergola
is a local landmark.*

be heard many nights of the week, from rock to blues and jazz. Be aware that Seattle's homeless problem is especially apparent in Pioneer Square, and nightlife can be seedy and rowdy.

Pioneer Square became the center for the settlers when they left Alki Point for the superior harbor at Elliott Bay. The **totem pole** is near to James A. Wehn's **bust of Chief Sealth**. Wehn arrived in Seattle soon after the 1889 fire and remained in the city until he died in 1953. He also designed the city's seal, which bears Chief Sealth's profile. When Chief Sealth died in 1866, he was buried on the Kitsap Peninsula, northwest of Seattle overlooking Puget Sound.

Historic buildings

At 1st Avenue and Yesler Way, the street is still surfaced with the original cobblestones. Pioneer Park Place has long been dominated by a **Victorian iron-and-glass pergola**

built in 1905 and which once sheltered the patrons of the 1.3-mile (2.1km) cable-car route which, until 1940, ran between Yesler and Lake Union, north of Downtown. The pergola was destroyed by a truck in 2001, but was so popular that a new cast-and wrought-iron one – with a safer and stronger steel structure – was unveiled 19 months later. Opposite is the **Merchant's Cafe** (http://merchants cafeandsaloon.com), the city's oldest restaurant, which in Gold Rush times served 5-cent beers to miners as they waited for their turn in the brothel upstairs. Seattle's Great Fire of 1889 (see page 35) wiped out almost all of the bar's neighbors in the Pioneer Square area.

Architect Elmer Fisher, who was responsible for at least 50 of the new structures, set the dominant style. A characteristic example of his work is the elegant **Pioneer Building** ❷ (600 1st Avenue) on the plaza. Its tenants included several dozen

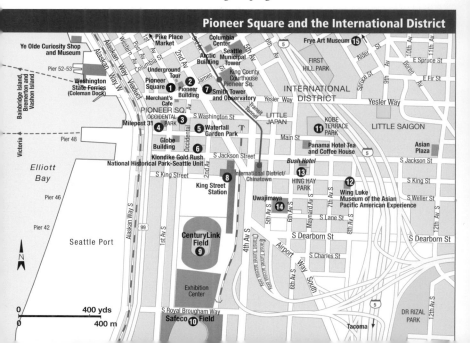

The Tlingit totem pole.

mining companies above a saloon, which was once operated by Dr 'Doc' David Swinson Maynard, who was among the area's first and pre-eminent settlers.

Underground Seattle

Doc Maynard's former saloon is now the starting point of the popular **Bill Speidel's Underground Tour** (608 1st Avenue; tel: 206-682 4646; www.undergroundtour.com; daily 9am–7pm), an inspection of the shops and rooms that were abandoned when this part of town was rebuilt. To eliminate what had been persistent flooding, some of the buildings were raised by as much as 18ft (5 meters) and the remaining subterranean city was sealed off, until Bill Speidel, an enterprising newspaper columnist, began conducting tours. The tour takes in a warren of the musty, debris-lined passageways and rooms that had been at ground level. Passing under the glass-paneled sidewalk at 1st and Yesler, the tour

ends at the **Rogue's Gallery**, where old photos, magazines, artifacts, and scale models depict the area as it was before the fire, when Yesler Way was three times as steep as it is today. On sale are books written by Bill Speidel.

Some of the guides in charge of the Underground Tour provide a refreshingly irreverent journey through Seattle's history. 'Henry Yesler had no moral or ethical values whatsoever,' one guide announced. 'Naturally he became our first mayor.' On another occasion the guide said, 'That's the true Seattle spirit – even if it's a lousy deal, we'll stick with it.'

Occidental Park ❸

Occidental Avenue gives way to a brick pedestrian mall-park between South Washington and Jackson streets. Enticing aromas drift out of the Grand Central Arcade into **Occidental Park** . The park boasts bocce (similar to *boules*) courts, chess tables, and **four cedar totem**

Entering the Underground Tour.

Occidental Square.

poles. The totems were carved over a 10-year period by Duane Pasco, a Washington State master carver with an international reputation, and are positioned following the tradition of having their faces to the sea and hollowed backs to the forest, though the forest is now the skyscrapers of the city. The tallest totem in Occidental Park – *Sun and Raven* – depicts the Raven bringing light to the world. Farther down the 35ft (11-meter) pole is the Chief of the Sky's daughter giving birth to the Raven, and the Chief himself holding the sun in his hands, and the box that holds 'light'.

The second totem, *Tsonoqua*, is a human figure with outstretched arms; the other two totems are *Bear* and *Man Riding on Tail of Whale*.

Also in Occidental Park is a memorial to Seattle firefighters who have died in the line of duty since 1889, when the city's Fire Department was formed after the Great Fire. The bronzed sculpture features four life-size firefighters in action.

Skid Row

In 1889, when the Great Fire destroyed hundreds of buildings, it burned deep into the commercial heart of the city. t was here, in 1853, that Doc Maynard and other settlers had donated land to Seattle's very first industry: a steam-powered lumbermill built by German-born Henry Yesler (see page 32). The sawmill was installed at the top of what is now **Yesler Way** – originally known as Skid Road, the steep ramp down which the lumber was slid to the sawmill. In Yesler's day, the mill ran day and night, employing almost half the city's working population.

According to Arthur Denny's account, Doc Maynard showed up drunk for a meeting to plan the street grid of Pioneer Square. Maynard insisted on orienting his streets to the compass points, but Denny and Carson Boren disagreed, which explains the strange turns at Yesler.

After World War II, Skid Road was a wasteland of cheap hotels and seedy activity. For at least a couple of generations, intersecting 1st Avenue was renowned for low-rent stores, prostitutes, X-rated bookstores, and taverns.

In the 1960s, artists began to establish studios in the low-rent lofts. Prevented from rebuilding by the city's rejection of wholesale urban renewal, property owners remodeled building interiors in wood and brass, setting the tone for the gentrification and regeneration that would follow later. Nowadays, despite the preserved historic character of the neighborhood and the many galleries and eateries, Pioneer Square retains its rough-and-tumble edge.

For those who want to know more about the history and geography of Pioneer Square, **Milepost 31 ❹** (211 1st Avenue; www.wsdot.wa.gov/Projects/Viaduct/Milepost31; Tue–Sat 11am–5pm; free) is an award-winning information center with artifacts and interactive exhibits exploring the neighbourhood.

The nearby, enclosed **Waterfall Garden Park ❺** (corner of South Main Street and 2nd Avenue South) is a charming miniature park, and a great place for a picnic. It was built in gratitude to the employees of the United Parcel Service (UPS), founded in Seattle in 1907 by 19-year old local

resident James Casey. The park's tables are set around flowers and trees in front of a glorious waterfall designed by Masao Kinoshita, which drops 22ft (6.7 meters) onto huge boulders and recycles 5,000 gallons (20,000 liters) of water every minute.

Klondike Gold Rush National Historical Park – Seattle Unit ❻

Address: 319 2nd Ave S; www.nps.gov/klse
Tel: 206-220 4240
Opening Hrs: daily 10am–5pm
Entrance Fee: free
Transportation: bus 62, 99

One block south, on the corner of Jackson and 2nd Avenue, is this fascinating museum with exhibits and photographs recounting the saga of the hectic 1890s, when half of Seattle caught Gold Rush fever.

Thousands, including the mayor, left jobs and homes to follow the call of gold. The rigorous journey 1,500 miles (2,400km) north to Alaska started with the steamship from Seattle to Skagway, and then continued onward by foot, over forbidding mountains and up treacherous

The Sun and Raven totem pole in Occidental Park.

Tourists inside Klondike Gold Rush National Historical Park.

Smith Tower

Though now dwarfed by modern skyscrapers, when L.C. Smith's tower was completed in downtown Seattle in 1914, it was touted as the tallest building in the West.

Picture postcards depicting the 500ft (150-meter) structure claimed that from 'the world-famous catwalk surrounding the Chinese temple may be seen mountain ranges 380 miles (600km) in the distance'. Well, not quite. The mountain ranges in view – the Olympics and the Cascades – are about 60 miles (100km) away. But 4,400 people flocked to the opening anyway, paying 25 cents each to speed past local government agency offices and to admire the view from the observation deck.

'A work of art worthy of the builders of the awe-inspiring cathedrals of the Middle Ages,' boasted the tower's historian, Arthur F. Wakefield, who revealed that New York's American Bridge Company had taken 20 weeks to make the building's steel, transported cross-country from their Pittsburgh, Pennsylvania, plant in 164 railcars.

Smith spared no expense. The $1.5 million building's 600 rooms had steel doors, teak ceilings, walls of Alaskan white marble or tinted Mexican onyx, elevator doors of glass and bronze and, on the 35th floor, an expensive Chinese Room decorated with bronze lanterns, oriental furniture, and 776 semi-porcelain discs. A throne-like Chinese chair, reputed to have been a gift from the Empress of China, was actually obtained from a waterfront curio shop but did spawn its own legend. One year after Smith's daughter posed sitting in the chair, she got married, convincing other would-be brides that to sit in the 'Wishing Chair' would bring them a husband.

Unusual visitors

One year after the tower's opening, some of the office tenants saw a one-armed parachutist floating down past their windows, and a year or two later watched Harry – The Human Fly – scale the building. 'I gave him a little help by hanging ropes over the cornices,' recalled William K. Jackson, just before his retirement as building superintendent in 1944. Jackson, then 72, had worked in the tower since it opened, during which time Seattle had changed from 'a friendly, clean little city to a town of strangers going so fast you can feel the tempo of wartime even in your own building'.

Stunts at the tower abounded. In 1938, two high-school students ran upstairs to the 36th floor in less than 10 minutes (and down again in four); four years later, a proud grandfather announced his new domestic status by running up a flag on the flagpole reading, 'It's a girl'.

The Smith Tower was bought in 1985 by a San Francisco firm, who remodeled it retaining the original (1914) copper, brass, and glass elevators. In 2015, the building changed hands again. Unico Properties LLC purchased the tower, converting it into a first-class tourist attraction.

Smith Tower under construction in 1913.

rivers. Few of the spur-of-the-moment adventurers struck it rich, however, since most of the valuable claims had already been staked long before the newcomers' arrival.

Many of those who stayed behind in Seattle did better. To ensure that prospectors could withstand the northern wastes, Canadian authorities insisted that they brought with them a year's supply of goods and provisions (400lbs/180kg of flour and 25 cans of butter, for example), and many of the city's early merchants did very brisk trade.

Smith Tower and Observatory ❼

Address: 506 2nd Avenue;
www.smithtower.com
Tel: 206-622 4004
Opening Hrs: Sun–Wed 10am–10pm (bar until 11pm), Thu–Sat 10am–11pm (bar until midnight)
Entrance Fee: charge
Transportation: bus 1, 2, 7, 14, 17, 18, 29 or 99

At the end of the 19th century, an inventor named Lyman Cornelius Smith arrived in Seattle. Already

wealthy from the sale of his gun company (later Smith & Wesson) and then his revolutionary new typewriter (later to be Smith Corona), Smith promptly bought several blocks around Main Street and 1st Avenue.

In 1901, he built the L.C. Smith Building. Goaded by the plans of a business rival, he then plotted the 42-story **Smith Tower**. When it was completed in 1914, this was the tallest building outside New York. The distinction was gradually diluted until, in 1962, its last remaining title – that of the tallest building in Seattle – was taken by the Space Needle.

Smith Tower remains a sentimental favorite, especially after a recent revamp. The 35th-floor **Observatory** offers sweeping views of the city from an open-air deck, as well as a speakeasy-inspired bar with a local menu and craft cocktails. You can also visit the Legends of Smith Tower exhibits (additional charge), which tell the story of Seattle and its tower, including how the city dealt with Prohibition and the impacts of accelerating technologies.

There are some other fine structures in Pioneer Square, but few are

Smith Tower as it appears today.

The Arctic Building (1916) at 206 Cherry Street was constructed to house a social club for people who had struck it rich in the Klondike Gold Rush.

more striking and noteworthy than the **Arctic Building** (3rd Avenue and Cherry Street), with its row of sculpted walruses adorning the upper levels. Believing the original terra-cotta tusks to be a potential danger to pedestrians walking below, the building's owners removed them some years ago and replaced them with epoxy versions. The building now houses a hotel.

Stations and stadiums

In 2008, handsome **King Street Station ❽** (2nd Avenue and King Street) was bought by the city of Seattle for a symbolic $10 and subject to a $50-million restoration, completed in 2013. The drop ceiling – with dreary panels and fluorescent lighting – was removed to reveal beautiful original plasterwork. Architecture enthusiasts and other observant visitors will spot the tower's resemblance to St Mark's campanile in Venice, after which it was modeled. It is the departure point for the fabulous 3.5-hour journey to Vancouver, British Columbia, where the train hugs the coastline most of the way. Much of the terrain around the station and Safeco Field is reclaimed land from what was once the bay. As much as 60-million cubic feet (1.7-million cubic meters) of earth was used for landfill and to raise the level of the city.

White, curvy **CenturyLink Field ❾** (formerly Qwest Field; corner of S King Street and Occidental Avenue; tel: 206-381 7582; www.centurylink field.com/tour-centurylink-field) is the home of the city's football team, the Seahawks. Ninety-minute tours of the state-of-the-art field take place three times a day (10.30am, 12.30pm and 2.30pm) from June to September, and on weekends from October to May.

For 22 years before CenturyLink and Safeco fields were built, the creaky and gloomy Kingdome on the same site was Seattle's sports venue, a skyline landmark since 1976. The Kingdome was demolished the year after **Safeco Field ❿** (corner of 1st Avenue S and Edgar Martinez Drive; tel: 206-346 4241; http://seattle.mariners.mlb.com/sea/ballpark), home to the Mariners baseball team, hosted its first baseball game. It is a retractable-roofed stadium, which opened at a final cost of just over half a billion dollars in 1999. With views of Puget Sound, cedar-lined dugouts, picnic areas, and a real field of Kentucky bluegrass and ryegrass, Safeco became one of baseball's most expensive stadium projects.

THE INTERNATIONAL DISTRICT

Known for more than a century as the city's Chinatown (Chinese were among the earliest residents), the **International District** has grown both geographically and culturally to include residents representing numerous Asian groups, especially Chinese, Japanese, Vietnamese, Filipino, Korean, and Southeast Asian. A branch of the Seattle Streetcar (opened in 2016) operates through the International District, connecting it to the First Hill and Capitol Hill neighborhoods, making this diverse area easily accessible.

In 1871, a man named Wa Chong built the third brick structure in the

Beautifully renovated King Street Station.

Safeco Field baseball stadium.

city and was also responsible for the first building to go up after the 1889 fire. The Wa Chong Tea Store, at the corner of Washington and 3rd Avenue, advertised in 1877 that contractors, mill owners, and others requiring Chinese labor 'will be furnished at short notice'. And, as an afterthought, the store offered 'the highest price paid for live hogs'. A front-page announcement in that same paper by Tong Wa Shing & Co., dealers in Chinese Fancy Goods, offered Asian specialties including tea, rice, and opium.

Japan Town

The area around **Kobe Terrace Park** ⑪ (221 6th Avenue South), at the top of the hill to the northern edge of the International District, is what began as Nihon-machi, or **Japan Town**.

This area lost most of its population to the US Government's internment policies of World War II, when Japanese-Americans were removed to camps in Idaho or eastern Washington. Presidential Order 9066, forcibly relocating Japanese-Americans on the mainland (most in Hawaii were left alone) to these internment camps, was signed by President Franklin D. Roosevelt in February of 1942. It was revoked in December of 1944. Of the Japanese interned during that period, about 7,000 were Seattle residents.

This area was later decimated by the construction of the Interstate 5 freeway. Kobe Terrace Park offers a panoramic view of Pioneer Square and Elliott Bay beyond. There's also a stone lantern donated by Seattle's sister city of Kobe, Japan.

Just outside the southwestern end of the park is the **Panama Hotel Tea and Coffee House** (605 South Main Street; tel: 206-223 9242). This building, where rooms are still rented out to travelers, dates from 1910 and served as a meeting place for generations of immigrants.

During World War II, the residents of the hotel stashed belongings in the basement before going to the internment camps. These unreclaimed relics are displayed in the hotel's café, and in the basement. Tours are also available of the old Japan Town bathhouse (by appointment), which is preserved at the base of the hotel.

Chinatown

By the turn of the 20th century, Seattle's **Chinatown** had become a city within the city, riddled with

At CenturyLink Field.

*The International
District's Chinese arc.*

secret passages and tunnels. Few white faces were seen, except for furtive opium smokers. Violent *tong* or gang wars were fairly common features. A 1902 story in the *Seattle Post-Intelligencer* described well-guarded Chinese gambling houses from which whites were barred.

But long before World War II, the community began to stabilize, largely under the influence of civic bodies like the Chung Wa Association, of which all prominent Chinese were members. The riotous and notorious gambling dens, though, survived until at least 1942.

Wing Luke Museum of the Asian Pacific American Experience ⑫
Address: 719 South King Street; www.wingluke.org
Tel: 206-623 5124
Opening Hrs: Tue–Sun 10am–5pm, first Thu of the month until 8pm
Entrance Fee: charge
Transportation: bus 7, 14, or 36
Named after the first Asian-American official elected in the Northwest, who joined Seattle's city council in 1962, this museum is in the historic East Kong Yick Building. Affiliated to the Smithsonian Museum, it focuses on the Asian Pacific American experience: its permanent collection includes historical photographs and artifacts

such as a 50ft (15-meter) dragon boat, used for festival races in China, and a mock-up of a Chinese apothecary. The museum also offers themed walking tours around the neighborhood, including Bruce Lee's Chinatown (advanced booking required). As a young Chinese immigrant, Bruce Lee washed dishes in Chinatown to pay the rent while he developed his street-fighting skills. The martial-arts star is buried in Capitol Hill (see page 125).

Chinatown highlights
Hing Hay Park ⑬ (423 Maynard Avenue South) has an ornamental arch dating from 1973 and designed in Taiwan by architect David Lin. The dragon mural is a larger-than-life depiction of local Asian events. The park is also the setting for occasional martial-arts exhibitions and Chinese folk dancing, and even a little early-morning t'ai chi. In 2017, it underwent a $3-million extension and renovation, which included the installation of colorful seats and steps.

A common sight in stores around here are rows of jars displaying herbs, flowers, and roots – peony, honeysuckle, chrysanthemum, ginger, ginseng, and especially licorice, which have been used for centuries to build strength and 'balance the body's energy'.

Brightly colored figures from legends cover the wall of the **Washington Federal bank** (6th and Jackson Street). A block away, at the corner of 6th and Weller, is the large department store **Uwajimaya** ⑭ (600 5th Avenue South; tel: 206-624 6248; www.uwajimaya.com), which stocks everything from cookware to fruit and exotic vegetables. The food court is a truly international district. Cuisines from Korea, Vietnam, China, Japan, and more are on offer, as well as desserts like ice cream and strange Bubble Tea.

Little Saigon
East of the freeway, the streets around the Japanese-owned Asian

TIP

When you're in Chinatown, take the chance to sample Bubble Tea. This 'smoothie' comes in a range of fruit flavors, and is characterized by the giant tapioca balls at the bottom of the cup. It's an acquired taste that is growing in popularity.

Plaza shopping mall at Jackson and 12th are sometimes known as **Little Saigon**, where many of the hundreds of Vietnamese-owned businesses in Seattle operate. Unlike the center of Chinatown, which houses mostly restaurants, gift shops, and just a few food shops, Little Saigon consists mainly of large grocery stores, jewelry shops, and just a few dining establishments. The district is still expanding to the north.

FIRST HILL

Several blocks northeast of the International District is the **First Hill** neighborhood, which is home to large hospitals and many health-care workers, giving it the nickname 'Pill Hill.' Sandwiched between Downtown and Capitol Hill, on some very steep streets, it is also home to St James Cathedral (804 9th Avenue). The main reason to come here is the wonderful Frye Art Museum.

Frye Art Museum ⑮

Address: 704 Terry Avenue; www.fryemuseum.org
Tel: 206-622 9250
Opening Hrs: Tue–Wed and Fri–Sun

11am–5pm, Thu 11am–7pm
Entrance Fee: free
Transportation: bus 3, 4, or 12

This First Hill Museum hosts frequently changing exhibits as well as poetry readings, chamber music, and other kinds of performance. The museum first showcased 19th-century German paintings from the late Charles and Emma Frye's collection. Exhibits are more diverse now, and include excellent salon paintings.

Hing Hay Park.

Late-night Chinatown shops.

AN ARTFUL BUS LINE

Seattle's Metro Transit bus company prides itself on its sponsorship of public art. Scores of works are shown in the stations of the transit tunnel, which is used by buses and light-rail trains. Art is chosen specifically for the station in which it is shown. Under Pioneer Square, there's a relic from the cable-car system that ran along Yesler Way: a cast-iron flywheel more than 11ft (3.5 meters) in diameter. There is also contemporary artwork, including a ceramic mural incorporating Indian baskets. The station for the International District has tiles created from designs by local children and an enormous origami work of painted aluminum. The open plaza above is tiled with symbols of the Chinese zodiac.

SHOPPING IN SEATTLE

Everything from couture to high-tech outdoor gear can be found in the birthplace of Nordstrom and REI.

Display at Glasshouse Studio in Pioneer Square, where artisans sell their wares.

The Emerald City is a wear-whatever-you-want kind of place. Its climate and outdoor life contributed to the success of Eddie Bauer, REI (www.rei.com), the North Face, and Patagonia, and many Seattle traditionalists look as if they've just stepped out of one of these sporty shops. But there's plenty more on offer, too. High-end boutiques are located in Downtown, especially along 5th Avenue and at Pacific Place Shopping Center, and in Bellevue's chic shopping centers on the Eastside. Here you'll find the likes of Tiffany, Cartier, Louis Vuitton, and Brooks Brothers. For quirky independent stores with interesting offerings, head to Belltown (hip shoe stores, galleries, and clothing boutiques) or Capitol Hill (clothing with attitude). In North Seattle, the University District caters to students with inexpensive clothing, music, and bookstores. Neighboring Wallingford and Fremont provide eclectic offerings, from retro furnishings to harps and hammered dulcimers. Ballard's historic Landmark District invites leisurely shopping, whether for costume jewelry, local clothes, or imported South American knitted hats or printed t-shirts. Outlet malls are also alive and well in Washington, the most prominent being in North Bend (east) and Tulalip (north). Retail realists should note that a 9.6 percent sales tax is added to any purchase price.

REI (Recreational Equipment Inc) sells biking and winter- and water-sports equipment. There is also a 65ft (19.8-meter) free-standing indoor climbing wall on site called The Pinnacle.

Pacific Place Shopping Center is home to 50 stores, as less as several restaurants and even a multi-screen movie theater.

Elliott Bay Book Company – a venerated literary institution with knowledgeable staff, an impressive selection, and big-name author readings.

SEATTLE MARKETS

Fresh veg at Queen Anne Market.

Seattleites love their markets, beginning with the famous Pike Place Market, which has small stalls selling gorgeous and inexpensive flower arrangements and a staggering assortment of the freshest fruit, vegetables, fish, and meats. Also on offer: the most delicious Northwest honey and jam, crafts and jewelry by local artisans, and Seattle-inspired t-shirts, framed pictures, and posters. It gets crowded there, so you're best off arriving early or visiting on weekdays. In addition, many neighborhoods have farmers' markets (www.seattlefarmersmarkets.org) that run from late spring to fall, including Capitol Hill and Columbia City; the University District and Ballard farmers' markets run year-round. These are fun and lively affairs with all the produce brought in by farmers within a four-hour drive of the city. Ready-to-eat food and live entertainment round out the offerings. The Fremont Market is more of a flea market with arts and crafts, clothing, vintage furniture, and food.

Some of the freshest and most interesting varieties of produce, from heirloom tomatoes to shitake mushrooms, tantalize the senses at farmers' markets throughout the city.

DOWNTOWN SEATTLE AND PIKE PLACE MARKET

Seattle's pleasant downtown area has hills, refined architecture, public sculpture, lapping waves, and one of the oldest public markets in the US.

North of Pioneer Square and the International District is Downtown, lined steep with skyscrapers, and unexpectedly pleasant with hills, sculptures, and peek-a-boo views of the sparkling water of Elliott Bay. Urban pioneers have moved in to occupy stylish lofts and apartment buildings, and restaurants, stores, and signature buildings have followed in their wake.

Along Elliott Bay itself, a comprehensive seven-year regeneration project (completion expected in 2020) is transforming the waterfront, adding parks, paths, and improving access routes.

DOWNTOWN

Seattle's tallest building – one of the highest in the West, in fact – is the 76-story **Columbia Center ❶** (701 5th Avenue), which rises 954ft (291 meters) and is served by 46 elevators. In 2015 it was sold to Hong Kong investors, and now offers the public an extraordinary view of the city from the observatory and café on the 73rd floor (www.sky viewobservatory.com; daily 10am–8pm). Below street level at the center are carpeted, picture-lined corridors. One leads to the **Seattle Municipal Tower** (700 5th Avenue) next door, and an attractive mall lined with shops, classy

The market at night.

snack bars, and tables. The Starbucks on the fourth floor is said to serve 500 customers an hour during its morning rush, and claims to be the world's busiest espresso bar, though a number of other Seattle espresso counters must surely be in contention.

Enormous skyscrapers began to rise in downtown Seattle in the 1960s and early 1970s, but the really big boom did not get underway until the following decade. Opinions about the esthetics of these newcomers vary, but the buildings have

Main Attractions
Central Library
Freeway Park
Seattle Art Museum
Pike Place Market
Seattle Aquarium
Belltown
Olympic Sculpture Park

Map
Page 100

Downtown to Seattle Center

Kerry View Point Park
Marketplace at Queen Anne
Roy St
Fremont
SOUTH LAKE UNION PARK
Maritime Heritage Center, Center for Wooden Boats
Valley St
Lake Union Park
Shurgard Building
Roy St

Mercer St
Marion Oliver McCaw Hall
KCTS-TV Studios
Mercer St
Broad St
Westlake & Mercer
Terry & Mercer
Mercer St

Seattle Repertory Theatre
Intiman Theatre
Exhibition Hall
24 Mercer Arena
The Bill and Melinda Gates Foundation
Republican St
CASCADE

Northwest Rooms
International Fountain
Memorial Stadium
22
Seattle Center Armory
23 Seattle Center
Museum of Pop Culture (MoPOP)
Harrison St
KING Studios (NBC)
Westlake & Thomas
Terry & Thomas
CASCADE PLAYGROUND

25 Key Arena
SEATTLE CENTER
Thomas St
Thomas St
Seattle Times Building

Seattle Center Pavilion
Fisher Pavilion
Children's Theatre
Chihuli Garden and Glass Museum
Space Needle
21
John St
John St

Myrtle Edwards Park
20
26
Pacific Science Center
IMAX Theaters
Denny Way
DENNY PARK
DENNY PLAYFIELD
John St

Bay St
Denny Way
Westlake & Denny
Denny Way

OLYMPIC SCULPTURE PARK
19 Pavilion
TILIKUM PLACE
4th Avenue
Westlake & 9th

Seattle Trade Center
Port of Seattle Headquarters
Monorail
18
BELLTOWN (DENNY REGRADE)
King Cat Theatre
Greyhound Bus Terminal
Westlake & 7th
Capitol Hill

Pier 70
REGRADE PARK
IA Theater
Plaza 600 Bldg
1600 Bell Plaza
Paramount Theater

Victoria
Victoria Clipper
Pier 69
Pier 68
Art Institute of Seattle
Cinerama
Westin Hotel
Westlake Hub
Pacific Place
Plaza 600

Pier 67
The Edgewater
Pier 66 (Bell St Pier) **17**
World Trade Center
Securities Building
Westlake Center **8**
Nordstrom
9

Bell Harbor International Conference Center
Moore Theatre
Westlake
Sheraton
Washington State Convention Center **4**

Odyssey Maritime Discovery Center
Bell St Pier
Market Place Tower
Soames Dunn Building
Inn at the Market
Olympic Tower
Century Square
US Bank Centre
7
5th Av Theater
Union Square **6**

Bell Harbor Marina
VICTOR STEINBRUECK PARK
The First Starbucks
Pike Place Market
PIKE PLACE MARKET HISTORIC DIST.
Macy's
Puget Sound Plaza
Rainier Square
FREEWAY PARK **5**

Pier 63
Pier 62
Piers 60&61
WATERFRONT
Benaroya Hall **10**
University St
Courthouse
3

Puget Sound
Seattle Aquarium **16**
Pier 59
WATERFRONT PARK **15**
Four Seasons Hotel
Seattle Art Museum **11**
Russell Investments Center
Central Library
US

Seattle Great Wheel
Gray Line Tours
Pier 57
Harbor Steps
Second & Seneca
2 Safeco Plaza
Seafirst Fifth Av Plaza

Port of Seattle
Pier 56
Pier 55
Bay Pavilion
Waterfront Place
Federal Office Building
Norton Bldg
Columbia Center **1**

Pier 54
Ye Olde Curiosity Shop & Museum **14**
Maritime Building
FINANCIAL DISTRICT
Seattle Municipal Tower

Victoria, Winston & Bremerton
Pier 53
Pier 52
Washington State Ferries (Coleman Dock) **13**
Pier 51
Pioneer Building
Pioneer Sq
Smith Tower

Joshua Green Fountain
Yesler Way
James St
PIONEER SQUARE

N
0 — 500 yds
0 — 500 m

been a boon for sculptures under the city's 'one-percent-for-art' ordinance, which requires that 1 percent of funds appropriated for municipal construction projects be set aside for art in public places.

In front of the Central Library, for instance, is the *Fountain of Wisdom* by George Tsutakawa, a 9ft (2.7-meter) sculpture that integrates water and bronze. Tsutakawa was a local artist whose works grace many of the city's public areas.

Another skyscraper with world-class art on its grounds is **Safeco Plaza** (formerly 1001 Fourth Avenue Plaza) **2**. The art is Henry Moore's haunting **Three Piece Sculpture: Vertebrae**, which belongs to the Seattle Art Museum. During its construction, the Plaza was nicknamed 'the box the Space Needle came in.' From the 46th-floor foyer, there's a great view of the skyline, the busy harbor, and the boats on Puget Sound.

Central Library **3**

Address: 1000 4th Avenue; www.spl.org
Tel: 206-386 4636
Opening Hrs: Mon–Thu 10am–8pm, Fri–Sat 10am–6pm, Sun noon–6pm
Entrance Fee: free
Transportation: bus 2, 12, 13 or 62

Directly behind Safeco Plaza is Seattle's jaw-dropping, state-of-the-art main library. Designed by Pritzker Prize-winning architect Rem Koolhaas, the 11-story exterior has a dazzling skin of glass and steel; the steel alone is said to outweigh the Statue of Liberty 20 times over.

The brightly colored interior is filled with light and open spaces. The carpets are woven in patterns of green that are designed to replicate the vegetation that grows on the other side of the glass, and art is integrated throughout the space.

For a while, it's possible to forget that you're in a library – until you realize that the spiral feature is actually presenting the entire non-fiction collection in one continuous run. Central Library is a place that all Seattleites – young, old, rich, poor – seem to use, and not just for the free Wi-fi. Hour-long general and architectural tours are available on a first-come, first-served basis (sign up at the Welcome Desk on level 3, check

The library's interior.

Seattle Public Library.

Outdoor café at the Westlake Center.

In Pacific Place.

website for times). There are also self-guided cell-phone tours if you prefer to do it on your own.

Constructed years earlier and so less cutting-edge, the airy, spacious, busy, and spotless **Washington State Convention Center ❹** (at the corner of 7th and Pike; www.wscc.com) also makes a feature of glass, looking as though it's built from green glass cubes. The center's ground-floor **Tourist Office** (tel: 206-461 5888; daily 9am–5pm, in winter only Mon–Fri) is a good place to pick up maps and brochures.

Hanging above a sterile walkway to Pike Street on the building's second level are bells from schools, churches, and other landmarks in each of Washington's 39 counties; due to complaints by local residents these are no longer played.

In the walkway park adjoining the convention center itself is the aluminum sculpture *Seattle George* by the local artist Buster Simpson, combining silhouetted heads of George Washington and Chief Sealth (Seattle).

Freeway Park ❺

The convention center segues into **Freeway Park** (700 Seneca Street; daily 4am–11.30pm), an oasis of greenery and waterfalls that, like the convention center, straddles the busy Interstate 5 in an imaginative use of air rights.

Tree-shaded paths wind past a multi-level 'canyon' in which invigorating cascades of water pour down sheer walls into pools, swirling, gurgling, and endlessly recycling. Freeway Park is one of the most restful oases in Downtown.

Near the park, **Two Union Square** is a pleasant office building with stores on the main level that forms part of **Union Square ❻**, an outdoor plaza with another waterfall.

An underground walkway runs from Union Square to **Rainier Square ❼** (1301 5th Avenue), two blocks west. The square is currently under construction, with a new skyscraper set to open in 2019. The new tower will be curved, and has been designed to complement its surroundings and to preserve existing views.

The most accessible collection of photographs of old Seattle is found along the carpeted walkway running under the **Skinner Building** (1326 5th Avenue), which forms part of the Rainier Square complex. The collection includes pictures of the Moran Brothers' shipyard in 1906, prospectors of the Alaska Gold Rush, and some that celebrate the history of Boeing (see page 179). The building is also home to the **Fifth Avenue Theatre** (www.5thavenue.org), one of the most beautiful in Seattle.

A major hotel area is half a dozen blocks northeast. Two of the biggest are the Westin Hotel (1900 5th Avenue; tel: 206-728 1000; www.westin seattle.com), whose distinctive twin towers double as a geographical landmark, and the 1,258-room Sheraton Seattle Hotel (1400 6th Avenue; tel: 206-621 9000; www.sheratonseattle.com). These are handily placed near to two shopping malls, **Westlake Center** ❽ (between Pine Street and Olive Way, and 4th and 5th avenues; tel: 206-467 1600; www. westlakecenter.com), and Pacific Place.

The southern terminus of the city's **Monorail** (www.seattlemonorail.com) is on the top floor of the Westlake Center, from where it powers north 1.3 miles (2.1km) to the Space Needle and Museum of Pop Culture. Like the Space Needle, the Monorail dates from the 1962 World's Fair.

Pacific Place ❾ (6th Avenue and Pine Street; tel: 206-405 2655; www. pacificplaceseattle.com) is an upscale mall with restaurants, a multi-screen movie theater, and high-end stores like Kate Spade and Tiffany & Co. keeping company with well-known chain stores. The overhead Skybridge connects the mall with the wonderful flagship branch of **Nordstrom** (http://shop.nordstrom.com), the department store that was founded in Seattle at the beginning of the 20th century and has since opened in cities throughout the US.

Music and art

A few blocks west toward the waterfront is **Benaroya Hall** ❿ (200 University Street; tel: 206-215 4747; www.seattlesymphony.org), home of the Seattle Symphony. The building is an architectural delight. Inside, the cylindrical lobby gives wonderful views of the Seattle Art Museum and Puget Sound, while outside, as the website says, 'at night, its surfaces of clear and frosted glass give the effect of a giant lantern illuminating the streetscape'. Classical music is piped onto the sidewalk outside during the day, lending a cultural air to the downtown bustle.

Seattle Art Museum ⓫

Address: 1300 1st Avenue; www.seattleartmuseum.org
Tel: 206-654 3100
Opening Hrs: Wed and Fri–Sun 10am–5pm, Thu 10am–9pm
Entrance Fee: charge, free first Thu of the month
Transportation: bus 2, 13, or 150

Architect Robert Venturi, winner of the prestigious Pritzker Prize, was credited with making the wry observation that 'less is a bore'. You can judge for yourself if you agree by visiting the museum he co-designed with his wife Denise Scott Brown. Commonly known as SAM, the downtown building is just one of the Seattle Art Museum's three sites; the other two

Nordstrom.

SEATTLE'S STONE AGE

Seattle's switch to stone instead of wood as a building material began after the 1889 fire that destroyed much of the city's downtown business district. Initially, local rock was used, quarried from the Puget Sound region, especially near Tacoma and Bellingham, and it was soon used for the construction of streets, walls, and foundations. As the city grew wealthier, though, builders sought out stone from Vermont and Indiana. Later still, with more economical transport and stone-cutting technology, local and regional stone became almost obsolete as contractors ordered stone from South Africa, Brazil, and Italy.

Walking through downtown Seattle is a tour along a geological time line, beginning with 1.6 billion-year-old Finnish granite at 1000 2nd Avenue ending up at the Seattle Art Museum and its young, 300-million-year-old limestone walls. Farther along, fossils, some up to 4 inches (10cm) long, are embedded in gray limestone at the Gap store on 5th Avenue. Around the corner and underground in the Westlake Center bus station is the burned oatmeal-colored travertine, deposited less than 2 million years ago near the Rio Grande River in New Mexico.

being the Seattle Asian Art Museum
(see page 125) – occupying the
Seattle Art Museum's former premises
in Volunteer Park – and the Olympic
Sculpture Park (see page 110).

The exterior of SAM is clad with
limestone, richly hued terra-cotta,
marble, and granite. *The Mirror*, a
2013 installation by Doug Aitken
outside the museum, reflects the surrounding life and landscape like a living kaleidoscope. Inside the museum,
the grand staircase and galleries also
uphold Venturi's belief that 'civic
architecture should be popular; it
should be liked by a range of people.
It should not be esoteric.'

Galleries in the museum are
devoted to collections that include
Japanese art, African art, and Pacific
Northwest tribal art, plus special exhibitions from around the world. SAM's
vast gallery space attracts large, high-
profile exhibitions, and it also houses
a restaurant and wonderful store.

Pike Place Market ⑫

A couple of blocks north, a number
of interlinking buildings on several
floors, all with knockout views of

*The 'Hammering Man' in front of Seattle
Art Museum.*

Puget Sound, form the spectacular
Pike Place Market (85 Pike St; tel:
206-682 7453; http://pikeplacemarket.org).
It runs between Virginia and Lenora
streets and envelops Pike Place, a short
avenue sandwiched between First and
Western avenues. Pike Place and Pike
Street intersect at the main entrance

*African sculptures in
Seattle Art Museum.*

to Pike Street Market. No need to worry – everyone here always confuses all the different Pikes.

As part of the Waterfront Seattle Program (see page 107), the market has grown westward toward Elliott Bay to include a brand new 'Market-Front', which opened in June 2017. The expansion features new small businesses, farmers selling their produce, and public art, as well as a dazzling neighborhood center.

Seattle's anchor and primary visitor destination began in 1907 with half a dozen farmers bringing produce to Seattle, to space that the city set aside for a commercial market in response to a public demand for lower prices. Over the years, the number of farmers has varied from a high of several hundred in the 1930s to a low of 30 in 1976. Developers wanted to demolish the market, but locals got the issue placed on the ballot and voted overwhelmingly to retain it.

Since then, the number of visiting farmers has stabilized at around

Rachel the Pike Place pig wearing the Rat City rollergirls' kit.

100, although that number is set to grow with the current expansion. Pike Place Market is the country's oldest continuously operated public market, though today it has become more famous for its other attractions – including charming, eccentric, and individually owned stalls.

Pike Place Market is the oldest continuously operating public market in the United States.

Market residents

Most of the colorful fruit and vegetable stalls, as well as those stacked with gleaming ice banks of fish, are in the semi-open arcade along Pike Place. They center around Georgia Gerber's life-size bronze piggybank **Rachel the Pig** (under the market sign at Pike Street and Pike Place) and on whose back there is nearly always a child posing for a photograph. Rachel, who gets sackloads of fan mail, arrived at the market in 1986 and annually collects between $6,000 and $9,000 for charities through the slot in her back.

Also near the entrance to the market is **Metsker Maps** (1511 1st Avenue; tel: 206-623 8747; www.metskers. com). This is the best place in the city to buy travel books, atlases, and maps. Among Metsker's many globes and maps is the Geochron, a map/clock that shows real time all over the world, with day and night indicated by a lighting and shading panel.

EAT

From June through September there are free cooking demonstrations at Pike Place Market on Sundays. Cooking classes are held all year round in the Pike Place Market Atrium Kitchen.

Not everybody comes to the market at the front entrance. Many approach from the waterfront, either via **Victor Steinbrueck Park**, on Western Avenue at Virginia and named for the architect who revived the market in the 1970s, or else up the Pike Street **Hillclimb** steps from Western Avenue.

Musicians gather at the market, perhaps because of the good acoustics. There are half a dozen other places where musicians with permits (around 50 are issued each year) are authorized to perform. Many of the regulars – among them a classical-music trio, a gospel singer, several bluegrass crooners, and a man who wheels around his own piano – can be found somewhere near the **neon billboard clock** at the market's main entrance, at Pike Street and Pike Place.

Just north of the entrance clock, around the uncovered stalls, craftspeople gather each morning to be allocated a place for the day. Some of them have been attending the market for years and seniority plays a role; there are hundreds of people on the waiting list who move up only

Buy fresh fish at Pike Place Market.

The Seattle Great Wheel on the waterfront.

if existing craftspeople turn up less than two days a week.

Eating, shopping, and fish

Eating at the market is a joy because there are so many choices: home-style diner cooking, fine dining with views of the bay, French cuisine, Bolivian fare, fresh-baked pastries, raw oysters at a casual bar, overstuffed sandwiches at a deli counter. The public buildings called **Corner Market**, **Post Alley Market** and **Sanitary Market** (the latter so-named because no horses were allowed) are joined by walkways with eating spots on all levels. Don't overlook the **Soames Dunn Building** (the city side of Pike Place between Stewart and Virginia), which also houses restaurants, as well as the planet's first **Starbucks** (1912 Pike Place), complete with old-school signage.

You might find it useful to obtain a map of the market, which you can get at the voluntarily manned **information booth** by the main entrance at 1st and Pike. This is where the major fish stalls are located. At **Pike Place Fish** – home of the 'flying fish'

– visitors with cameras can outnumber the customers.

If you want to take some of the Northwest's fresh fish back home (within the US), stop at the market en route to the airport and arrange to have your salmon packed in ice for the trip.

Individual touches

Under the Pike Street Market's main arcade (on the water side of Pike Place) is a labyrinth of corners, corridors, cubbyholes, shops, stalls, stairs, and empty spaces. Magic tricks, old posters, talking birds, Australian opals, Turkish pastries, books, funky clothes… these are but a few of the thousands of items for sale. No chain stores or franchises are allowed, so everyone's an individualist, and there's no shortage of characters.

Even the tiles on the floor are eccentric. Locals were invited to pay $35 for their own design some years ago; a mathematician's wife listed all of the prime numbers under 100. The floor of the main arcade is covered in tiles with hundreds of monikers of Seattleites who paid for their names to be immortalized underfoot at the market.

According to merchants, the market is also home to a few ghostly inhabitants. The **Market Ghost Tours** (www.seattleghost.com; May–Nov only) go under and around this popular attraction, retelling stories of hauntings and sightings told by workers and residents. The tour ends – appropriately – at Seattle's first mortuary.

It seems the only thing you cannot find in the six-block market area is a parking space. Leave the car behind and come by the Downtown bus. In case you can't bear to leave at all, the popular 70-room **Inn at the Market** (corner of 1st Avenue and Pine Street; tel: 206-443 3600; www.innatthemarket.com) has pretty rooms (some with spectacular waterfront views), and an outdoor deck, perfect for watching the sunset.

ALONG THE WATERFRONT

Seattle's waterfront is where you'll find fantastic seafood, some fine stores, and a stunning aquarium; and its future looks ever brighter. It is currently in the middle of a seven-year regeneration program (the Waterfront Seattle Program; set for completion in 2020), prompted by the replacement of the Elliott

The marketplace's information booth.

SOUND FERRIES TO EVERYWHERE

The Washington State Ferry System (www.wsdot.wa.gov/ferries) is a vital link for both Puget Sound and Seattle residents and travelers. Among the thousands of islands and inlets that dot the coastlines of the Sound, sea travel is often the quickest, least costly, and most popular means of getting from place to place.

Washington State Ferries range from small boats to jumbo ferries. The Bainbridge Island and Bremerton ferries carry over 200 cars and 2,000 people each, and have large, comfortable lounges and food services. Major ferry routes have hourly departures during daylight hours, with fewer boats at night. On most routes, frequency is greater during the summer months; in winter, check schedules before making plans if time is tight. The privately owned Victoria Clipper, for instance, which travels between Seattle and Victoria, BC, has a greatly abbreviated timetable in winter.

If you plan to use the ferries to island hop around Puget Sound, make sure that you reserve accommodations on the smaller islands in advance, as these tend to get booked up.

A lovably irascible character, Seattle-born Ivar Haglund (1910–1985) began his career playing guitar and singing on local radio and TV. He later made a fortune with his seafood restaurants, Ivar's (www.ivars.com), including the one on the waterfront, which collectively sell a quarter of a million clams each year.

The Window on Washington Waters at the Seattle Aquarium.

Bay Seawall. The extensive program will redevelop the waterfront from Pioneer Square all the way to Belltown, and will include improved street surfaces, new parks, paths, better access to Elliott Bay, and a new face for Pike Place Market.

The **Washington State Ferries Terminal (Colman Dock)** ⑬ (Pier 52) at the waterfront end of Yesler Way may be the US's busiest waterbound commuter route. The 29 ocean-going boats of the Washington Transportation Department's Maritime Division each year carry more than 26 million passengers and more than 11 million cars. About half of them cross Puget Sound to or from island homes, often in less than 35 minutes. Fares collected cover only 60 percent of the operating costs.

The **Joshua Green Fountain** outside the ferry terminal at Pier 52, on Alaskan Way, is named after the late centenarian, who, arriving in Seattle in 1886, operated steamboats on Puget Sound and helped establish one of the city's first banks. The fountain is by local sculptor George Tsutakawa, who is also responsible for the fountain outside the former

Seattle Post-Intelligencer building topped by the globe about a mile farther north along Elliott Avenue in Belltown. In 2009 the long-running and much loved Seattle broadsheet printed its last edition; it continues as an online publication only (www.seattlepi.com).

Ye Olde Curiosity Shop and Museum ⑭

Address: 1001 Alaskan Way; www.yeoldecuriosityshop.com
Tel: 206-682 5844
Opening Hrs: open daily, hours vary based on season
Entrance Fee: free
Transportation: bus 99

On Pier 54 is **Ye Olde Curiosity Shop and Museum**, with bizarre carnival attractions like Siamese twin calves, mummies, shrunken heads, shark jaws, and pins engraved with the Lord's Prayer. The shop-museum is owned by descendants of Joe Standley, who opened it in 1899, later selling his ethnological collection to New York's Museum of the American Indian. Sharing Pier 54 is a bronze statue by Richard Beyer, *Ivar Feeding the Gulls*, of the late restaurateur Ivar Haglund.

Waterfront Park ⑮

What was once Pier 57 is now **Waterfront Park** (1301 Alaskan Way), a relaxing place to sit or to watch the sun set. Iconic green and white Foss tugs – almost all tugboats on the Sound belong to the Foss company – ply the waters of the Sound, hauling timber, sand, and gravel as they have for a century. Norwegian immigrant Thea Foss started the company with her husband by renting boats to fishermen. Foss was thought to be the model for Norman Reilly Raine's *Tugboat Annie* in the series of 1930s movies.

The **Seattle Great Wheel** (1301 Alaskan Way; https://seattlegreatwheel.com; hours vary by season) was built over the water in 2012. It offers fantastic panoramic views from a maximum height of 175ft (53 meters).

Seattle Aquarium ⑯

Address: 1483 Alaskan Way; www.seattleaquarium.org
Tel: 206-386 4300
Opening Hrs: daily 9.30am–5pm
Entrance Fee: charge (free for children under 3 years)

In the Underwater Dome at Seattle Aquarium.

Transportation: bus 99

A cruise ship traveling through.

The **Seattle Aquarium** is a family-friendly attraction on Pier 59, just west of Pike Place, which features 200 varieties of fish native to Puget Sound. There are also environments simulating the region's rocky reefs, sandy sea floor, eelgrass beds, and tide pools. A working fish ladder illustrates the salmon life cycle and other exhibits show the paths that water travels on its way to Puget Sound. See the website for details of talks offered.

Vividly striped lionfish, lethal electric eels, chameleon-like flatfish, octopus, dogfish, and salmon dart by, side by side with irresistibly entertaining otters and seals. The twice-daily oceanic tides flood Puget Sound and mix with ample fresh water from rainfall to nurture 'an unequaled estuarine haven for plants, animals, and humans', as one of the educational captions says.

Seattle Aquarium includes a three-story great hall with educational kiosks and conservation exhibits, though the main attraction here is the enormous tank filled with fish, sea anemones, and other marine life. The aquarium's most recent addition was a harbour seal exhibit (opened in 2013), and there are more plans to expand as part of the city's ambitious programme of the waterfront revitalization.

Heading north from Downtown

Pier 66, also known as the **Bell Street Pier ⑰** (2225 Alaskan Way), is the

FACT

The mummies at Ye O de Curiosity Shop, Sylvester and Sylvia, are for real. A CT scan revealed that Sylvester is extremely well preserved.

'Ivar Feeding the Gulls' is a tribute to the late restaurateur Ivar Haglund.

'Angie's Umbrella' decorates the Belltown area, standing 20ft (6-meters) high and as if in a perpetual storm.

site of a busy cruise-ship terminal, with a steady stream of passengers from cruise lines that ply the waters up to Alaska. Here, too, are a conference and events center, a small craft marina, and several places to eat.

BELLTOWN ⑱

A couple of blocks north of Downtown and Pike Place Market, along 1st through 5th avenues, is the trendy **Belltown** area, once better known as the Denny Regrade. Denny Hill was removed to provide much of the landfill to raise Downtown's muddy streets. The Regrade is now home to stylish condos and cool media offices, like those of TV stations and the makers of video games.

In recent years, Belltown has become a nightlife hub. It has fine restaurants, a couple of hotels, interesting shops, and popular bars and clubs. With the influx of residents, the area, once known for illicit activities, has been somewhat cleaned up. There is a small, dog- and family-friendly park, **Regrade Park**, at the corner of 3rd and Bell. Belltown also gave birth to 'grunge' music. It was in tiny, sweaty, hot spots here that bands like Nirvana, Pearl Jam, and Soundgarden first got noticed. **The Crocodile** (www.thecrocodile.com), a music venue that has been around for years, rocks out at the corner of 2nd Avenue and Blanchard.

Nearby you will find the Seattle Art Museum's third venue, the **Olympic Sculpture Park** ⑲ (between Broad and Bay streets; free). The Z-shaped 9-acre (3.6-hectare) park opened in early 2007, and added green space, 574 trees, and a lovely stretch of man-made beach to Seattle.

In the process, it restored what had formerly been the contaminated soil of an industrial area into an open park and recreation zone with a salmon-friendly sea wall, where visitors can enjoy strolling among works of art. The park's 22 sculptures include Richard Serra's *Wake*, Claes Oldenburg's *Typewriter Eraser*, and Alexander Calder's 39ft (12-meter) *Eagle*. There's also a glass pavilion that reveals the beauty of the Olympic Mountains and Puget Sound beyond and provides a space for performances and events. Additionally, the amphitheater serves as a venue for movie screenings, as well as an outdoor play area for children.

Another fascinating part of the Sculpture Park is the Neukom Vivarium, a living piece of sculpture, architecture, and education in the form of a giant feeder log that supports a wide array of plant and insect life. Volunteers are on hand to provide information about this micro-ecosystem.

Myrtle Edwards Park ⑳ (3130 Alaskan Way) is adjacent to the Olympic Sculpture Park and runs alongside the railroad tracks. Rippling along the waterfront, the park offers another spot with lovely views of the Olympic Mountains, Mount Rainier, and Puget Sound. There is also a winding cycle and walking trail that runs along Elliott Bay. Picnic tables are sited in perfect positions for dining alfresco and enjoying the stunning views.

The striking Olympic Sculpture Park.

The Space Needle was built in 1962.

SPACE NEEDLE AND SEATTLE CENTER

The city's iconic Space Needle was built for the 1962 World's Fair, but Seattle Center's museums and theaters are definitely 21st century.

Just north of Downtown is the ever-popular **Seattle Center**. This 74-acre (30-hectare) park and arts and entertainment center was developed for the 1962 Century 21 Exposition (World's Fair) and contains many Seattle landmarks, including the Space Needle, the northern terminus of the Seattle **Monorail**, the Pacific Science Center, the Chihuly Garden and Glass Museum, and the Museum of Popular Culture (MoPOP). It is also the place where the city's biggest festivals are held.

Space Needle ㉑

Address: 400 Broad Street, Seattle Center; www.spaceneedle.com
Tel: 206-905 2100
Opening Hrs: Sun–Thu 9.30am–9.30pm, Fri–Sat 9.30am–10.30pm
Entrance Fee: charge
Transportation: bus 3, 4, or 82; monorail

Only one World's Fair was the setting for an Elvis Presley movie (*It Happened at the World's Fair*) and that was the one held in Seattle in 1962. However, most Seattle residents are proudest of the fair's most tangible legacy: the internationally recognized Space

Needle. Built in 1962, the 605ft (184-meter) **Space Needle** was a marvel of design and engineering that cost $4.5 million. The centerpiece of the fair, the flying-saucer shape (an idea, according to local lore, first sketched on a placemat in 1959) was chosen from many designs. Construction was speedy, but the three elevators that transport visitors from the ground to the Needle's restaurant and observation deck were last to arrive; the final one got to Seattle just a day before the fair opened.

Main Attractions
Monorail
Space Needle
MoPOP
International Fountain
Pacific Science Center

Map
Page 100

The Space Needle observation deck has telescopes which can be used for free to get closer views of Seattle.

The Space Needle is the city's most famous landmark.

In 1993, two of the elevators were replaced with computerized versions that travel at 10mph (16kmh); the third, which is mostly used to transport freight, moves at 5mph (8kmh).

With a restaurant 500ft (152 meters) above ground and an observation deck just above, the Space Needle offers some of the city's best views: to the east are Lake Union, the immensely larger Lake Washington and the distant Cascade Range; westward, Elliott Bay opens into Puget Sound in front of the Olympic Mountains; and southeast is the snowcapped peak of 14,410ft (4,392-meter) Mount Rainier, 60 miles (100km) away. The revolving restaurant, **SkyCity**, provides a 360-degree view. As diners enjoy tasty – if expensive – Northwest cuisine, the restaurant completes a rotation every 47 minutes with the aid of a 1.5 horsepower motor.

One floor up, the **Observation Deck** level has free-to-use telescopes on the outside deck, and a variety of graphic displays inside to help visitors orient themselves. Also inside is a coffee counter and bar to help warm up in cold weather.

Back on the ground, directly east of the Space Needle is the Seattle Center's **Sculpture Garden**, which has four distinctive artworks by different artists. Perhaps the best

Taking in the view at dusk.

known of the four is *Olympic Iliad*, a huge red-and-orange sculpture made of gigantic industrial tubes, designed by Alexander Lieberman, former editorial director of Condé Nast Publications.

Northwest of the Needle is the **Seattle Center Armory ㉒**. Originally built as an armory in 1939, the building housed half-ton tanks and the 146th Field Artillery. It was remodeled in 2012 and now contains an impressive array of popular eateries like Eltana Wood-Fired Bagels, Pie, and Mod Pizza, as well as the Seattle Children's Museum, and a performance area where 3,000 free public performances are held each year.

Seattle Children's Museum

Address: Center House, Seattle Center, 305 Harrison Street; www.thechildrensmuseum.org
Tel: 206-441 1768
Opening Hrs: Mon–Fri 10am–5pm, Sat–Sun 10am–6pm
Entrance Fee: charge

Transportation: bus 3, 4, or 82; monorail

Of particular interest to families is the **Children's Museum** on the first floor of the Armory. The 22,000-sq-ft (2,043-sq-meter) space features hands-on, interactive, and child-size exhibits on world culture, art, technology, and the humanities.

Chihuly Garden and Glass Museum

Address: Center House, Seattle Center, 305 Harrison Street; www.chihulygardenandglass.com
Tel: 206-753 4940
Opening Hrs: Sun–Thu 10am–7pm, Fri–Sat 10am–8pm
Entrance Fee: charge
Transportation: bus 3, 4, or 82; monorail

For an esthetic escape, slip into the **Chihuly Garden and Glass Museum** between the Space Needle and the Seattle Center Armory. The museum, chronicling the work and inspiration behind legendary glass artist Dale Chihuly, includes eight galleries, a magnificent 4,500-sq-ft

WHERE

Skateboarders and music fans will want to check out the skate park at Seattle Center. Designed by skateboarders themselves, it was developed with the help of a $50,000 gift from Pearl Jam.

Illuminated Chihuly Garden and Glass installation at night.

TIP

One of around 20 monorail systems in North America, Seattle's Monorail (www.seattle monorail.com) travels on its 1.3-mile (2.1km) single-rail elevated track between Westlake Center (at 5th Avenue and Pine Street) and the station next to the Space Needle. The trains depart every 10 minutes, can carry up to 450 passengers and pass through – yes, through – the MoPOP.

The Monorail passes through the futuristic MoPOP building.

(418-sq-meter) glass house holding a 100ft (30-meter) sculpture, a theatre, and a stunning garden featuring installations and major works.

Museum of Popular Culture (MoPOP) ㉓

Address: 325 5th Avenue N; www.mopop.org
Tel: 206 770 2700
Opening Hrs: daily June–Aug 10am–7pm, Sept–May 10am–5pm
Entrance Fee: charge
Transportation: bus 3, 4, or 82; monorail

Downtown may have landmark buildings by Rem Koolhaas and Robert Venturi, but Microsoft co-founder Paul Allen brought the artistic eye of California-based architect Frank O. Gehry to the Seattle Center with the **Museum of Popular Culture (MoPOP)**, previously the EMP. No one can ignore the structure clad in psychedelic shades of aluminum and stainless steel (see page 120).

The rock 'n' roll building, originally solely an interactive music museum, has branched out to house

Enjoying a sunny day by International Fountain.

exhibits that span popular culture, covering film, TV, and even gaming, as well as music. State-of-the-art technology is combined with a world-class collection of artifacts from artists such as Jimi Hendrix and Nirvana, and from films and TV series including *Star Wars*, *Star Trek*, *Blade Runner*, *Men in Black*, and many more.

For something out of this world, visit the Science Fiction and Fantasy Hall of Fame exhibit, celebrating the most impactful science fiction and fantasy creators as well as their works. You can see Luke Skywalker's severed hand from George Lucas' The Empire Strikes Back, the Staff of Ra headpiece from Steven Spielberg's Raiders of the Lost Ark, author Isaac Asimov's typewriter, and the 'Right Hand of Doom' from Guillermo del Toro's film Hellboy.

As you exit the MoPOP and head north, stop to admire *The Reeds*, an

art installation by John Fleming. The 110 laminated orange and yellow steel rods stand 30ft (9 meters) tall and sway gently with the breeze.

Centers for the arts

Performance halls line Mercer Street between 4th Avenue and Warren. The $127-million **Marion Oliver McCaw Hall** ㉔ (www.mccawhall.com) covers 295,000 sq ft (27,406 sq meters) and includes a 2,900-seat auditorium, a glass lobby, a public plaza, and more. Home to the Seattle Opera and Pacific Northwest Ballet, it often hosts concerts, festivals, conventions, and other events.

At Mercer and 2nd is the **Intiman Theatre**, whose Swedish name means 'the Intimate'. It seats 446 people around a 3,110-sq-ft (289-sq-meter) stage. One of the state's oldest theater institutions, Intiman is recognized nationally for its programs and its fresh approach to classics as well as new productions.

A little farther west on Mercer are the three theaters of the **Seattle Repertory Theatre** (www.seattlerep.org), known locally as 'The Rep'. The non-profit group is internationally recognized for its productions and also delivers workshops and educational programs. The best-known and largest of the Rep's three stages, the **Bagley Wright Theatre**, seats 842; the Leo K and the tiny PONCHO Forum seat 282 and 133, respectively.

The **Key Arena** ㉕ (1st Avenue between Thomas and Republican; www.keyarena.com) is a 17,000-seat arena which hosts big rock concerts as well as family shows and is also the home stadium for the city's women's basketball team, the Seattle Storm, and the city's roller derby team, Rat City Rollergirls.

The playfully designed **Seattle Children's Theatre** (SCT; www.sct.org) produces family-friendly performances on two stages, the Charlotte Martin and Eve Alvord theatres. Performances

The Weeknd performing at Key Arena.

have included classics such as *Goodnight Moon* and *The Diary of Anne Frank*. The theater company also develops and teaches educational programs in theater arts, including drama courses, residencies, and workshops.

Just east of the SCT is the **Mural Amphitheatre**, another great spot

In Marion Oliver McCaw Hall.

The Model Railroad Show at the Pacific Science Center.

Interactive exhibits and games for all ages at the Pacific Science Center.

for a picnic. During festivals, the amphitheater features live musical acts. Its mural backdrop by Japanese artist Paul Horiuchi provides a lovely setting. In summer, the amphitheater hosts 'Movies at the Mural,' a well-attended series of free outdoor evening movies.

International Fountain

Originally built in 1961 for the World's Fair, the **International Fountain** is in an open area near the heart of the Seattle Center. Rebuilt in 1995, the fountain features a bowl with a diameter of 220ft (67 meters), a 10ft (3-meter) -tall dome and 274 nozzles spraying mist and shooting jets of water (the highest reaches 120ft, or 37 meters). The nozzles are also set to play 12-minute water shows, choreographed to different pieces of music. On sunny days, families picnic on the grassy area around the fountain, and children flock to the fountain bowl to dart and dance among the jets.

Pacific Science Center

Address: 200 2nd Avenue N; www.pacificsciencecenter.org

Tel: 206-443 2001
Opening Hrs: Mon–Fri 10am–5pm, Sat–Sun and hols 10am–6pm; call for times of laser and IMAX shows
Entrance Fee: charge
Transportation: bus 1, 2, 3, 4, 8, 13, 24 and D Line; monorail

Under five white arches at the corner of 2nd and Denny is the nonprofit **Pacific Science Center** ㉖, the first US museum founded as a science and technology center. With the goal of advancing public knowledge and interest in science, the PSC's five buildings contain interactive exhibits, two **IMAX theaters**, the **Butterfly House**, an excellent **planetarium**, and laser shows.

Hands-on math and basic science exhibits delight school-age children, and other exhibits excite the inquiring mind with demonstrations of virtual reality, computer science, and robotics. Two of the many exciting permanent exhibits are 'Dinosaurs: A Journey Through Time,' which features eight full- and half-size robotic dinosaurs that roar; and the 'Insect Village,' inhabited by live and robotic insects, and a beehive.

FESTIVAL TIME

Often called 'Seattle's living room,' Seattle Center is host to many of the city's biggest festivals. Major music events Bumbershoot and the Northwest Folklife Festival are the crown jewels in the line-up, but other favorites include the excuse for gorging known as Bite of Seattle, the Northwest's largest PrideFest, and the many cultural festivals held throughout the year – with the Arab Festival, the Live Aloha Hawaiian Cultural Festival, and the Irish Festival among the best offered. Eating and shopping are major components of every festival, with local craftspeople and mouthwatering food booths jockeying to lighten attendees' pocketbooks. Do yourself a favor and give in – bring cash and an empty stomach – beer gardens, haberdasheries and Thai food await.

'Rocky Mountain Express' movie showing at the Boeing Imax Theater in the Pacific Science Center.

MOPOP

With undulating steel ribs and a rippling, multi-colored skin, it's pretty hard to miss the Museum of Popular Culture, or MoPOP.

The Museum of Popular Culture (MoPOP), founded as the EMP Museum, was the brainchild of Microsoft co-founder Paul Allen. The original project drew a good deal of its inspiration from Seattle-born guitar virtuoso Jimi Hendrix, and a sizeable exhibit is still dedicated to the rock legend.

Allen commissioned Frank Gehry as the architect of the distinctive, sinuous structure, all 180,000 sq ft (16,722 sq meters) of it. The skin was designed on an aerospace computer system made in France for jet planes and assembled from more than 21,000 shingles of aluminum and stainless steel. The materials were milled in Germany, and the colors of the stainless steel were applied with an 'interference coating' by a specialist company in England. The panels were shipped to Kansas City to be cut and fabricated, before being taken to Seattle and attached to the 280 steel ribs that shape the construction. No two panels are the same shape.

The finished structure, in billowing folds of red, blue, purple, silver, and gold, houses a range of impressive exhibitions covering music, film, TV, and even gaming, making use of the newest technologies and displaying some remarkable artifacts.

THE ESSENTIALS

Address: 325 5th Avenue N, www.mopop.org
Tel: 1-877-367 7361
Opening Hrs: June–Aug daily 10am–7pm, Sept–May daily 10am–5pm
Entrance Fee: charge
Transportation: bus 3, 4, or 82; monorail

An exhibition pays tribute to Jim Henson, whose puppets have delighted audiences for generations.

Luke Skywalker's Lightsaber, used by Mark Hamill in 1977.

The Nirvana exhibiton at the museum.

The 'If VI was X:Roots and Branches' sculpture.

SEATTLE ROCKS

The modern interior of the MoPOP which is packed with interactive exhibits on popular music, film, TV and more.

Washington State has certainly played its part in the development of contemporary music, but the birthplace of crooner Bing Crosby and folk singer Judy Collins never glimmered with such resonance as it did in the 1990s. In addition to the feminist girl-punk mini-quake that was Riot Grrrl, exemplified by the band Bikini Kill, there was a sound called grunge.

A meld of heavily distorted punk and heavy metal, with a penchant for lyrics that made the Doors sound like light entertainment. Soundgarden, Alice in Chains, Mudhoney and Mother Love Bone (later Pearl Jam) personified the Belltown club sound of the 1980s and 1990s, along with their compatriots from Aberdeen, WA, Nirvana.

Nirvana achieved worldwide success with their record *Nevermind*, but had a difficult relationship with MTV and the growing trend toward censorship in US chain stores like K-Mart. The tragic death of songwriter Kurt Cobain in 1994 brought Nirvana to an end, but drummer Dave Grohl went on to form Foo Fighters, and producer Butch Vig teamed up with Scottish singer Shirley Manson to form Garbage who, among many achievements, performed the theme song for the James Bond movie *The World is Not Enough*. Soundgarden singer Chris Cornell also sang a Bond theme, *You Know My Name*, for *Casino Royale*.

Visitor engaging with the museum's attractions.

Skateboarder in Capitol Hill.

CENTRAL NEIGHBORHOODS

Neighborhoods like Capitol Hill, Queen Anne Hill, Madison Park, and Magnolia show the great diversity of Seattle's spirited, sophisticated personality.

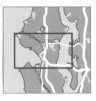

Seattle is a city of many neighborhoods with well-defined identities. East of Downtown is vibrant Capitol Hill, a walkable neighborhood of apartments, 19th-century mansions, and lots of bars and restaurants. Farther east along Madison Street is quirky Madison Valley, continuing to Madison Park on Lake Washington, where you can experience upscale dining and shopping, and admire multimillion dollar homes. Lake Union is another focus of eclectic neighborhoods. Eastlake has a thriving houseboat community and postage-stamp parks from which you can watch kayaks, sailboats, and floatplanes. South Lake Union is a booming mixed-use residential and commercial neighborhood that is home to cutting-edge biomedical research companies. Queen Anne Hill, west of Lake Union, is a pleasant, largely residential neighborhood. Farther west lies Magnolia, known for the vast Discovery Park and stunning views of Puget Sound.

Capitol Hill ❶

North of the International District and east of Downtown, **Capitol Hill** gets its name not from any seat of government, but from Denver, Colorado. Real-estate promoter James A. Moore,

whose wife was from that city, gave it the name – after the Capitol Hill in Denver – in 1901. The area is culturally, economically, and racially mixed, and the hill is home to a large gay and lesbian population. A concentration of condos does little to detract from the charm of the mansions nestled throughout the leafy neighborhood.

The end result is a refreshing mix of tree-lined streets with elegant homes and excellent museums, alongside a vibrant street scene. Great clubs, coffeehouses, and restaurants

Melrose Market.

TIP

It's hard to find parking in the high-density Capitol Hill neighborhood, so consider taking a Metro bus or taxi. Alternatively, it's only a 20- or 30-minute walk to or from Downtown (with hills).

complete the picture. With two colleges and a university nearby, Capitol Hill stays up later than most 'early to bed' neighborhoods.

On Broadway

Broadway (Pine Street to E Roy Street) is one of the hill's main thoroughfares and commercial districts; it is also one of the few places in town where casual strollers are seen on the street at midnight, even on weeknights. The **Egyptian** (805 E Pine Street) is a handsome reminder of earlier cinema eras. It specializes in first-rate foreign-film presentations and hosts shows during the annual Seattle International Film Festival (May and June).

Traffic is heavy on Broadway at almost any time of day and parking is tough, but the ever-changing street scene of shops and restaurants makes this a good place for walking. Walkers can even learn some traditional dances from artist Jack Mackie's **bronze**

footsteps embedded in the sidewalk, part of the city's public-art program.

Follow Broadway south to Pike and Pine streets (which run parallel to one another) and you'll find the hippest zone in Seattle; the Pike-Pine Corridor is where the action is, from the Elliott Bay Book Company (www.elliottbaybook.com) to Neumos (a concert venue; www.neumos.com) to some of the best dining on Capitol Hill, including Cascina Spinasse.

Several blocks east, **15th Avenue East** is another Capitol Hill shopping district, albeit one that's less congested and less flamboyant than Broadway, with a handful of good restaurants representing varied cuisines, several interesting shops, and the ubiquitous coffee shops.

Volunteer Park ➋

Address: 1247 15th Avenue E; www.seattle.gov/parks/find/parks/volunteer-park
Tel: 206-684 4075

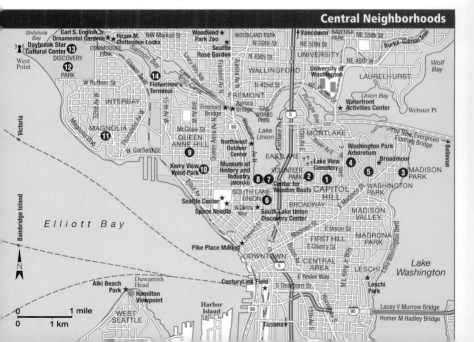

Central Neighborhoods

Opening Hrs: daily 6am–10pm
Entrance Fee: free
Transportation: bus 10

A few blocks north of the retail district on 15th Avenue East is one of Seattle's loveliest neighborhood parks, 48-acre (19-hectare) **Volunteer Park**. Originally a cemetery for the city's early pioneers, the land became Lake View Park when it was decided in 1887 to site a reservoir at the southern part of the property. The graves were moved north to what is now **Lake View Cemetery**, the final resting place of Seattle notables such as Doc Maynard and his wife Catherine, Henry Yesler, Hiram M. Chittenden, and John Nordstrom, as well as martial-arts legend Bruce Lee. In 1901, the park was renamed Volunteer Park in honor of the Seattle men who served in the 1898 Spanish-American War.

With an elevation of 445ft (135 meters), the park has magnificent views on rare sunny days of the Space Needle, Puget Sound, and the Olympic Mountains. The park's attractions are the **Volunteer Park Conservatory** (tel: 206-322 4112; Tue–Sun 10am–4pm; free first Thu and Sat of the month), with its five lush greenhouses, and the **Seattle Asian Art Museum** (tel: 206-654 3210; www.seattleartmuseum.org; currently closed for renovation until 2019). When the Seattle Art Museum moved to Downtown in 1991, the Art Deco (1932) building in Volunteer Park was renamed and

Cafe Vita on Capitol Hill.

Volunteer Park Conservatory.

In the Japanese Garden at Washington Park Arboretum.

Boats on Lake Union.

renovated to display the museum's extensive Asian art collections, including 14–16th-century ceramics from Thailand and netsuke from Japan.

Madison Park ❸

East of Capitol Hill is Madison Valley. The area west from Lake Washington Boulevard to 23rd Avenue E along both sides of Madison Street underwent a transformation in the 1980s and 1990s, and two-story retail complexes now anchor the intersection of Madison and Lake Washington Boulevard. A few consistently top-rated restaurants, an expansive gardening store, and a number of pleasant delis and cafés, along with numerous new condominiums lining the hillside, signal the resurgence of this formerly overlooked neighborhood.

At the eastern foot of **Madison Street** – Seattle's only waterfront-to-waterfront street, running west to east from Elliott Bay to Lake Washington – is the unmistakably affluent community of **Madison Park**, once the western terminus of a passenger-boat line connecting Seattle to the east side of Lake Washington. Here are restaurants that range from trendy to a local-favorite bakery, as well as a village of shops. The park itself has floodlit all-weather tennis courts and a beach, thronged on hot summer days by a lively urban mix from surrounding neighborhoods.

Washington Park Arboretum ❹

Address: 2300 Arboretum Drive E; https://botanicgardens.uw.edu/washington-park-arboretum
Tel: 206-543 8800
Opening Hrs: daily dawn to dusk
Entrance Fee: free
Transportation: bus 43 or 48

Adjacent to Madison Park is the **Washington Park Arboretum**, a 230-acre (93-hectare) public park and botanical research facility for the University of Washington. One of the highlights is **Azalea Way**, a wide, grassy strip winding through the park and lined by azaleas, dogwoods, and flowering cherry trees. It was developed by the Public Works Administration in the 1930s, the federally funded 'right to work' scheme that was begun during the Great Depression.

Another of the arboretum's highlights, the 3.5-acre (1.4-hectare) formal **Japanese Garden** (tel: 206-684 4725; summer daily 10am–7pm, closes earlier and on Mondays in spring and fall, closed winter), has tea-ceremony demonstrations in summer and guided tours April through October.

WASHINGTON PARK, MADRONA, AND LESCHI

Adjacent to Madison Park is the wealthy neighborhood of **Washington Park ⑤**. A showcase for this residential area of stately homes and doted-upon lawns is the majestic thoroughfare on **36th Avenue E**, extending south between Madison and E Mercer streets. Towering trees arch toward each other high above the street from both sides of 36th Avenue to form Seattle's most magnificent natural cathedral.

Follow the sparkling waterfront neighborhood south of Madison Park along the western shore of Lake Washington and you'll find neighboring **Madrona** and **Leschi**, the latter named after the Native American leader who enjoyed camping here. Leschi was said to have been among those who planned an attack in 1856 on the city of Seattle, during the so-called Indian Wars. Conflict broke out after some local tribes signed treaties and were moved to reservations. The first automobile ferry, the *Leschi*, named after him, started regular service from here to the east side of Seattle in 1913.

At one time considered a social hot spot, Leschi is today a quiet neighborhood of waterfront homes, condominiums, and apartment buildings, with a public beach, small-sailboat marina, and the lushly green **Leschi Park** – once an amusement park at the terminus of the Yesler Street cable-car line. There are a couple of attractive restaurants that offer waterfront dining. Madrona, up the hill from Leschi, is equally quiet and lovely – perfect for a sunny-day stroll. You can end your walk at 34th Avenue near Union Street, where there are eateries, alehouses, and cafés.

EASTLAKE

Cut off from Capitol Hill by Interstate 5 and north of Downtown along the east side of Lake Union, the **Eastlake** area is a lively mix of large historic homes, multi-family dwellings, and a thriving houseboat community. The residential neighborhood shares

Knot-tying at the Center for Wooden Boats.

The boat-making station at the Center for Wooden Boats.

The Museum of History and Industry.

space – uneasily at times – with ever-changing commercial and industrial properties. The Boeing Company got its start here in 1915, when William Boeing began building seaplanes in a hangar at the foot of Roanoke Street, that he tested on Lake Union. Boeing moved the company to the south end of the city two years later, but the hangar remained here until 1971. It was demolished to make way for an abortive condominium project, which was defeated after a fierce 13-year legal battle fought by determined neighborhood groups. A few notable restaurants and some bakeries and small parks call this quirky area home.

SOUTH LAKE UNION ⑥

The south end of **Lake Union**, once an exclusively industrial area, has seen an explosion of developments and residents in recent years. The **South Lake Union Discovery Center** (101 Westlake Avenue N; tel: 206-342 5900; www.discoverslu.com; Mon–Fri 9am–5pm; free) serves as a community center for this rapidly changing neighborhood, as well as a sales center for the many condominium and commercial projects springing up. Millions of square feet of residential and business property has been developed, with much more planned and under construction.

RESEARCH FOR LIFE

Health care is a big deal in Seattle, since it accounts for tens of thousands of jobs in the city's hospitals, health-care services, and biomedical research. The city has one of the nation's highest concentrations of biotechnology research, centered around South Lake Union, with organizations like Fred Hutchinson Cancer Research Center, ZymoGenetics, the University of Washington's Department of Global Health, and the Seattle Biomedical Research Institute. The South Lake Union headquarters of the Bill & Melinda Gates Foundation, with its high-profile focus on local and global health care, brings a philanthropic aspect to this powerful contingent of leading-edge health-care organizations.

The district has long been a magnet for biomedical research, with nationally acclaimed institutions at the forefront of medical research in cancer and genetics. This area is also a hot spot of philanthropy in health care and education, led by the Bill & Melinda Gates Foundation, whose headquarters are based here – the amazing visitor center at 440 5th Avenue North is open Tuesday to Saturday. 10am to 5pm (no admission charge). In 2010 Seattle-based online retailer Amazon moved its headquarters from the Beacon Hill neighborhood into brand new buildings here (tours Wed at 10am and 2pm; www.amazonhqtours. com). The area is in a constant state of change, as the older buildings give way to new, modern, high-rise ones. A slew of galleries, restaurants, and cafés has followed, making this neighborhood a great place to spend the day.

For years the city has been laying the infrastructure for the planned growth of both public and private transportation. The South Lake Union line of the Seattle Streetcar connects the area with Downtown. The streetcar was initially named the Seattle Lake Union Trolley, with the unfortunate acronym SLUT, which delighted the press and soon led to the streetcar being renamed. Roads, too, are being redesigned to improve traffic flow, especially Mercer Street, which has been referred to as the Mercer Mess for years.

Lake Union Park (860 Terry Avenue N; www.atlakeunionpark.org) occupies a prime location at the south end of the lake, with a great vantage point for watching the nautical life of the lake, including the seaplanes. As part of a plan to embrace the maritime history of the region, the park incorporates a Historic Ships Wharf, boat-building and boat rentals, and education for all ages. In 2012 the Museum of History and Industry (MOHAI) moved here into the Naval Reserve Building.

Center for Wooden Boats ❼

Address: 1010 Valley Street; www.cwb.org
Tel: 206-382 2628
Opening Hrs: summer Tue–Sun

TIP

Harbor cruises of Lake Washington and Lake Union are available from Argosy Cruises (tel: 1-888-623 1445). Ask the guide to point out Tom Hanks' Lake Union floating home from the movie *Sleepless in Seattle*.

Exploring the Museum of History and Industry.

10am–8pm, fall–spring Wed–Sun 10am–5pm
Entrance Fee: free
Transportation: bus 40, 62, 70, 83, or C Line; streetcar

Adjacent to Lake Union Park, this is a nostalgically charming maritime museum with some 100 sailboats and rowboats, many of which are available for rent. Rowing or paddling is the most enjoyable way to appreciate the lake, and is the only chance to get close to the **houseboats and floating homes** that bob along the northeast and northwest shorelines. The museum has a second branch at Cama Beach State Park.

Lake Union is also the home of a number of commercial seaplane services, including Kenmore Air (950 Westlake Avenue N; tel: 1-866-435 9524; www.kenmoreair.com), which offers flights around the city, to the San Juan Islands, and to the Canadian cities of Vancouver, Victoria, and other places on Vancouver Island.

On the west side of the lake, the **Northwest Outdoor Center** (NWOC; 2100 Westlake Avenue N; tel: 206-281 9694; www.nwoc.com; Apr–Sept Mon–Fri 10am–8pm, Sat 9am–6pm, hours vary during other months) offers kayak rentals by the hour.

Museum of History and Industry (MOHAI) ❽

Address: Lake Union Park; www.mohai.org
Tel: 206-324 1126
Opening Hrs: daily 10am–5pm
Entrance Fee: charge, free first Thu of the month
Transportation: bus 40, RapidRide C; streetcar

This intriguing museum contains thousands of items related to the development of Seattle and the Puget Sound area, and is much more interesting than its dry-sounding name might suggest. Its 50,000 sq ft (4,645 sq meters) of exhibit space means plenty of room for fascinating exhibitions, performances, and hands-on fun. Kids and families love this museum, and its proximity to the Seattle Center and more doesn't hurt.

Queen Anne Hill ❾

Northwest of Downtown, perched above the Seattle Center to the west

of Lake Union, is the area known as **Queen Anne**: Lower Queen Anne is mainly made up of condos and apartments, and the graceful residential streets of **Queen Anne Hill** are a steep climb uphill from there. An interesting array of shops, coffeehouses, and restaurants occupy Roy and Mercer streets, as well as Queen Anne Avenue just south of Mercer.

Queen Anne Hill, in the words of Seattle photo-historian Paul Dorpat, 'is cleansed by winds, girdled by greenbelts, and topped by towers and mansions'. The hill rises sharply on all four sides to a summit of 457ft (139 meters), the second-highest elevation in the city (35th Avenue SW in West Seattle reaches 514ft/ 157 meters). Seattle pioneer Thomas Mercer, who arrived in 1853, filed the first claim on Queen Anne Hill and had to cut through a forest in order to build a home.

The hill got its name from Rev. Daniel Bagley, who referred to it as 'Queen Anne Town', a jocular reference to the lavish mansions some of the city's prominent citizens built on the hill in the 1880s in an American variation of the Queen Anne architectural style in England.

Bounded by Mercer Street on the south, Lake Union on the east, Lake Washington Ship Canal on the north, and Elliott Avenue on the west, the Queen Anne district is home to more than 50,000 residents. Because of its height, the hill has spectacular views (weather permitting) of Puget Sound, the Olympic Mountains, and dramatic sunsets to the west; Lake Union, Capitol Hill, and the Cascade Range to the east; Elliott Bay, Downtown, and Mount Rainier to the south; and the Ship Canal and Mount Baker to the north.

Getting to the best viewpoint requires a walk, drive, or bus ride through some of the loveliest residential streets in the city. Head west on Highland Drive from Queen Anne Avenue, about halfway up the hill. Gracious apartment buildings line both sides of the street. **Kerry View Point Park ⑩** is a narrow stretch of green with spectacular wide-open views of the Space Needle, Downtown office towers, the Elliott Bay harbor, and Mount Rainier.

Queen Anne Hill houses.

Head to the Fishermen's Terminal, or a restaurant nearby, for fresh seafood.

West of Kerry View Point Park, mansions line both sides of Highland Drive, which ends in tiny, secluded **Parsons Garden**, a beautiful public park.

Magnolia ⑪

In 1856, a captain in the US Coast Survey named the southern bluff overlooking Puget Sound for the magnolia trees growing along it. But the trees turned out to be madrona trees. The community liked the name Magnolia better than Madrona and decided to keep it.

Northwest of Downtown, affluent **Magnolia** is a well-ordered, conservative neighborhood of mostly single-family homes nestling on expansive lots. Magnificent waterfront properties along the western edge, south of Discovery Park, are protected from view by vegetation and long driveways. The main shopping area, **Magnolia Village** (W McGraw Street between 32nd and 35th avenues), has fashionable stores and watering holes.

Discovery Park ⑫

Address: 3801 Discovery Park Boulevard; www.seattle.gov/parks/find/centers/discovery-park-environmental-learning-center
Tel: 206-386 4236
Opening Hrs: daily 4am–11.30pm
Entrance Fee: free
Transportation: bus 24 or 33

At 534 acres (216 hectares), **Discovery Park** is Seattle's largest green open area. The park was named for the ship of the English explorer Captain George Vancouver, who, during his 1792 exploration of Puget Sound, spent several days with the HMS *Discovery* at anchor within sight of this land.

A 2.5-mile (4km) loop trail around the park winds through thick forests and crosses broad meadows and high, windswept bluffs with spectacular views of Puget Sound and the Olympic Mountains. Wildlife is abundant here, with bald eagles regularly seen in the treetops, as well as sightings of falcons, herons, beavers, and foxes. In 1982, a mountain lion was encountered in Discovery Park.

The **Daybreak Star Cultural Center** ⑬ (tel: 206-285 4425; Mon–Fri 9am–5pm; www.unitedindians.org; free) is a local attraction sponsoring Native American events, and exhibiting contemporary Indian art. Discovery Park also has picnic areas, playgrounds, tennis, and basketball courts.

Fishermen's Terminal ⑭

Fishermen's Terminal, on W Thurman Street on Magnolia's northern side, provides an opportunity to admire the boats of a major fishing fleet. This is the home port for more than 700 commercial fishing vessels, many of which fish for salmon, halibut, or crab in Alaskan waters. Visitors can sample the day's catch at the restaurants, or by purchasing from the fish market at the terminal.

Parsons Garden.

NORTH SEATTLE

From the pleasant University of Washington campus to the cageless Woodland Park Zoo, North Seattle blends lovely outdoor scenery with cool neighborhoods like Fremont and Ballard.

he 8-mile (13km) -long **Lake Washington Ship Canal** ❶ separates the northern neighborhoods of Seattle from the city center. Completed in 1917, the canal winds through the Ballard, Fremont, Wallingford, and University districts linking salty Puget Sound with the fresh waters of lakes Union and Washington. A series of locks raise and lower ships making the transit. Six bridges cross the canal, leading into a cluster of neighborhoods born as independent townships in the 19th century that retain distinctly individual characteristics.

THE UNIVERSITY DISTRICT

The **Burke-Gilman Trail** is a 27-mile (43.5km) biking and walking route, beginning in Ballard, swinging along Lake Union past Gas Works Park, winding through the University of Washington campus before coursing north on the left bank of Lake Washington (stay on the trail to continue all the way to Marymoor Park in Redmond).

The **University District** is an eclectic commercial center thriving on the cultural, educational and athletic amenities afforded by the University of Washington. **University Way Northeast**, affectionately called 'the

Ave' by locals, is a busy strip of shops, theaters, newsstands, bookstores, pubs, and eateries. Some Seattleites treat this animated district with caution, as an increasing number of panhandlers, rebellious young people, and homeless bring with them a sometimes shadowy subculture. But the diversity of the community, made up of students, businesspeople, academics, and vagrants, certainly has a verve and vitality. The **University Bookstore** (4326 University Way NE; tel: 206-634-3400; www.bookstore.washington.edu), a

Main Attractions
Burke-Gilman Trail
Burke Museum of Natural
  History and Culture
Henry Art Gallery
Gas Works Park
Woodland Park Zoo
Hiram M. Chittenden Locks

Map
Page 136

Gas Works Park.

TIP

A plethora of cultural events takes place at the University of Washington throughout the year, from classical concerts to big-name author readings to social commentators. Events are announced on the excellent university radio station KUOW 94.9FM (http://kuow.org), in the local newspapers, and on the Campus Events Calendar: www.washington.edu/calendar.

stalwart of 'the Ave' since 1925, has a huge selection of contemporary fiction as well as textbooks, school and art supplies, and T-shirts.

University of Washington ②

A few blocks to the east is the 640-acre (260-hectare) **University of Washington** campus itself. Over 46,000 students and more than 20,000 staff come here to the state's finest public university, best known for its medical and law schools, and for fine research facilities. Pick up a self-guided walking tour brochure from the **Visitors' Information Center** (022 Odegaard; tel: 206-543 9198; www.uw.edu/visit).

Much of the original campus was designed by the Olmsted family, famous for New York's Central Park. **Drumheller Fountain** sits at the top of the Rainier Vista Mall, the gateway to the Gothic-style Quad, where in April rows of cherry trees burst into pink or white blossoms.

The addition of the **Allen Library**, made possible by a $10-million donation from Paul Allen, co-founder of Microsoft, expanded by 40 percent the capacity of the Gothic-style **Suzzallo Library**, which was opened in 1927 and dubbed the soul of the university by then-president Henry Suzzallo. The red-tiled plaza adjoining Suzzallo is known as Red Square. On summer evenings at the **Theodor Jacobsen Observatory** (tel: 206-685 7856; http://depts.washington.edu/astron/outreach/jacobsen-observatory; variable hours; free) visitors can gaze at the heavens through one of the observatory's telescopes, and hear talks given by the university's undergrads.

Husky Stadium ③ is in the southeast corner of the campus. It is one of the largest in the Pacific Northwest, with a capacity for 72,000 spectators to watch its extremely popular football games. Renovations to the original stadium have added seismic reinforcements, extra seating,

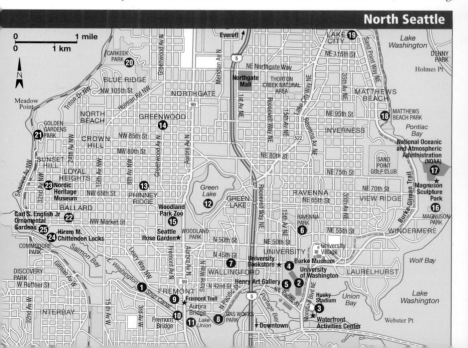

North Seattle

and a newer concourse. Adjacent to Husky Stadium is the dazzling Sound Transit light-rail station, opened in 2016 and connecting riders with Downtown and further on Angel Lake. Just below the stadium, on Union Bay, weekend water warriors rent rowboats or canoes at the **UW Waterfront Activities Center** (boat rental daily May–Oct 10am–6pm, until 9pm in summer; tel: 206-543 9433; www.washington.edu/ima/waterfront), while others bring their own beer and boats.

Burke Museum of Natural History and Culture ❹

Address: corner of 17th Avenue NE and NE 45th Street; www.burkemuseum.org
Tel: 206-616 3962
Opening Hrs: daily 10am–5pm, first Thu of the month until 8pm
Entrance Fee: charge, free first Thu of the month
Transportation: bus 44, 45, 49, 7C or 71

The Burke is the Northwest's premier museum of natural and cultural history. It has the only dinosaur skeletons in the Pacific Northwest, as well as the region's most comprehensive collection of native art from the Northwest coastal tribes.

The impressive anthropology, geology, and zoology collections when combined total more than 3 million specimens and artifacts. The museum has a 'walk-through' volcano, in addition to two permanent exhibits. One illustrates 500 million years of regional history, while the other highlights Pacific Rim cultures.

Henry Art Gallery ❺

Address: 15th Avenue NE and NE 41st Street; www.henryart.org
Tel: 206-543 2280
Opening Hrs: Wed, Fri–Sun 11am–4pm, Thu 11am–9pm
Entrance Fee: charge, free on Sun
Transportation: bus 43, 44, 48, 49 or 70

Cherry blossom at the University of Washington's Quad.

Not far from the Burke, this gallery has 46,000 sq ft (4,300 sq meters) of exhibit space to show its 24,000 pieces of 19th- to 21st-century art, including Japanese ceramics and the American and European painting collection of Horace C. Henry, a real-estate and railroad magnate for whom the museum was named in 1927.

Ravenna Park ❻

Seattle is young enough that residents still wistfully imagine the land as it was over a century ago – a wilderness of virgin forests and crystal waterways. Just north of the University of Washington is lush **Ravenna Park** (daily 6am–10pm; www.seattle.gov/parks/find/parks/ravenna-park), an unspoiled, deep, and wooded gorge far from the cosmopolitan life. Standing in silence next to a towering tree or a spill of green fern, it is not hard to imagine early settlers meeting a grizzly bear on the track or gathering herbs for healing. Both the town and the park were named Ravenna

View from Gas Works Park.

Machineries at Gas Works Park.

after the city on Italy's northern coast, which also stood on the edge of an ancient forest. The park offers tennis courts, a children's playground, a soccer field and picnic areas, as well as walking trails.

Wallingford ❼

West of the University District, Wallingford has a residential history steeped in memories of the sounds and stench that arose from the gasworks at the bottom of the neighborhood.

The district attracted working-class people who took a special pride in their schools. The earliest school in the area, Latona, was founded in 1889. The Home of the Good Shepherd, a girls' orphanage started in 1906 by the Sisters of Our Lady of Charity, is now a cultural and community center. Many of the neighborhood's old houses are elegant showpieces today. The historic 1904 Interlake Public School at the corner of 45th and Wallingford was converted into a mixed-use complex in 1983. Now **Wallingford Center** (www.wallingfordcenter.com), it has restaurants and shops, with apartments above. Shops and cafés line **45th Avenue** for several blocks, and you can find bakeries, bars, coffee- and teashops, as well as little specialty stores. The street even has two small movie theaters.

Gas Works Park ❽

Address: 2101 N Northlake Way; www.seattle.gov/parks/find/parks/gas-works-park
Tel: 206-684 4075
Opening Hrs: daily 6am–10pm
Entrance Fee: free
Transportation: bus 32

Hulking specters of a bygone age dominate **Gas Works Park**, situated on a southerly knob of land jutting into Lake Union and the front door to North Seattle. The Seattle Gas Light Company began to produce heating and lighting gas in this refinery on the 20-acre (8-hectare) knoll in 1906, fueling a rapidly growing city while earning a reputation as a filthy, foul-smelling killer of vegetation and wildlife. The plant closed its valves for good in 1956.

When the site was proposed as a park in the early 1960s, the city council hired landscape architect Richard Haag to create a lush, arboretum-type park. Instead, Haag submitted a plan incorporating much of the old gas plant. His design – with the rusting hulks of the gasworks in the middle of an undulating lawn – triumphed after a storm of controversy from those wishing for a more traditional park.

Kites fly high over the park's **Grand Mound**, a grassy hill built west of the park's core from abandoned industrial waste. Picnickers and joggers share the space along an incline, and at the crown, visitors admire a mosaic astrological sun and moon dial. The crest offers a great panorama of inner Seattle – Downtown, Queen Anne Hill, the Aurora Bridge (where Highway 99 crosses the Lake Washington Ship Canal) to the west, and Capitol Hill to the east.

Fremont 9

No bridge in the state opens more often than the **Fremont Bridge** 10, which was constructed in 1917 over the Lake Washington Ship Canal. You can watch boats go under the blue and orange drawbridge from a peaceful overlook at the **Fremont Canal Park**, a walkway on the north side of the waterway that features outdoor public art. Just east of the bridge on the north side is the headquarters of **Adobe Software**.

Fremont, strategically located at the northwest corner of Lake Union, was once a busy stop on the 1880s Burke-Gilman's SLS&E Railway, which carried lumber, coal, and passengers between Downtown and Ballard.

During Prohibition, Fremont's thriving taverns and hotel salons were closed, though the basement speakeasies flourished in spite of the frequent police raids. The **Aurora Bridge** 11 opened in 1932, bypassing Fremont.

By the 1960s, hippies and unemployed drifters had taken over the Fremont and Triangle hotels, but the 1970s brought a long-awaited local

Taking in the view of the skyline.

renaissance. Artists moved into the cheap brick studios in lower Fremont, setting up the kind of eclectic galleries, shops, and cafés that define the neighborhood today. Fremont got funky. Longtime Seattleites, however, view the current 'Fremont funkiness' as a little forced. Countless condo projects, which followed the offices of companies like Adobe and Google, pushed Fremont real-estate values up, and pushed out many of the artists and other folks who gave the neighborhood its charm.

These days, its stores are likely to be chic boutiques rather than hippie havens, but they *are* individually owned and fun to visit.

Fremont's tavern life has survived during these changes, and options have even expanded. Choices now range from a biker atmosphere to young adults on the prowl, to pubs serving microbrews and almost-nightly live music. Good restaurants

The 'Troll Under the Bridge' sculpture in Fremont.

Statue of Lenin in Fremont.

former mayor), all supposedly waiting for the electric trolley, which until the 1930s ran north to the town of Everett. All three sculptures are regularly and humorously decorated by the public, and Lenin is ceremoniously lit for the winter holidays.

GREEN LAKE, PHINNEY RIDGE, AND GREENWOOD

The shimmering waters of **Green Lake** ⑫ ripple against grassy shores in the high-density neighborhood of the same name.

It's a lake in a city surrounded by water, an algae-tinged reservoir born of glacial gougings 15,000 years ago. Runners and inline-skaters zip along the busy 2.8-mile (5km) perimeter path in all weather conditions. Rent a pair of blades or admire the occasionally aggressive ducks at the **Waldo Waterfowl Sanctuary** (commonly known as Duck Island). Also keep a look out for great blue herons and an eagle.

A community center and its environs offer facilities including football fields, tennis courts, a swimming pool, gym, rowboat and canoe rentals, a large playground, and a beach.

dish up cuisine ranging from vegetarian fare to Asian, to Greek, to upscale fine dining.

It is perfectly possible to take a tour of a chocolate factory, distillery, and brewery on the same day. The neighbourhood is also famous for its lively festivals, including Oktoberfest (http://fremontoktoberfest.com) and First Friday Artwalk (www.fremont firstfriday.com).

Fremont is home to some of the city's most beloved sculptures, including the **Fremont Troll**, an 18ft (5.5-meter) sculpture of a troll clutching a real Volkswagen beetle under the Aurora Bridge on Troll Avenue, and **The Statue of Lenin**, a 16ft (5-meter) bronze sculpture of Vladimir Lenin outside a gelato shop on the corner of Evanston Avenue and 36th Street. *Waiting for the Interurban*, on 34th Street, just north of the Aurora Bridge, features five life-size adults, a baby in arms, and a dog (said to have the face of a

A bird trainer at Woodland Park Zoo.

Restaurants around the lake range from trendy watering holes to fine Italian dining, to fish and chips.

The neighborhoods of **Phinney Ridge** ⑬ and **Greenwood** ⑭ blend easily together. Greenwood Avenue, once touted as Seattle's Antiques Row, mixes traditional antiques and secondhand stores with modern merchants and specialty food shops. There are galleries with contemporary Northwest art, home-style cafés, and several popular drinking establishments along the ridge.

Woodland Park Zoo ⑮

Address: 5500 Phinney Avenue N; www.zoo.org
Tel: 206-548 2500
Opening Hrs: daily May–Sept 9.30am–6pm, Oct–Apr 9.30am–4pm
Entrance Fee: charge
Transportation: bus 5 or 44 (from Ballard/University District)

Almost 300 animal species inhabit the hills between Phinney Ridge and Green Lake at the **Woodland Park Zoo**. The former wilderness estate of Guy Phinney, a leading Seattle real-estate developer in the 1880s, this 92-acre (37-hectare) park pioneered the concept of creating naturalistic habitats for animals.

The zoo demonstrates a true commitment to cageless animal care. Eight bioclimatic zones provide comfort for the animals and encourage natural behavior. The Asian Elephant Forest and African Savannah have earned international recognition, and the Northern Trail area is a visitors' favorite. Near the southeast exit, take time to smell the roses in the magnificent **Seattle Rose Garden** (free), originally laid out in the 1890s by old man Phinney himself.

ALONG LAKE WASHINGTON

On the southern stretch of the **Sand Point** peninsula, which juts out into Lake Washington north of the university, at least 87 species of birds and innumerable kinds of wildlife frequent the re-contoured terrain of

EAT

The best coffeehouse around is Zoka (2200 N 56th Street, Green Lake). Open from 6am to 9pm Sat–Thu and until 7pm on Fri, Zoka roasts its own beans, serves yummy baked goods, and plays host to live music.

Lion at Woodland Park Zoo.

Magnuson Park ⓰ (www.seattle.gov/parks/find/parks/magnuson-park), once a naval air station and now adorned with bluffs, sports fields, trails, and long, serene stretches of beach. On the same delta extending into Lake Washington, Bill Boeing flew his first airplane in 1916. In 1921, the first around-the-world flight began and ended here – four Navy aircraft left on April 6 and three arrived back on September 28.

In 1974, the city of Seattle granted the **National Oceanic and Atmospheric Administration** ⓱ (NOAA) the northern 114 acres (46 hectares) of what had been the naval air station for NOAA's Western Regional Center. It is now the largest federal center for atmospheric and oceanic research in the United States. Many of the facilities are open to the public through tours, but arrangements should be made first through the National Weather Service (tel: 206-526 6087) or the Pacific Marine Environmental Lab (tel: 206-526 6239).

Walkers are invited (upon advanced booking) to enter through NOAA's main gate and stroll through

the eerie and stunning **Magnuson Sculpture Park**, featuring six pieces along a half-mile stretch of prairie. The artists combined earth, wind, and water among their media: a concrete spiraling dome gives views in every direction; a viewpoint over the lake with chairs and sofas is cut from boulders; a bridge is lettered with excerpts from Moby Dick; and a 'sound garden' of lacy towers and tuned organ pipes makes music from the wind – this beloved sculpture was the inspiration behind the band name Soundgarden. For details and information on security measures, go to www.wrc.noaa.gov.

About a mile to the north of Magnuson Park is Seattle's largest freshwater bathing beach (a lifeguard is on duty) at **Matthews Beach Park** ⓲ (www.seattle.gov/parks/find/parks/matthews-beach-park), just off the Burke-Gilman Trail. At the south end, cross the footbridge above Thornton Creek to reach the tiny, charming **Thornton Creek Natural Area**, where wildlife finds a convenient retreat from the noisy, urban melee.

Sailboat preparing to dock at the canal.

In the tiny hamlet of Pontiac, a railroad worker once hung a sign saying just 'Lake' on a shed near the tracks of Northern Pacific Railroad. The name stuck, and **Lake City** ⑲ was annexed by Seattle in 1954. Here, the blur of car lots, gas stations, and supermarkets lining Lake City Way may not make a huge impression, but the region has a few spots of distinction. A flagpole dedicated to World War II veterans sits in the smallest official city park, and a **Will Rogers Memorial** (12501 28th Avenue NE) honors the Oklahoma-born wit and philosopher, who spent one of his last days playing polo here. He then left Seattle for Alaska, and was killed in a plane crash.

Heading west

If access to the jeweled shores of Puget Sound means prosperity, then Seattleites are rich indeed, for 220-acre (89-hectare) **Carkeek Park** ⑳ (www.seattle.gov/parks/find/parks/carkeek-park), on the coast of Puget Sound and northwest of Green Lake, winds and plunges down into a maze of wooded pathways, over the railroad tracks, and onto an unfettered stretch of beach. The park was named for Morgan and Emily Carkeek, early Seattle contractors and philanthropists. Locals have successfully labored to re-establish the park's Piper's Creek as a salmon-spawning site.

Following the railroad tracks south leads toward the proud-hearted neighborhood of Ballard. The tracks run through **Golden Gardens Park** ㉑ (on Seaview Place NW; www.seattle.gov/parks/find/parks/golden-gardens-park), neatly dividing it into two distinct sections: a forested hillside and a golden beach stretching along **Shilshole Bay**, Seattle's coast of blue. Sunbathe, scuba dive, dig for clams, or watch the sailboats breezing out toward the Puget isles. Wind up Golden Gardens Drive and go south until a 'scenic drive' sign at NW 77th denotes the aptly named **Sunset Hill**.

At the underwater fish-viewing area at Ballard Locks.

Ballard ㉒

Scandinavians were drawn here by the fishing, lumber, and boat-building opportunities found in such a majestic and watery region, much like their homeland. When downtown Seattle was rebuilt after the great fire of 1889 and Washington entered the Union as the 42nd state, Gilman Park, with nearly 2,000 residents, hurried to be the first to incorporate, naming their boomtown **Ballard.**

Early Ballard was a bastion of pioneer revelry, said to hold 27 saloons on a four-block strip. It has fewer today, but Ballard still sports its share of bars and plays a key role in Seattle's music scene. It's a fun neighborhood, with independently owned stores and businesses, a booming culinary scene, and a mix of fisherman and hipsters thronging the streets.

Nordic Heritage Museum ㉓

Address: 3014 NW 67th Street; www.nordicmuseum.org
Tel: 206-789 5707
Opening Hrs: Tue–Sat 10am–4pm, Sun noon–4pm

Entrance Fee: charge, free first Thu of the month
Transportation: bus 17X

The exhibits at this heritage center tell a graphic story of Scandinavian immigrants' travel to the new land and the impact those immigrants had on the Pacific Northwest. Three floors in a former elementary school describe the cultural legacy of Sweden, Norway, Iceland, Finland, and Denmark.

Hiram M. Chittenden Locks ㉔

Address: 3015 NW 54th Street; www.nws.usace.army.mil
Tel: 206-764 3742
Opening Hrs: locks daily 7am–9pm; Visitor Center daily 10am–6pm, until 4pm in winter, closed Tue–Wed, Oct–Apr
Entrance Fee: free
Transportation: bus 17, 29, or 44

Every year, about 100,000 commercial and pleasure vessels navigate through the 1917-era **Hiram M. Chittenden Locks** – also known as the **Ballard Locks** – two masonry gates on the north bank of the canal and opposite Discovery Park, which raise and lower boats between the level of the saltwater of Puget Sound and the freshwater of Lake Washington. A fascinating Visitor Center explains the history and workings of the locks.

About 500,000 sockeye, chinook (king), and coho salmon use the same channel to get to their spawning grounds in Lake Washington and streams farther along in the Cascade Range to the east, climbing a 21-level fish ladder built to preserve the migrating runs. In summer, visitors can watch their passage upstream through six lit underwater viewing windows, a moving portrait of creatures driven by a mandate of nature and against all odds back to their birthplace.

Within the grounds are the terraced lawns and roses of the waterside **Carl S. English Jr Ornamental Gardens** ㉕ (daily 7am–9pm). Named after one of the region's top horticulturalists in the early 1900s, the gardens make an excellent picnic spot.

Fresh and salt water passing through the Hiram M. Chittenden Locks.

Lottie's Café in Columbia City.

WEST AND SOUTH SEATTLE

The 'birthplace of Seattle' has views, parks, and sandy beaches, while South Seattle is the place for new homeowners and urban pioneers.

It was on the windswept shores of what is now Alki Beach that Seattle's pioneers first built a community. The area's early settlers, led by Arthur Denny, came from the state of Illinois, in the American Midwest, seeking a better life. After one blustery winter on Alki (pronounced Al-kai, rhymes with 'pie'), however, most of the Denny party moved away from the beach's winds to the shelter and deeper anchorage of Elliott Bay.

That exodus seems surprising given Alki's current popularity. In summer, the sandy beach is a mass of tanned bodies, and year-round, the footpath and its adjacent bike-and-skating path are crowded with promenading, strutting, jogging people.

WEST SEATTLE

Southwest of Downtown, West Seattle is located on a peninsula separated from the mainland by the Duwamish River and reached via the massive West Seattle Bridge, which arches over busy Harbor Island. The manmade island, located at the river's mouth where it empties into Elliott Bay, operates as a storage depot for much of the equipment that serves the busy Port of Seattle. It is home

to shipyards and containership loading facilities, and a steady stream of trucks hauling containers.

There is something about crossing the bridge and arriving in West Seattle that feels like an escape from the city. With its relaxed, seaside kind of a vibe, life seems a little slower than in other parts of the city.

Another fun way to reach West Seattle is by the King County Water Taxi (from Pier 55 on the Downtown waterfront to Seacrest Marina), which takes about 12 minutes. From the

Main Attractions
The Junction
Alki Beach
Schmitz Park
Lincoln Park
Columbia City
Georgetown
Seward Park

Map
Page 148

Alki Point Lighthouse on Puget Sound, with Mount Rainier behind.

A King County Water Taxi departing for a trip across Elliott Bay.

marina it's a short walk to Alki Beach, or you can take the free shuttle van, which operates between the Admiral District, Alki Point, and the Junction.

The Junction ❶

The main commercial district of West Seattle is better known as **The Junction**. It's centered around California Avenue SW, and SW Alaska Street. There's a mix of boutiques, second-hand stores, and restaurants and bars. Easy Street Records (4559 California Avenue SW; tel: 206-938 3279; www. easystreetonline.com; Mon–Sat 9am–9pm, until 7pm Sun) is one of the anchors and important in the local music scene, showcasing live artists and staging album release parties.

The Junction's murals are remarkable. More than half a dozen wall-sized paintings decorate the retail and commercial buildings, most depicting the area as it was over a century ago. The best of these is on the wall at California and Edmunds,

and looks as if one could walk right into a 19th-century street scene.

North of The Junction on California is the rolling **Admiral District**, named for Admiral Way, which climbs the hill from the West Seattle Bridge on the east and slides down to Alki Beach on the west. The district is home to the last of West Seattle's movie theaters, the historic **Admiral Theatre**, which reopened in 2017 after a remodeling and an extension and now boasts four modern screens. A lovely old brick public library is here with some restaurants, coffeehouses, and West Seattle High School.

This part of Seattle is on two hills, Gatewood and Genesee, which give it plenty of view-enhanced property. Homes on the west sides of both hills overlook Puget Sound and the Olympic Mountains, while those on the east have views over Downtown and Harbor Island. At the top of Genesee Hill are scenic outlooks

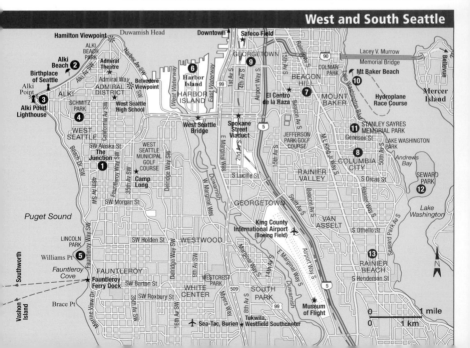

including **Hamilton Viewpoint**, at the north end of California Avenue, and **Belvedere Viewpoint**, which is on Admiral Way.

Alki Beach ②

The closest thing the city has to a Southern California outdoor scene is **Alki Beach**, which, for many years, was a summer place where teenagers brought their cars. Anti-cruising laws were enacted to restrict drivers to a single pass along the beach's Alki Avenue every four hours, cutting down considerably the noise and traffic nuisance that so irked local residents – many of them occupants of the condo complexes across from the beach.

In summer, though, Alki still attracts a good crowd of shiny cars, bronzed bodies in bikinis, and teenagers out to see and be seen. Beach volleyball courts are usually bouncing with players and lined with spectators.

In the fall, winter, and spring, Alki is a wonderful place for a beach stroll under swirling clouds and squawking seagulls. If the wind and rain that drove the Denny party across the bay do get to be too much, the area also offers plenty of shelter and places to eat, ranging from bakeries and delis to a chain seafood restaurant with an excellent view of the Downtown skyline.

The oldest landmark here is a concrete column marking the beach as the 'Birthplace of Seattle'. It was presented to the city in 1905 by Arthur Denny's daughter and stands now at 63rd Avenue SW and Alki Avenue. In 1926, when the column was moved from its original location on the other side of the street, a hunk of the Plymouth Rock, the Massachusetts boulder that the Pilgrims steered toward in 1620, was embedded in its base.

Alki Point Lighthouse ③

Address: 3201 Alki Avenue SW
Tel: 206-841 3519
Opening Hrs: June–Aug Sat–Sun

View across Elliott Bay from Alki Beach.

The lighthouse on Alki.

1pm–4pm; guided tours by appointment
Entrance Fee: free
Transportation: bus 37, 56 or 57

At the southern end of the beach – just before it becomes residential – is the **Alki Point Lighthouse**, established in 1881. The present lighthouse, standing on a small reservation behind apartments and condominiums, dates from 1913.

Schmitz Park ④

Address: 5551 SW Admiral Way;
www.seattle.gov/parks/find/parks/
schmitz-preserve-park
Tel: 206-684 4075
Opening Hrs: daily 6am–10pm
Entrance Fee: free
Transportation: bus 50 or 56

Just east of Alki is this 53-acre (21-hectare) nature preserve with narrow trails through thick woods, but no picnic areas or playgrounds. The old-growth trees provide a wonderful canopy for birds and quiet contemplation. Just off 35th Avenue SW, the hillside West Seattle Municipal Golf Course offers views of downtown Seattle, Elliott Bay, and the Duwamish

waterway. The 18-hole, par-72 golf course was laid out here in 1940.

Continue along the waterfront, which becomes **Beach Drive**, passing beachside homes both extravagant and funky, as well as apartment buildings and open spaces such as Emma Schmitz Memorial Park. Beach Drive culminates in the lower part of Lincoln Park, at the foot of Gatewood Hill. Alki Beach Park may be the most visible of this area's city parks, but it is certainly not the only one.

Lincoln Park ⑤

Address: 8011 Fauntleroy Way SW;
www.seattle.gov/parks/find/parks/
lincoln-park
Tel: 206-684 4075
Opening Hrs: daily 4.30am–11.30pm
Entrance Fee: free
Transportation: bus 550, 554, or C

Lincoln Park has miles of wooded and waterfront trails within its 135 acres (55 hectares). It's hard to believe you're in a large metropolitan area when you take in the uninterrupted views over Puget Sound, toward the Olympic Mountains. The park really is one of Seattle's gems. Colman Pool

Schmitz Park.

is a heated 164ft (50-meter) Olympic-size outdoor pool open only in summer. Filled partly with chlorinated freshwater and part saltwater, Colman Pool is accessible only on foot; the roads through the park are restricted to park vehicles. At the south end of Lincoln Park is the **Fauntleroy Ferry Dock**, where boats depart for Vashon Island and Southworth. Either destination makes a pleasant day trip. Vashon, just 20 minutes from the dock, is a charming rural area far from the rush of city life. Many residents farm as a hobby and make the daily commute to Seattle or Tacoma via ferry; a few have found work on the island itself, in bucolic pursuits like orchid growing.

One of the city's few parks to offer overnight facilities, **Camp Long** (just off 35th Avenue SW at Dawson; tel: 206-684 7434; www.seattle.gov/parks/find/centers/camp-long/schurman-rock-at-camp-long) is 68 acres (27 hectares) of wilderness. Open to organized groups and the public for camping and wilderness-skills programs, Camp Long is a popular site for weddings and also features Schurman

Colman Pool was originally a saltwater pool with mud sides. The existing structure was built in 1941, thanks to a donation from local businessman Kenneth Colman.

Rock (Tue–Sat 10am–6pm), a decent rock wall for climbing instruction and practice.

Harbor Island 6

Located between Downtown and West Seattle, and beneath the West Seattle Bridge, **Harbor Island** is home to the city's shipyards and loading facilities for freighters. It is a landfill of more than 25 million cubic yards (19 million cubic meters), all of it dredged up and reclaimed from the bottom of the Duwamish River.

When it was completed in 1912, Harbor Island was the largest man-made island in the world. Shortly after the island was created, the meandering Duwamish was straightened, allowing much greater space along its banks for industrial development. South from Elliott Bay, past busy Harbor Island and through Seattle's industrial corridor, the river passes salvage ships, commercial shipping lanes, Boeing Field, and the town of Tukwila.

SOUTH SEATTLE

Overlooked for many years, South Seattle has been discovered by 'urban pioneers' and is now a destination itself. Three neighborhoods in particular – Beacon Hill, Columbia City,

A FARMERS' MARKET

Seattle is a city of farmers' markets, there's no doubt, starting with Pike Place – the crown jewel. While the Ballard and University District markets get a whole lot of attention, it's the Columbia City Farmers' Market (www.seattlefarmersmarkets.org) that's got the city charmed. More than 40 vendors set up in a long line next to an expansive, rolling lawn in front of the neighborhood library – particularly popular with children, who happily frolic and shriek until the sun starts to set. Live music and cooking demonstrations are on offer, as well as prepared food, including Indian curries and Mexican tacos. Check the website for the market schedule, but generally it's held Wednesdays from 3pm to 7pm, May through October.

WHERE

Seattle's **White Center** was named for George W.H. White, a partner in the railroad that served this part of the city when it was a rugged logging district. Government housing projects went up after World War II, and later, taverns were built just outside the city limits, earning White Center the nickname Rat City in the 1960s. Nowadays, it is one of the few places left with affordable real estate for first-time homebuyers.

TIP

The ethnic diversity of South Seattle provides an interesting mix of shopping and eating opportunities.

and Georgetown – are areas to consider visiting. A light-rail link from Downtown to Sea-Tac Airport, with stations in Beacon Hill, Mount Baker, Columbia City, and Rainier Beach, provides easy access to South Seattle.

Beacon Hill ❼

On the east side of Interstate 5 is **Beacon Hill**, an affordable residential area with a diverse ethnic mix. The view from Beacon Hill itself is fantastic, stretching out over Downtown all the way down to Seattle's waterfront. The city-owned Jefferson Park Golf Course, where pro Fred Couples perfected his swing, is located here. For many years Beacon Hill was home to success-story **Amazon**, which was headquartered in a tall Art Deco building – a towering landmark near the top of the hill that was part of an old hospital – until it relocated to South Lake Union neighborhood in 2010.

Columbia City ❽

Another neighborhood that has been gentrified in recent years is **Columbia City**. The area now has a small cinema, a good bakery, several popular restaurants and watering holes – even a wine bar. Older houses are sporting fresh coats of paint and attention is being paid to detail, a sure sign that real-estate values are buoyant. The gorgeous weekly summer farmers' market is the main reason to visit.

Georgetown ❾

To the northwest is **Georgetown**, which has seen a surge in countercultural types. With some of the city's more affordable real estate, the area has sprouted artists' studios, parks, and museums, as well as the requisite coffeehouses and a microbrewery. There are also several interesting independent shops, such as Georgetown Records and Fantagraphics. A lively 'Art Attack' (http://georgetownartattack.com) featuring art, music, and community events is held on the second Saturday of each month.

LAKE WASHINGTON SHORES

Lake Washington is lined by various neighborhoods. East of Beacon Hill is the comfortable neighborhood of **Mount Baker**, which has fine old homes, a few interesting shops, and a diverse population. Wind down the hill through Mount Baker and you're on the shores of Lake Washington. At **Mount Baker Beach ❿**, a large, blue boathouse holds rowing shells, which are taken out daily by rowers young and old.

Along the west side of the lake runs **Lake Washington Boulevard**, which begins at the University of Washington in North Seattle and continues all the way down to Seward Park. The road gives eastward views of the Cascade Range and meanders past the string of grassy Lake Washington beachfront parks. An adjacent cycle path follows the road for miles.

A speedboat on Lake Washington.

On scheduled Sundays from May through September the road is closed to automobile traffic in observance of Bicycle Sunday (May–Sept 10am–6pm; more details at http://parkways.seattle.gov/2016/05/04/join-us-for-bicycle-sundays-along-lake-washington-blvd). It's a beautiful ride any time, but the event makes it even more appealing.

The stretch of lake shoreline from just south of the bridge – which carries Interstate 90 to Andrews Bay – is hydroplane race heaven during the annual Seafair celebration, which was first staged in 1950. The event draws thousands of spectators despite the noise of engines on 150mph (240kmh) boats. Seafair's official viewing beach is **Stanley Sayres Memorial Park** ⓫, where the hydro pits are, but many fans watch from homes along the lake, and hundreds pay a per-foot charge to moor their boats along the challenging course.

The Lake Washington parks culminate in **Seward Park** ⓬, 300 acres (121 hectares) of greenery, trails, and waterfront. Bald eagles have bred here, and there's plenty of other wildlife, too. The park has an art studio, a playground, an outdoor amphitheater, and a short lakeside trail for cyclists and runners.

RAINIER VALLEY

In **Rainier Valley**, named for the views of Mount Rainier that it enjoys, the old Sicks Stadium once stood, home successively to baseball teams the Seattle Rainiers and the Seattle Pilots. Neighborhoods near the Duwamish River as it winds south from Elliott Bay include Holly Park, Highland Park, South Park, Beverly Park and, farther southwest, Burien. To the east on the edge of the lake is **Rainier Beach** ⓭.

Limited real estate in the city's International District lured Asian immigrants to search out new areas for development, including the area south of Safeco Field. This neighborhood now has a substantial Asian population, mostly Vietnamese, and some good restaurants. Many more Asian restaurants line Pacific Highway South toward Sea-Tac International Airport.

A local Starbucks in Columbia City.

Fall colors in Bellevue, with the Seattle skyline visible on the other side of Lake Washington.

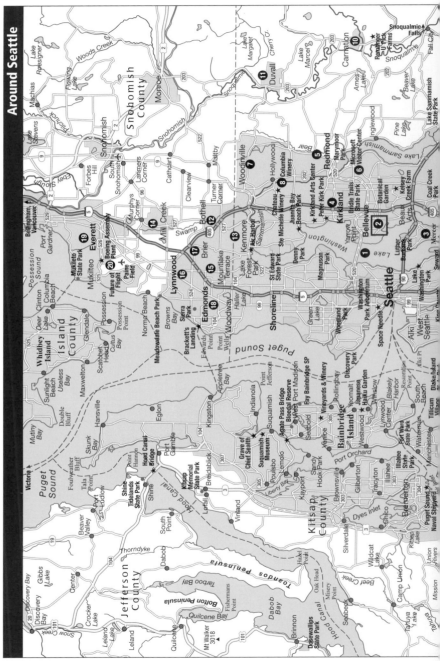

EASTSIDE

The Eastside – east of Lake Washington – is a lush location of big homes, fine wineries, and high-tech, high-profile companies like Microsoft.

The Eastside is smooth and sleek, well-heeled, and well-connected. The presence of globally known technology firms has brought an international flavor to the area, attracting workers from many different parts of the world. Stroll along the Kirkland waterfront, espresso in hand. Stop for an outdoor lunch on a sunlit deck overlooking Lake Washington. Head to downtown Bellevue for an afternoon at the arts museum. Visit the velodrome in Redmond's Marymoor Park and cheer on champion cyclists. Drive into Issaquah for an evening of theater, or head out to Woodinville for an afternoon of wine tasting and music at Chateau Ste Michelle.

Although these scenes are taken for granted by Eastsiders, they are often overlooked by visitors intent on seeing just the sites of Seattle's city center.

ACROSS LAKE WASHINGTON

It wasn't long ago that visiting the Eastside from Seattle meant packing a picnic lunch and going for a drive in the country. Today, all of that has changed. Seattleites zip back and forth across Lake Washington to the east side of the lake (20 minutes

one-way, if the traffic gods are with you, over an hour if they're not) with regularity. In fact, increasing numbers that can afford it pack up and move to the Eastside permanently, making the trip across the lake twice a day as commuters.

Some don't even need to commute. Formerly sleepy cities like Bellevue, Redmond and Kirkland now have high-profile identities as financial or technology centers, or, like Woodinville, as increasingly sophisticated recreation centers.

Main Attractions
Lake Washington
Bellevue Square
Kirkland's Carillon Point
Redmond
Microsoft Visitor Center
Woodinville Wineries

Map
Page 156

Bellevue Arts Museum.

Bellevue shopping mall just before Christmas.

Many high-profile companies have made the Eastside their home. Microsoft has long held its headquarters there, while global companies like Google, Nintendo of America and T-Mobile USA have placed their North American headquarters east of Seattle. It's **Lake Washington** ❶ that provides the frame of reference for the term 'Eastside', a designation that applies to the cities, towns, and rural areas that dot the hills and valleys to the east of the lake. Navigating the waterways and highways of the Eastside requires a few reference points, and the most useful are the bridges that run east and west across Lake Washington. The new **Evergreen Point Floating Bridge** (SR 520) opened in 2016 to replace its old and earthquake-prone predecessor of the same name. It connects Seattle from just south of the University District in North Seattle to Kirkland and continues on to Redmond – but trips across this bridge come with a price (toll charges).

Both the **Lacey V. Murrow Memorial Bridge** and the **Homer M. Hadley Bridge** on Interstate 90 connect South Seattle with southern

The New Evergreen Point Floating Bridge.

Bellevue via Mercer Island, a residential community about midway across Lake Washington.

The main north-south route on the east side of the lake is Interstate 405, which runs the length of the state and goes directly through Bellevue, Kirkland, and north on to Bothell and Woodinville. Interstate 405 eventually leads farther north to the Canadian border and to Vancouver, British Columbia.

In many ways the Eastside owes its development to the bridges that connect it to Seattle in a truly love-hate relationship. As well as some of the most spectacular scenic views, these bridges can be the scenes of horrendous traffic congestion. It may be, in fact, that the scenery contributes to the traffic problems. Residents rarely seem blasé about Lake Washington, or the spectacular vistas of Mount Rainier, also visible from the bridges.

BELLEVUE ❷

Given the beauty of Lake Washington and the finite aspect of its waterfront, it's no surprise that from **Bellevue** north to Bothell, waterfront property is prime real estate. Properties with private docks, private beaches, and multi-level houses cascading down the hills can be seen from the highways; they look even more spectacular from the water.

Bellevue's **Meydenbauer Bay** is an area of luxury homes and condominiums on the lake west of Bellevue's downtown area and was named for William Meydenbauer, a Seattle baker. North of Meydenbauer Bay, the exclusive communities of Medina, Yarrow Point and Clyde Hill are other prominent Bellevue-area waterfront places. Public-beach access to the lake around Bellevue is limited, but **Chism Beach** (1175 96th Avenue SE) offers swimming, trails, and picnic facilities. Other reasonable beaches in Bellevue include Meydenbauer, Newcastle, and Enatai.

Bellevue Square ❹

Address: NE 8th Street and Bellevue Way; http://bellevuecollection.com
Tel: 425-454 8096
Opening Hrs: Mon–Sat 9.30am–9.30pm, Sun 11am–7pm
Aside from Lake Washington, the strongest attraction in Bellevue for visitors is **Bellevue Square**, known to locals as **Bel Square**. Opened in 1946 as one of the first suburban shopping centers in the country, the upscale mall now has some of the area's trendiest shops.

Bellevue Arts Museum ❺

Address: 510 Bellevue Way NE; www.bellevuearts.org
Tel: 425-519 0770
Opening Hrs: Wed–Sun 11am–5pm, first Fri of the month 11am–8pm
Entrance Fee: charge, free first Fri of the month
The Bellevue Arts Museum is across from Bellevue Square. The museum specializes in the decorative arts.

Lincoln Square ❻

Address: 700 Bellevue Way NE;

A view of Bellevue.

Luxury homes on Mercer Island.

http://lincolnsquareexpansion.com
Tel: 425-454 8096
Opening Hrs: Mon–Sat
9.30am–9.30pm, Sun 11am–7pm

Also in the area is the **Lincoln Square** complex, featuring a shopping center on the ground floor with a home-related focus. It also has fine restaurants as well as a billiards club and a 16-screen movie theater. But much of Lincoln Square's space is rented out as offices for companies including Microsoft and Eddie Bauer. A new addition is the Two Lincoln Tower, housing, among others, premier offices and luxury residences, and the W Bellevue hotel.

The Bravern

Address: 11111 NE 8th Street;
www.thebravern.com
Tel: 425-456 8795
Opening Hrs: Mon–Sat 10am–8pm,
Sun noon–6pm

This outdoor, European-inspired shopping center makes for a classy, upscale shopping experience. Stores include the Neiman Marcus, Louis

Vuitton, Jimmy Choo, and Salvatore Ferragamo. There are various dining options, including the acclaimed Wild Ginger.

Performance and roses

Lovers of the performing arts are also very well catered for in the **Meydenbauer Center** (11100 NE 6th Street; tel: 425-637 1020; www.meydenbauer.com). This convention facility features a 36,000-sq-ft (3,350-sq-meter) exhibition hall and a 410-seat performing-arts theater.

Across the street from the southern side of Bel Square is Bellevue's **Downtown Park and Rose Garden** (10201 NE 4th Street; open dawn until 11pm), a 20-acre (8-hectare) site in the heart of the shopping district. It includes a high, cascading waterfall, a canal enclosing a large meadow, and an ice rink, November through January.

Just south of the park is **Old Bellevue** (http://visitoldbellevue.com), the city's first shopping district before the arrival of Bel Square. The two-block precinct includes cafés, delis, restaurants and several independent shops. Keep in mind that in Bellevue 'old' means dating to about 1940.

Bellevue Botanical Garden

Address: 12001 Main Street; www.bellevuebotanical.org
Tel: 425-452 2750
Opening Hrs: daily dawn to dusk
Entrance Fee: free

An urban refuge comprising 53 acres (21 hectares) of cultivated gardens, restored woodlands, and natural wetlands is one of Bellevue's most popular attractions. In December, it hosts the Garden d'Lights Festival (www.gardendlights.org), when more than half a million lights transform the garden into 'a blossoming winter wonderland'.

Kelsey Creek Farm

Address: 410 130th Place SE; www.farmerjayne.com
Tel: 425-452 7688
Opening Hrs: daily 9.30am–3.30pm
Entrance Fee: free

Bellevue's Kelsey Creek Farm has pigs, horses, chickens, goats, and rabbits, as well as walking trails, picnic tables, and plenty of room to roam.

MERCER ISLAND ❸

Named for Aaron Mercer, one of the first local homesteaders, **Mercer Island** sits directly west of Bellevue, about midway in Lake Washington between Bellevue and the southern part of Seattle. A thriving community of over 22,000, it was incorporated in 1960. There are still people around who remember Mercer Island as a summertime vacation area, accessible only by ferry. Interstate 90 and the bridges that linked the island to Seattle and the Eastside changed all that.

Today, it's a residential community known for some incredible luxury homes, including the enormous compound built by Microsoft co-founder and Vulcan Inc. supremo Paul Allen, and an excellent theater. Worth a stop is **Luther Burbank Park** (2040 84th Avenue SE). Originally a private estate, the park has 77 gorgeous acres (31 hectares) of lake front, tennis courts, an outdoor amphitheater, and a playground for kids. The sandy beach completes this great spot for summer.

KIRKLAND ❹

Just north of Bellevue, with much of its shopping, restaurants, and

TIP

Public boat launches in both Bellevue and Kirkland make Lake Washington accessible to all kinds of floating craft, from sailboats and motorboats to cabin cruisers and canoes. If you're taking the organized lake cruise, ask the pilot to point out Bill Gates' multimillion-dollar waterfront house in Medina.

The Kirkland Arts Center.

Microsoft Visitor Center exhibits.

then left onto Juanita Drive. This county-run beach has summertime lifeguards, roped-off swimming areas, and a snack bar. The park is open year-round and has several picnic areas, a children's playground, and a number of piers jutting into the lake.

Other Kirkland beach parks include O.O. Denny, Waverly, and Houghton. **Bridle Trails State Park** (5300 116th Avenue NE; http://parks. state.wa.us/481/Bridle-Trails), right in the middle of residential neighborhoods, is a heavily wooded haven for horseback riders and hikers who don't mind sharing the trails with horses. The park is located in south Kirkland near the Bellevue border and can be accessed off 132nd Avenue NE. Joggers and walkers can also make use of the 11.5-mile (18.5km) -long Kirkland Cross Corridor Trail (www.kirklandwa.gov/ CrossKirklandCorridor), which follows the old railway line from Yarrow Woods to Totem Lake.

Local arts, retail, and recreation

Kirkland Parkplace (on 6th Street and Central Way) has movie theaters,

commercial areas hugging the shore of Lake Washington, is **Kirkland**. This city of nearly 90,000 has a remarkable amount of public access to waterfront through parks, open space, and walkways. Public access to the waterfront has been a priority here since the city was first incorporated in 1905. A walk along **Lake Street** passes by a number of green, grassy parks which provide public access to the lake and to its waterfront restaurants.

Kirkland parks

A central part of Kirkland's Downtown is **Peter Kirk Park** (202 3rd Street), with tennis courts, a ball field, one of the few public outdoor swimming pools on the Eastside, and a children's playground. On summer evenings, the floodlit baseball field is a big draw. A few miles north of Downtown is the **Juanita Beach Park** (9703 NE Juanita Drive). To reach the park, head to the northern end of Lake Street, turn left onto Central Way, right onto Market, and

MORE AT MARYMOOR

Lush, sprawling Marymoor Park isn't just 640 acres (259 hectares) of good, green fun: it's also home to Washington's one and only velodrome, a 400-meter bicycle-racing track. A local association keeps the velodrome in top condition, with classes, workshops, and events held regularly. Also at this favorite Eastside Park is one of the best off-leash pet areas in the city. Its 40 acres (16 hectares) have been dubbed 'Doggy Disneyland' by the Seattle Parks Department. Add to the mix plenty of playing fields, Clise Mansion (an early 1900s residence now on the National Register of Historic Places), and a concert series every summer at the park's 5,000-person concert venue, and it becomes clear: Marymoor definitely makes the cut.

gift shops, a bookstore, a gym, and a great selection of places to eat.

A good place to see art is the **Kirkland Arts Center** (620 Market Street; tel: 425-822 7161; www.kirkland artscenter.org; Tue–Fri 11am–6pm, Sat 11am–5pm; free), which offers classes and exhibits for children and adults and has a changing roster of 'happenings'. Kirkland also has numerous outdoor art works.

Carillon Point (4100 Carillon Point, on Lake Washington Boulevard at Lakeview Drive; www.carillon-point. com) is a waterfront complex that includes a luxury hotel, restaurants, waterfront walkways, and docks, as well as shops and restaurants, a mile or two south of Downtown. Two large office towers and a hillside of condominiums initially drew complaints from nearby residents, but the views from the hotel, the restaurants, and the docks *are* spectacular.

REDMOND ⑤

In the past two decades **Redmond** has tripled its population to over 57,000 residents (the number climbs 100,000 during the workday) and shows no signs of slowing.

Fortunately, there's still enough open space in the city for one of the signature activities, hot-air ballooning. Look out toward the northern part of the city along the Sammamish River on just about any summer or fall evening and chances are you'll see colorful hot-air balloons drifting peacefully in the sky. Balloon rides are available from several companies and in a variety of styles: some offer 'red carpet' romantic rides complete with champagne and gourmet lunches or dinners; others offer family prices.

At the Microsoft Visitor Center.

Captain piloting his sailboat off the shores of Kirkland.

Washington wines

The Northwest's pioneering spirit extends to its wine industry. Local wineries have reached a global market in just a few decades.

In 1980, Washington state had fewer than 20 wineries; today it is the nation's second-largest producer of wine (after California), with more than 900 wineries and 14 distinct American Viticultural Areas. This is good news for wine lovers, though this *can* make the choice of what to buy and where to visit a little overwhelming.

While often processed in the Seattle region (specifically Woodinville), Washington-grown grapes are mostly nurtured on the eastern side of the Cascades in an arid environment that has long, warm, sunny days and cool nights. The state has ideal geography and conditions for growing premium *vinifera* wine grapes. More than 43,000 acres (17,000 hectares) in the state are currently planted with wine grapes of more than 60 different varieties. Leading red varieties include merlot, cabernet sauvignon, syrah, cabernet franc, malbec, pinot

In the tasting room of the Chateau Ste Michelle winery.

noir, lemberger, and sangiovese; white varieties include chardonnay, riesling, sauvignon blanc, pinot gris, gewurztraminer, semillon, chenin blanc, and viognier.

Washington's potential for premium wine was discovered in 1966 when renowned wine critic Andre Tchelistcheff first sampled a homemade Washington gewurztraminer and called it the best produced in the US. In 2001, *Wine Enthusiast Magazine* cited Washington as 'Wine Region of the Year' for quickly emerging as a global wine industry recognized for quality.

In 2006, the state's Quilceda Creek Vintners (coincidentally owned by Tchelistcheff's nephew, Alex Golitzen) made history by earning its second consecutive 100-point wine rating from Robert Parker's *Wine Advocate* for its cabernet sauvignon.

Seattle-area wineries

Though most of the state's wineries are situated closer to where the grapes are grown, on the east side of the Cascade Mountains, a certain number are in the Seattle area, primarily on the Eastside. Chateau Ste Michelle (www.ste-michelle.com), the largest winery in the Pacific Northwest, has its headquarters in Woodinville. Across the street is Columbia Winery (www.columbia winery.com). The majority of the state's wineries are smaller, family-owned operations, however, many of which have tasting rooms open to the public on weekends, if not more frequently. Other Woodinville wineries worth a visit include Chatter Creek (www.chatter creek.com), Cuillin Hills (www.cuillinhills.com), Novelty Hill-Januik Winery (www.noveltyhill januik.com), and Di Stefano (www.distefano winery.com). Also in the Seattle area are Northwest Cellars (www.northwestcellars.com) in Kirkland, Hedges Family Estate (www. hedgesfamilyestate.com) in Benton, and Wilridge (www.wilridgewinery.com) near Yakima.

About 50 wineries are within a couple of hours' drive of the city. Two of the most accessible are Bainbridge Island Vineyards and Winery (www.bainbridgevineyards. com), on one of the main ferry routes to the Olympic Peninsula, and the Mount Baker Winery (www.mountbakervineyards.com), just outside Bellingham.

The **Sammamish River** (often called the Sammamish Slough) winds its way south from Bothell to Marymoor Park, passing through Redmond and Woodinville. An asphalt pathway alongside the slough makes a perfect path for cyclists, and on weekends the place gets a mix of visitors with a wide range of bicycling skills.

Toward the southern end of Redmond, the river drifts past **Marymoor Park** (6046 West Lake Sammamish Parkway NE; 8am–dusk), a pretty 640-acre (259-hectare) county-operated park which includes ball fields, bicycle and hiking trails, and the largest off-leash dog area in the state. The park features a 5,000-person concert venue (www.marymoorconcerts.com) which hosts a popular summer concert series. The park is also the home of the **Marymoor Velodrome**; the banked racing course attracts professional cyclists from all around the world.

Microsoft Visitor Center

Since the 1980s, Redmond has probably become best known as the headquarters of **Microsoft**. The company employs more than 114,000 people worldwide, but it all began – and continues – here. Locally, Microsoft occupies office space in 120 buildings in Redmond, Bellevue, Seattle, and Issaquah, most of them numbered accordingly, ie, Building 33, Building 34, etc. In the Puget Sound area, there are some 41,000 Microsoft employees.

Unfortunately for the curious, the ambitious, or the simply digitally desperate, its campuses are closed to the public and guarded around the clock. There is, however, the **Microsoft Visitor Center ❻** (1510 NE 36th Street, Building 92; tel: 425-703 6214; Tue–Fri 9am–7pm, Mon from 10am: www.microsoft.com/en-us/visitorcenter) in Redmond. Here, visitors can learn all about the company's history via a timeline, and see technological advances from the earliest PC computer to the latest research. Visitors can also play in the Video Games Room with tech toys like multiscreens, the Xbox, and screen interfaces controlled by hand

Relaxing in the sunshine at Chateau Ste Michelle Winery.

movements. They can also learn about the latest Windows apps.

Although the software giant dominates Redmond, video-game company **Nintendo of America** (4900 150th Avenue NE) has its headquarters for the Western hemisphere right down the street.

To complete the tech trio, search-engine giant **Google** has a recently expanded campus in Kirkland (777 6th Street S) in addition to their Seattle office.

WOODINVILLE ❼

There are several attractions in **Wood-inville**, including important wineries.

Chateau Ste Michelle

Address: 14111 NE 145th Street; www.ste-michelle.com
Tel: 425-488 1133
Opening Hrs: daily 10am–5pm
Entrance Fee: free

The best-known Washington winery is Chateau Ste Michelle, just west of the Sammamish River and a frequent stop for bicyclists on the slough route.

The winery, the largest in the state of Washington, has 87 acres (35

A marching band at the Salmon Days Festival Parade.

hectares) of picnic grounds, a pond with ducks and swans, a tasting room, and test vineyards. The attractive facilities are popular for weddings, receptions, and a successful summer concert series. Tours of the winery's operations (the main vineyards are actually in eastern Washington) are offered daily, along with wine tastings. Premium tastings can also be arranged for a fee.

Columbia Winery ❽

Address: 14030 NE 145th Street; www.columbiawinery.com
Tel: 425-482 7490
Opening Hrs: daily 11am–6pm, open until 7pm on Fri
Entrance Fee: free

Just a few hundred feet away, in a large, gingerbread-style building, is another excellent regional wine producer. **Columbia Winery** also gives daily tours for a small fee, with wine tastings. Private tours with tastings of signature wines are another possibility. Although best known for white grapes, the wineries of western Washington are increasingly producing fine table wines, both red and white.

Salmon navigating a fish ladder.

Redhook Ale Brewery

Address: 14300 NE 145th Street;
www.redhook.com
Tel: 425-483 3232
Opening Hrs: call ahead for tour times
Entrance Fee: charge

The brewery and **Forecasters Public House** are next door to the Columbia Winery. Redhook was founded in 1981 and is one of Seattle's original microbreweries (although it was originally located in Ballard on Leary Way and Fremont, where Theo Chocolate now resides). It brews ESB, an India Pale Ale; Hefe-Weizen; and other beers in this Eastside facility. The Forecasters pub is open every day (and night) and features live music on weekends. A tour of the brewery can be taken and the small fee includes tastings and a souvenir glass. Children are welcome.

From Woodinville, hikers can walk the **Tolt Pipeline Trail**, either westward to Bothell or eastward to the Snoqualmie Valley. Its wooded and open terrain makes this a very popular pastime.

Issaquah ❾

Southeast of Bellevue and nestled in a valley between Squak, Tiger and Cougar mountains is the woodsy city of **Issaquah**. The developers chose a country theme for the town shopping center. They scoured the vicinity for old clapboard-style homes, then moved and arranged them into a village setting at the edge of Downtown. Then they built wooden boardwalks, planted flowers, and set to work attracting a particular kind of retailer. **Gilman Village** (317 NW Gilman Boulevard; www.gilmanvillage.com) is the result, a 'destination shopping center' of specialty shops and restaurants which draws people from many miles around.

Also in Issaquah, the **Village Theatre** (303 Front Street N; tel: 425-392 2202; http://villagetheatre.org/issaquah) puts on regular dramatic performances, popular with locals. A few blocks east of Gilman Village is **Boehm's Candies** (255 NE Gilman Boulevard; tel: 425-392 6652; https://boehmscandies.com). a family-owned confectionery that has been in Issaquah since 1956. Swiss-style chocolate candies are still hand-dipped here the old-fashioned way.

Local parks

Lake Sammamish State Park (2000 NW Sammamish Road), just north of downtown Issaquah, provides access to the trails, baseball

WHERE

Every fall crowds gather to watch salmon head up Issaquah Creek via a fish ladder at the Issaquah Salmon Hatchery (125 W Sunset Way; tel: 425-392 1118; www.issaquahfish.org). The early October Issaquah Salmon Days Festival celebrates their return.

fields, picnic tables, and barbecue spots of the lake's south shore. Lake Sammamish is popular for boating in summer, despite the noise of water-skiers' speedboats.

Cougar Mountain Zoological Park

Address: 19525 SE 54th Street; www.cougarmountainzoo.org
Tel: 425-391 5508
Opening Hrs: Wed–Sun 9.30am–5pm
Entrance Fee: charge

Wildlife enthusiasts enjoy this tiny zoological park, with its emphasis on endangered species and education.

SNOQUALMIE VALLEY

Past Issaquah, the scene around Interstate 90 becomes more rural the farther east one travels. Bears have been seen in the region, and Carnation and Fall City have enough attractions to fill a whole weekend's visit, Snoqualmie Falls especially.

In the heart of the Snoqualmie Valley in **Carnation** ⑩ is the popular 574-acre (232-hectare) **Tolt Mac-Donald Park** and Campground (31020 NE 40th Street), spanning

both sides of the Snoqualmie River. The park has camping (including tent, RV, yurt, and even shipping container sites), play fields, picnic shelters, and meandering bicycle and hiking trails. The 40-minute tour can be topped off with a picnic in the park. From May through October, **Remlinger U-Pick Farms** (32610 NE 32nd Street, Carnation; tel: 425-333 4135; www. remlingerfarms.com; May–Oct, see website for details), south of Carnation, is a great place to prove to the kids that there is a connection between the land and the food they eat. Remlinger has fruits and vegetables aplenty, a restaurant, a petting farm, and seasonal events and entertainment.

The valley's **Duvall** ⑪ is the outer limits of the Eastside; its one-street Downtown has several antiques stores. The town celebrates its rural atmosphere with many fun annual events, including a Duvall Days parade and pancake breakfast in June, Movies in the Park in August, and a Farmers' Market each Thursday during the summer.

For sites and attractions farther east, see page 218.

Snoqualmie Peak.

Keeping fit in the Snoqualmie Valley, just south of Carnation.

NORTHWESTERN WILDLIFE

The fascinating wildlife of the Pacific Northwest ranges from red-tailed hawks, colorful snails, woodpeckers, and black bears to salmon, seals, bald eagles, and beautiful hummingbirds.

Despite Seattle's urban – and suburban – growth, wildlife is still at home in this corner of the Northwest. Though expanding residential areas have shrunk the number and extent of natural wild habitats, many species have adapted and made their homes in Seattle's parks and fertile green spaces.

Inside the city limits, the most common creatures are eastern gray squirrels, opossums, raccoons and a range of birds including robins, seagulls, pigeons and crows. Beaver and otter sightings are also not uncommon, and harbor seals are the highlight of most cruises around the port. A little farther away – in the suburbs – chances increase of spotting cougar, deer or coyotes (they occasionally make a meal of someone's cat or small dog). Black bears are seen at Tiger Mountain, near Issaquah.

Even closer to home, in November 2009, a cougar was captured in Discovery Park, after roaming the neighborhood for days. Two nesting pairs of bald eagles are known to reside in the Seattle area, and are occasionally spotted near Green Lake and Seward Park. Popular places for birds in the city include Lake Union, as well as Discovery Park and the Washington Park Arboretum, home to shorebirds and freshwater ducks.

Though wild in the area, the best places to find sea otters (Enhydra lutris) are Woodland Park Zoo or the Seattle Aquarium.

A child feeding Canadian geese in a West Seattle park, with the Downtown skyline visible in the distance across Elliott Bay.

Watch for the black dorsal fins of killer whales (Orcinus orca) in Puget Sound. The Sound was designated a critical habitat for orcas in 2006; they are most commonly sighted in the San Juan Islands.

Bears are frequently spotted on Tiger Mountain, east of Issaquah on Interstate 90, in the Seattle suburbs. Black bear cubs are agile climbers, and, unlike most young mammals, will follow their mother sometimes for as long as two years. Bear cubs tend to be alert, with a developed sense of smell and exceptional hearing, though they have only moderate eyesight.

Bald eagles (Haliaeetus leucocephalus) can sometimes be seen in Seattle's Green Lake area, Discovery Park, and Seward Park.

SWIMMING FOR HOME

Salmon seen through the underwater viewing window at Ballard Locks.

Five species of salmon migrate through Puget Sound. King, sockeye, coho, chum and pink salmon all return from the saltwater to spawn in rivers and streams from early June through November.

Their most spectacular appearance in Seattle is in early July, when thousands of sockeye salmon fight their way from Puget Sound up the fish ladder at Ballard's Hiram M. Chittenden Locks, heading for the Cedar River and other streams. The fish ladder bypasses the locks, and viewing windows are provided for the public, along with an explanation of the salmon's life cycle.

Issaquah's annual Salmon Days Festival (www.salmondays.org) is held in the first week of October. In Seattle, the Salmon Homecoming event is celebrated around the second week of September, with Northwest tribal gatherings, powwows, sacred sites exhibits, cedar-canoe events and an environmental fair. There is a huge salmon bake every day from mid-morning till evening.

The northern elephant seal or 'sea elephant' (Mirounga angustirostris) is an occasional visitor to Puget Sound, and usually travels solo.

A Puget Sound ferry from Edmonds beach.

HEADING NORTH

Within easy reach of the city, set amidst beautiful scenery, and growing in popularity, the lure of towns like Bothell, Edmonds, and Everett is palpable.

Shortly after Seattle was named America's 'most livable city' by *Money* magazine for the first time, scores of young, affluent people settled the suburbs just outside the city, searching for that prize of prosperity known as 'quality of life'. From the northern frontier of Seattle at 145th Street to the city of Everett, 25 miles (40km) north on Gardner Bay, a stretch of satellite communities with award-winning parks and progressive public schools seem to offer the modern suburban idyll. The presence of the Boeing plant and the aerospace industry doesn't hurt, either.

With a population of more than 600,000 people and rising, the commuter communities on these great expanses of verdant rolling hills, lakes, and sparkling streams on the northern tip of King County and the southern stretch of Snohomish County are among the nation's fastest-growing regions. Thanks to improvements along Interstate 5 and the Sounder commuter rail services, the journey out here is easy.

Technology Corridor

The very earliest European settlers – mill owners, homesteaders, and land developers – relied on the Mosquito Fleet steamship line for transportation

up and down Puget Sound, but railroads and electric trolleys soon followed to speed the flow of goods and passengers. Today's commuters head to jobs in downtown Seattle or, more likely, to one of the business parks in the Technology Corridor, a path of commercial communities stretching along Interstate 405 between Bothell and Everett. Hundreds of businesses in electronics, software, telecommunications, and computing cluster in campus-like neighborhoods where high-tech execs cycle along groomed

Bothell's biking and hiking trail.

TIP

See Seattle from the air on one of Kenmore Air Harbor's tours. Highlights include the Space Needle, Green Lake, and the campus of the University of Washington (tel: 866-435 9524 or 425 486 1257; www.kenmoreair.com).

cycle paths at lunch or work out in the company gym after hours.

Bothell is the gateway to the corridor, a town of 33,000 people northeast of Lake Washington and nestled in the winding Sammamish River Valley, only 30 minutes' drive from Seattle or the Boeing plant in Everett. The Sammamish River biking and hiking trail joins the Burke-Gilman Trail in Bothell and curves along 33 acres (13 hectares) of a natural wildlife habitat south of the river, and continues uninterrupted to Marymoor Park on the east side of Lake Washington. The trail connects by a pedestrian bridge to the north side of the river, where **Bothell Landing**, with its historic buildings, serves as a focal point for the community.

Kenmore Air Harbor

Also in the vicinity is **Kenmore** , known for water sports, a spectacular view of Lake Washington, and the **Kenmore Air Harbor** (6321 NE 175th Street; tel: 425-486 1257; www.kenmoreairharbor.com), the country's largest seaplane base, with scenic flights over Seattle and scheduled flights to Victoria and Vancouver in British Columbia.

Mill Creek began as a designed community in 1976, with almost

3,000 homes developed around a country club, a private 18-hole golf course, tennis courts, swimming pools, and a nature preserve. It was incorporated as a city in 1983, and remains very popular.

Mountlake Terrace

The National Park Service awarded a commendation for the parks of **Mountlake Terrace** – a lavish sprinkling of little neighborhood parks on Lake Ballinger. The largest and one of the fastest-growing commercial and manufacturing centers in the north is **Lynnwood** , with a large middle-class population, a good percentage of whom are commuters to Seattle.

The only truly rural community is **Brier** , a small town of approximately 6,300 people. A strict no-growth policy keeps stores and traffic to a minimum.

Edmonds

Flower boxes and hanging planters dot the main street of **Edmonds**, the self-proclaimed 'Gem of Puget Sound,' a modern community of around 40,000 on the shore 11 miles (18km) north of Seattle.

Property values here are such that few people under 40 can afford the taxes, much less the mortgage payments. Few big business interests bother with this growth-resistant town either, but artsy-craftsy Edmonds doesn't mind. Residents know that their prestigious Amtrak station, ferry terminal, waterfront shops, restaurants, and stylish parks draw plenty of weekend visitors. Travel writer, broadcaster, and general celebrity Rick Steves also makes Edmonds his home; his Travel Center (www.ricksteves.com) is at 130 4th Avenue N.

One of three waterfront parks in Edmonds' **Brackett's Landing** (just north of the Edmond/Kingston Pier) includes the oldest and most popular **underwater park** in Washington, dedicated as a Marine Preserve in

At Kenmore Air Harbor.

Brackett's Landing in Edmonds.

1970. Divers can explore the 300ft (90-meter) -long De Lion dry dock, which dropped to the sandy bottom in 1935, and a number of other sunken structures. The dock is a maze-like haven for schools of fish and aquatic plant life.

Visitors are encouraged to feel the texture of leaves, needles, and tree bark at **Sierra Park** (190th and 81st avenues W). The park was innovatively designed around the aroma and fragrance of plants, and created with the blind in mind, providing braille signs for sight-impaired visitors.

Views from Marina Beach include the former Unocal oil refinery loading dock at Edwards Point just off the beach to the south and the port of Edmonds to the north. The whole area around the old oil refinery is currently being cleaned up and readied for new development. The Puget Sound Express (www.pugetsoundexpress.com), located in the nearby marina, organises whale- and bird-watching cruises. At Olympic Beach, be sure to see the sea-lion sculpture and watch the activities at the **Edmonds Fishing Pier**, open year-round for fishing. And at the nearby **Cascadia Art Museum**

(www.cascadiaartmuseum.org; Wed–Sun 11am–6pm, free 3rd Thu of the month 5–8pm), located in a beautifully converted old Safeway supermarket, you will find a celebration of Northwest art and excellent temporary exhibitions.

Other parks along this stretch of waterfront include the woodsy **Meadowdale Beach Park** (6026 156th SW) and the high, sandy cliffs of Norma Beach Boathouse. Among Edmonds' cultural attractions are a community theater and a symphony orchestra.

Everett ⑲

Tacoma lumberman Henry Hewitt hoped the Great Northern Railroad would site its western terminus where **Everett** sits today. He persuaded investors to develop an industrial lumber site on Port Gardner Bay, and although the town boomed in 1891, it went bust almost immediately. This cycle continued to haunt the lumber mill town through the next century. In 1966, the **Boeing Assembly Plant** was constructed in Everett. Boeing was the world's largest maker of commercial aircraft in the second half of

Divers at Brackett's Landing.

the 20th century, and the area's prime employer; for some time, Seattle's economy was intimately linked to Boeing's – the company still employs about 30,000 workers in Everett and the Everett plant remains the world's largest building by volume.

Starting with Boeing, Everett's emphasis on lumber shifted to an economy based on technology, and while Boeing remains the largest employer, the city has a vibrant mix of public and private industry. There is also a significant military presence, thanks to the state-of-the-art Naval Station Everett. The base is home to the aircraft carrier USS *Nimitz* and six other ships. Everett is the county seat of Snohomish County, and also

Bird's-eye view of Everett.

home to the AquaSox minor-league baseball team.

Future of Flight ⓴

Address: 8415 Paine Field Boulevard, Mukilteo; www.futureofflight.org
Tel: 1-800 464 1476
Opening Hrs: daily 8.30am–5.30pm; tours 9am–3pm
Entrance Fee: charge (includes aviation center and tour)

Upon entering the main lobby of Boeing's **Future of Flight**, the first sight is of an aircraft flying directly above, while further along the runway, a 727 is poised nose-up for takeoff. Interactive programs explain the finer points of the design and technology.

Visitors are given the opportunity to digitally design and test an airplane of their own. Other interactive exhibits include flight simulators, a virtual tour of the 787 flight deck, plane components to touch and examine, a multimedia presentation of the 787, and more.

This is also the place to join the 90-minute **Boeing Tour**, which gives a firsthand view of the company's planes – including the 787 Dreamliner – in construction. Visitors see airplanes at various stages, including manufacture and flight testing. Please note that Boeing does not allow photography, reservations are suggested, and children must be at least 4ft (1.2-meters) tall to go on the tour.

Another interesting aviation museum in Everett is the **Flying Heritage and Combat Armour Museum** (www.flyingheritage.com; June–Sept daily 10am–5pm, Tue–Sun rest of the year) featuring restored combat aircrafts from World War II. Art lovers should head to the award-winning **Schack Art Center** (www.schack.org; Mon–Fri 10am–6pm, Sat 10am–5pm, Sun noon–5pm; free) where you can see works by international and local artists and get immersed in the fabulous world of glass-blowing at the centre's state-of-the-art shop.

Boeing

The world's largest commercial airline manufacturer started right here in Seattle. Though its headquarters moved to Chicago in 2001, Boeing still plays a significant role in the area's economy.

Bill Boeing, the company's founder, was a prosperous Seattle lumberman who developed a fascination with planes. In 1916 he asked Navy engineer George Westervelt to design one – the resulting spruce-and-linen pontooned biplane was called the B&W for the two men's initials. Only two B&Ws were built, but they impressed the government and earned the fledgling Boeing Company new contracts to build military trainers in World War I.

During World War II, Boeing supplied huge numbers of the successful B-17 and B-29 bombers. Over the following decades, the company moved from strength to strength, and in 1958 unveiled the 707, the first commercial airliner in the United States. By the 1970s an airline recession and severe cutback of the Apollo program had a profound impact on Boeing and the area's economy. Thousands of families packed up and left. A billboard on the outskirts of Seattle exhorted 'Will the last person leaving Seattle please turn off the lights?'

Changing fortunes

Boeing won back commercial dominance in the 1980s but lost its lead to the European consortium Airbus by the end of the 1990s. For four decades, Boeing and Airbus have battled for supremacy in the global market. Downturns have been the result of a number of influences, significantly including the 1990s meltdown of the Asian economies, and the impact of the 9/11 terrorist attacks of 2001.

With soaring oil prices and mounting pressure over the need to reduce carbon dioxide (CO_2) emissions, the battleground is increasingly over fuel efficiency. To this end Boeing introduced the 787 Dreamliner, first

rolled out in 2007, which is made from lighter composite materials, resulting in reduced fuel use and CO_2 emissions. Airbus, meanwhile, added the A350 as a direct rival to the 787.

By late 2008 and 2009, the worldwide economic downturn caused a slump in air travel, shrinking orders for new airplanes while Boeing's defense unit felt the pinch as the Pentagon cut back on spending. Since then, despite significant company job cuts between 2012 and 2017, an increased demand for aircraft and a string of high-profile contracts have seen Boeing profits boom. Boeing reigns supreme as the largest exporter in the US (dollar value) and the world's second-largest defense contractor (based on 2015 revenue).

In Everett you can see for yourself one of the world's biggest industrial enterprises. The original airplane hangar, built in 1968 for the 747, enclosed 200 million cubic feet (5.7 million cubic meters). At that time, it was the world's largest building; it has since doubled in size. Tours are offered daily at the Future of Flight.

Boeing 747 jets in production

Union Station's historic restoration, turned into a federal building, has spurred the growth of urban renewal in this previously depilated section of Tacoma.

UNION STATION

HEADING SOUTH

South of Seattle are superlative mountain views, glassworks as great as any in the world, museums, and one of the prettiest state capitals in the US.

Southof Seattle is a rapidly developing region with equal parts natural beauty and urban sprawl, with some first-rate attractions.

Museum of Flight

Address: 9404 E Marginal Way S, Seattle; www.museumofflight.org
Tel: 206-764 5700
Opening Hrs: daily 10am–5pm
Entrance Fee: charge, free first Thu of the month

For a fascinating dip into Seattle's aviation history, consider setting aside an afternoon for the **Museum of Flight** ㉑ at Boeing Field, just south of the city. The museum is a stalwart local favorite, predating the Future of Flight Aviation Center (see page 178) by several years. The impressive collection of aircraft and aviation ephemera represents the entire aerospace industry, not only Boeing's contribution. It occupies the original 1909 Boeing building, known as the **Red Barn**, which was part of a shipyard along the Duwamish River, and the adjacent Great Gallery, added in the 1980s. Inside the Red Barn are restored early planes, as well as historical photographs and drawings. The main-hall gallery has appropriately high ceilings and an assortment of flying

craft, ranging from hang-gliders to fighter jets, including an F-104 Starfighter and a Russian MiG 21.

Other interesting exhibits include an airplane car that looks like (and in fact is) a shiny, red sports car with wings; a flight simulator (actually, a simulation of a simulator); and, just outside the gallery, the country's first presidential jet, a Boeing 707, and a supersonic Concorde. The museum also offers a view of Boeing's airfield.

Most visitors arrive in the Seattle area by air, touching down in one of

Main Attractions
Museum of Flight
Tacoma
Museum of Glass
Washington State History Museum
Point Defiance Park
Olympia
State Capitol

Maps
Pages 156, 182, 138

The Museum of Flight charts aviation history.

In the Museum of Flight.

Washington's newer cities – aptly, if unpoetically, named **SeaTac**, after the **Sea-Tac International Airport ㉒**. The cumbersome name is a combination of the names of the two cities the airport serves, Seattle and Tacoma.

RENTON AND BEYOND

Renton ㉓, a city of more than 97,000 residents at the southern end of Lake Washington, is home to the Boeing facilities where the 737 and 757 jets were produced, and has its own municipal airport. Attractions include **Liberty Park** by the Cedar River (the site of the annual Renton River Days) and **Gene Coulon Memorial Beach Park** on the lake.

Renton History Museum

Address: 235 Mill Avenue S, Renton; www.rentonwa.gov/rentonhistorymuseum
Tel: 425-255 2330
Opening Hrs: Tue–Sat 10am–4pm
Entrance Fee: charge, free first Wed and third Sat of the month

Plane exhibits at the Museum of Flight.

Not far from Liberty Park, this museum recounts the city's beginnings as a coal-mining community called Black River Bridge. On view are more than 15,000 historical photographs, as well as thousands of objects, including mining equipment, newspapers, books, and fire-fighting equipment. Maps show the mining shafts that crisscross underneath the expensive homes that now perch on Renton Hill.

The valley around **Kent ㉔**, south of Renton, formerly produced much of the Puget Sound area's agriculture; now it sprouts manufacturing plants and warehouses. To the east are the waterfront communities of **Normandy Park** and **Des Moines**, named by a founder from Des Moines, Iowa, who persuaded friends in the Midwest to finance his venture in 1887.

Federal Way ㉕, south of Seattle along Interstate 5 and named for the federally funded Highway 99, is home

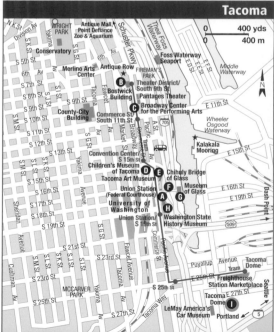

to **Dash Point State Park** (http://parks.state.wa.us/496/Dash-Point) and the **Wild Waves Theme and Water Park** (www.wildwaves.com), popular summer attractions for children.

Rhododendron Species Botanical Gardens

Address: 2525 S 336th St, Federal Way; www.rhodygarden.org
Tel: 253-838 4646
Opening Hrs: Tue–Sun 10am–4pm
Entrance Fee: charge

The world's largest collection of rhododendrons is another Federal Way attraction. The 24-acre (10-hectare) gardens (at their best from March through April) feature more than 450 varieties of Washington's state flower – from the 100ft (30-meter) -high trees of the lower Himalaya to the ground-hugging species of Tibet and China.

TACOMA 26

Just south of Federal Way and an hour's drive south of Seattle, **Tacoma** is the state's third-largest city, with more than 200,000 people. Approaching the city with the bay in front and Mount Rainier behind, it's easy to understand why the city founders had such high hopes for Tacoma. It is one of the few cities with a setting that rivals – surpasses, locals would argue – Seattle in beauty. In the quality and variety of its architecture, Tacoma also stands out; just about every major architectural style of the past 100 years is represented in the city.

It began as a 19th-century timber boomtown that in its 1890s heyday rivaled Seattle in importance, but the city went bust in the nationwide slump of 1893 and has been trying to catch up ever since. In the last couple of decades, quietly and without too much fuss, Tacoma has transformed itself from a blue-collar mill town with a gang problem to an economically diverse and environmentally aware city with a vibrant cultural life. Tacoma serves as a major port facility

Tacoma's Union Station is now the federal courthouse.

in the Pacific Northwest and as a gateway to two of the Northwest's most popular attractions: the Olympic Peninsula (see page 201) and Mount Rainier National Park (see page 217).

An effort to revive the downtown area has brought commerce and culture back to the city center. An energetic preservation movement is writing new leases on life for Tacoma's old buildings. The movement began with the transformation of the long-vacant Beaux Arts **Union Station A** into an elegant venue for the federal courthouse. Across the street, once-empty warehouses serve as the locale for a University of Washington campus.

On Broadway, at the entry to so-called **Antique Row**, the triangular-shaped **Bostwick Building B**, built in 1889 as a hotel, has turned its downstairs into a coffeehouse and jazz club. The upper floors have been converted into apartments to let; antiques stores and specialty shops occupy the rest of the block. A brass plaque on the Bostwick makes a claim to fame: that here, in 1893, Civil War veteran Russell O'Brien

TIP

To visit the grave of a legend, make a trip to Greenwood Cemetery at 350 Monroe Avenue NE, in Renton, the final resting place of Jimi Hendrix. His tomb is permanently adorned with letters and flowers from fans.

At the Tacoma Museum of Glass.

Children's Museum of Tacoma

Address: 1501 Pacific Avenue. Tacoma; www.playtacoma.org
Tel: 253-627 6031
Opening Hrs: Wed–Sun 10am–5pm, Tue play days for children with special needs 10–11.30am
Entrance Fee: donation

Young ones (aged zero to eight) will love the **Children's Museum**, with its early learning programs and activities, playgrounds, and art installations. The idea here is learning through play, and the five 'playscapes' (Woods, Water, Voyage, Becka's Studio, and Invention) aim to develop life-long skills including creativity, social and emotional sensitivity, motor skills, and early literacy.

Tacoma Art Museum

Address: 1701 Pacific Avenue, Tacoma; www.tacomaartmuseum.org
Tel: 253-272 4258
Opening Hrs: Tue–Sun 10am–5pm
Entrance Fee: charge, free third Thu of the month 5–8pm

The **Tacoma Art Museum** was designed by architect Antoine Predock. It features major traveling exhibitions, TAM's permanent collection, interactive activities, and a café. The museum is building a top collection of works by Northwest artists, and on permanent display is a collection of early glass works by world-renowned and Tacoma-born glass artist Dale Chihuly.

Dale Chihuly has done much to raise the profile of the city. The dazzling **Chihuly Bridge of Glass** over the Thea Foss Waterway that connects the Museum of Glass with Union Station and the Art and State History museums is the most famous contribution. The sculptures nearest Union Station make up the **Seaform Pavilion**; the middle section has the glittering *Crystal Towers*; while the walkway nearest to the Museum of Glass is the breathtaking Venetian Wall, featuring 109 Chihuly sculptures.

started the tradition of standing for the national anthem.

Art and glass

A lively arts scene has also contributed to the revival of Downtown. The excellent **Broadway Center for the Performing Arts** (901 Broadway; tel: 253-591 5894 for tickets; www.broadwaycenter.org) puts on dance, music, and stage productions at the restored **Rialto Theater** and **Pantages Theater**, and at the postmodernist **Theatre On the Square**. A 1,100-seat vaudeville palace dating back to 1916, Pantages was designed by B. Marcus Priteca, a European-trained architect known for his neoclassical style and the designer of more than 150 theaters throughout North America. A Tacoma Museum District Pass (www.washingtonhistory.org/visit/wshm/museumdistrict) will give you entry to six town museums: Tacoma Art Museum, Washington State History Museum, the Museum of Glass, LeMay-America's Car Museum, Foss Waterway Seaport, and the Children's Museum of Tacoma.

Museum of Glass **G**

Address: 1801 Dock Street, Tacoma;
www.museumofglass.org
Tel: 866-468 7386
Opening Hrs: summer daily 10am–
5pm, Sun noon–5pm, winter Wed–Sat
10am–5pm, Sun noon–5pm
Entrance Fee: charge, free third Thu
of the month 5–8pm

'Hot glass. Cool art' is the catchphrase
of the **Museum of Glass**. This is one
of the few museums in the country
to concentrate on contemporary
glass art. Glass-blowing techniques
are demonstrated in the fascinating
Hot Shop Amphitheater, housed in
a 90ft (27-meter) -tall stainless steel
cone with both hot- and cold-glass
studios. Several cozy galleries show
up-and-coming glass artists.

Washington State History Museum **H**

Address: 1911 Pacific Ave, Tacoma;
www.wshs.org
Tel: 1-888 238 4373 or 253 272 9747
Opening Hrs: Tue–Sun 10am–5pm,
third Thu of the month until 8pm
Entrance Fee: charge, free third Thu
of the month 2–8pm

In a handsome brick building next
to Union Station, this museum has a
substantial collection of pioneer and
Native American exhibits. Theatrical
displays and hands-on exhibits – like
the History Lab Learning Center –
make this a fun spot for children.

Other Tacoma attractions

Popular culture and sports have
a venue at the **Tacoma Dome ❶**.
Built in 1983, the 152ft (46-meter)
-tall dome, one of the world's largest wooden-domed structures, is well
known for its acoustics. A popular
venue for rock acts, the arena seats
up to 23,000 people and has hosted
events ranging from the Billy Graham
Crusade to truck-and-tractor pulls, to
Lady Gaga. Its first major concert was
David Bowie in August 1983.

Opposite the dome is **LeMay
America's Car Museum** (www.americas-
carmuseum.org; daily 10am–5pm), which
celebrates the American love affair with
the automobile. It features more than
350 exhibits including a 1925 Ford

TIP

Walking tours of sites
created by or which
inspired glass artist Dale
Chihuly are organized by
the museum. Go to:
https://museumofglass.org/
event-calendar.

*The Museum of Glass
focuses on contemporary
and Pacific Northwest
glass art.*

TACOMA'S NAMES

The town was originally named 'Commencement City' after its large bay of the
same name, which itself was named after
the starting point of an 1841 surveying
expedition. The name 'Tacoma' comes
from the Nisqually and Puyallup tribal
name for Mount Rainier. In the heady, early
days, Tacoma dubbed itself the 'City of
Destiny', but for much of the 20th century,
this nickname seemed amusingly at odds
with reality. The smelly 'Tacoma Aroma'
caused by pulp-mill emissions wafted
across Puget Sound, and the crime rate
and defunct Downtown made it the butt of
Seattle jokes. Nowadays environmental
and social regeneration is even beckoning
some Seattleites to move south.

TIP

Tacoma has a lovely stretch of waterfront along Ruston Way that acts as a magnet for joggers and walkers. A number of restaurants are located along here, too, with splendid views of Commencement Bay.

The Puyallup Fair is a 17-day event held every September.

Model T and the 1994 Flintmobile, built for the motion picture.

The three-block-long building, **Freighthouse Station Marketplace** (2501 D Street; https://freighthouse square.com), was, for a long time, a mom-and-pop shopping mall. This early 1900s former freight house for the Milwaukee/St Paul Railroad now contains small specialty stores, New Age health services, and an international food court with everything from Korean barbecue to Greek salads. A section of the historic building had to be demolished to make way for the brand new Amtrak railway station scheduled to open in 2017.

Located on Dock Street, **Foss Waterway Seaport** (http://fosswaterway-seaport.org; Wed–Sat 10am–4pm, Sun noon–4pm), a century-old wooden wheat warehouse located at the waterfront, displays historic boats and delves into the maritime history of Tacoma.

The oldest residential neighborhood, **North End**, is evidence of Tacoma's glory days when the new city on the hill held promise of becoming the West Coast's center of industry and finance. Stroll along broad, tree-lined **Yakima Avenue** past colonnaded

mansions built by Tacoma's 19th-century industrial barons. The neighborhood's best building (at 111 North E Street) is a French chateau lookalike, complete with towers and turrets.

The building was commissioned by the Northern Pacific Railroad in 1891 as a hotel for its passengers after Tacoma became the terminus for the railroad. But before it was finished, the railroad went bankrupt and the hotel became (and still is) **Stadium High School**. Scenes were filmed at Stadium for the movie *Ten Things I Hate About You*, a 1990s teen take on *The Taming of the Shrew*.

Below the North End, along the south shore of Commencement Bay, **Ruston Way** has trails, parks, and piers, as well as enough waterfront restaurants to earn it the nickname **Restaurant Row**. Follow Ruston Way inland a few miles, and plan to spend some time on one of Tacoma's most engaging landmarks. At 700 acres (280 hectares), **Point Defiance Park** ㉗ (5400 N Pearl Street) is one of the largest urban parks in the United States. It occupies a finger of land jutting out into Puget Sound and has formal gardens, a swimming beach, a

replica of a 19th-century trading post, a children's storybook park, a zoo and aquarium, and a logging camp, complete with a 1929 steam train.

Point Defiance Zoo & Aquarium

Address: Point Defiance Park, 5400 N Pearl Street, Tacoma; www.pdza.org
Tel: 253-404 3689
Opening Hrs: June–Sept daily 9.30am–6pm, hours and days vary at other times of year
Entrance Fee: charge

The zoo, founded in 1888, is both animal- and people-friendly; it isn't unusual to encounter a llama, a pig, or even an elephant with its keeper on an afternoon walk. With a Pacific Rim focus, the zoo is known for its humane and innovative approach. Aquarium Encounters and polar bear talks are among the weekly offerings.

AROUND TACOMA

On the west side of Tacoma, the **Tacoma Narrows Bridge** ㉘, a pair of twin suspension bridges, has a total length of nearly 6,000ft (1,828 meters). The first bridge, opened in 1940 across the Tacoma Narrows, was called 'Galloping Gertie' for the undulating winds that whip through the narrows. Gertie galloped too much, though, and just a few months after opening, collapsed. Pieces of the old bridge shelter marine life, and entice scuba divers into the waters. The first bridge was rebuilt in 1950, and due to a large increase in traffic, the second bridge was completed in 2007.

Just over the Narrows Bridge is **Gig Harbor** ㉙, a pleasant harbor town with old-fashioned shops, restaurants, and bed-and-breakfasts.

Puyallup ㉚

Although much of the surrounding farmland has been lined with strip malls, **Puyallup** is still primarily a farming community. This is one of those Washington place names where

Tacoma Narrows Bridge.

the pronunciation separates locals from outsiders: it's pronounced 'pyew-all-up'. The Native American tribe of the same name now has numerous casino interests in the area.

In the 1880s, this fertile valley was a huge producer of hops, used for brewing beer. Most were exported to Europe. Hop yards were later converted to berry and rhubarb farms. Today, the area produces daffodils, tulips, and Christmas trees. A revival of the downtown area has brought back some of the small-town ambiance, lost when a mall was built on the outskirts of town. Contributing to the effort is the Arts Downtown program, a changing exhibit of outdoor art by local and outside artists. Shown in parks, shops, and on public buildings, pieces range from a sculpture of a pet pig made from scrap metal to a Russian-born artist's elegant bronze tribute to a mother's love.

The 17-room Italianate **Ezra Meeker Mansion** (312 Spring Street; tel: 253-848 1770; www.meekermansion.org; Mar–mid Dec Wed–Sun noon–4pm) was built in 1890 by Puyallup's first mayor for his wife.

Steilacoom

A 20-minute drive southeast of Tacoma, **Steilacoom** ㉛ (pronounced 'stilla-cum') is Washington's oldest

TIP

Even if you don't live locally, you can be a part of Olympia's thriving arts scene. The cute website www.buyolympia.com not only has unusual mail-order gifts, but also lists events.

incorporated town. It is hard to believe that this small waterfront village once was a busy frontier port and seat of government. It was one of the first places in the area to develop a sense of its own historic importance: years ago, its preservation-minded citizens registered the downtown area as a national historic site, ensuring that Steilacoom was protected from development.

The town's old drugstore, Bair Drug and Hardware, was built in 1895. The traditional combination pharmacy, hardware store, post office, and gathering place has been turned into the delightful **Bair Bistro** (1617 Lafayette St; tel: 253-588 9668; www.thebairbistro.com; Tue–Sun 8am–2pm, Fri–Sat until 8pm). Among the historic furnishings is a 1906 marble-topped soda fountain.

The **Steilacoom Historical Museum** (1801 Rainier Avenue; tel: 253-584 4133; www.steilacoomhistorical.org; Sat–Sun 1–5pm) documents early town life with realistic displays of an 1880s living room, kitchen, and parlor.

At the other end of the block, **Steilacoom Tribal Cultural Center and Museum** (1515 Lafayette Street; tel: 253-584 6308; www.facebook.com/SteilacoomTribe; Sat 10am–4pm) is one of the few tribal-run museums in the state of Washington, and tells the story of Native American life, and Pacific Northwest and local history, from the point of view of several native tribes (including the Steilacoom Tribe).

OLYMPIA ㉜

Thirty miles (50km) south of Tacoma at the southernmost point of Puget Sound, the Washington state capital of **Olympia** brings to mind a comment made about another capital, Washington, DC – that is, it's a city for people who don't like cities. The city's low-rise architecture and leisurely pace gives the place a friendly, small-town feel, while Evergreen State College, a progressive liberal arts college established in 1972,

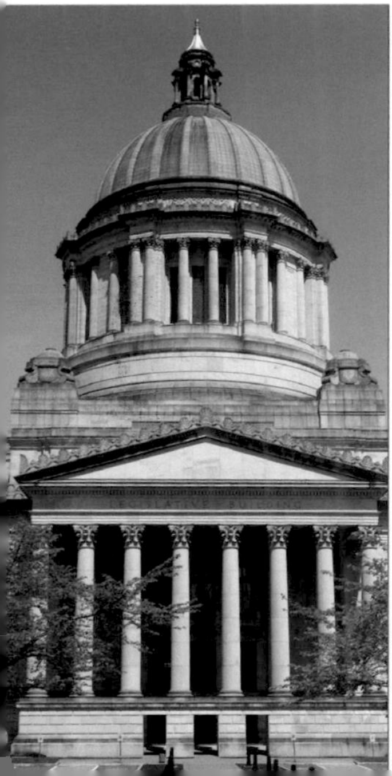

The Olympia Capitol building.

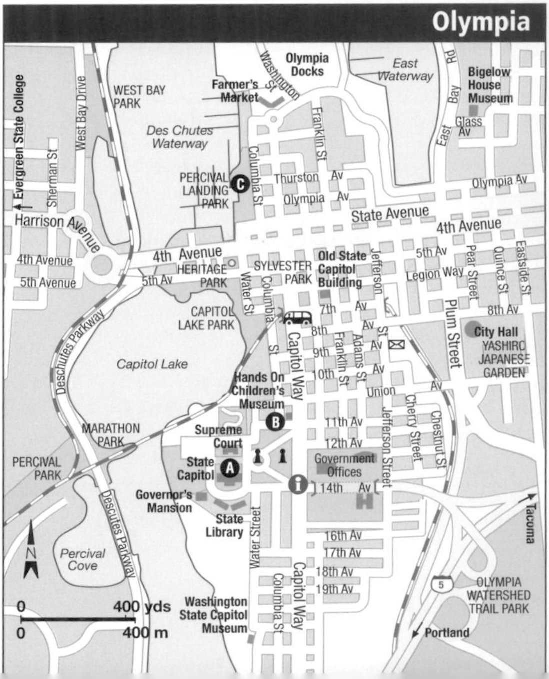

provides enough of a countercultural edge to keep the city interesting.

It wasn't until 1890 that Olympia was officially named Washington's state capital, and it took another 60 or so years for it to wrestle several state government offices away from Seattle. It's easy to forget that Olympia is Washington's state capital until you see the beautifully landscaped grounds and stately buildings of the **State Capitol Ⓐ** set on a hill overlooking the water, with the snowcapped Cascades in the distance. Olympia has one of the loveliest and most impressive capitol sites in the country. Dominating the 55-acre (22-hectare) campus is the Washington State **Legislative Building**.

Constructed in 1927, the handsome Romanesque structure, with its 287ft (87-meter) dome, brings to mind the capitol building in Washington, DC. The chandelier hanging in the rotunda was designed by Louis Tiffany, the American artist and designer who established a firm in New York specializing in glasswork and whose father founded the venerable Tiffany and Co.

Embedded in the floor underneath it, the state seal bears an image of George Washington worn smooth by the feet of visitors. During a visit to the capitol in the late 1940s, President Harry S. Truman objected to the image being defaced in this way, and the state seal has been cordoned off ever since.

Other notable buildings in the State Capitol compound include the handsome **Governor's Mansion**, the **State Library**, which houses a collection of artworks by Northwest artists, and the **State Greenhouse**, which provides all the flowers and plants for the capitol complex. War memorials and sculptural works also grace the lovely grounds.

Guided hour-long tours of the Legislative Building (tel: 360-902 8880; http://des.wa.gov) are provided on a daily basis. More detailed information,

Capitol Lake, Olympia.

including special appointments for group tours, is available from the **Visitor Center** (tel: 360-902 8880).

Hands On Children's Museum Ⓑ

Address: 141 Jefferson St NE, Olympia; www.hocm.org
Tel: 360-956 0818
Opening Hrs: Tue–Sat 10am–5pm, Mon and Sun 11am–5pm
Entrance Fee: charge, free first Fri of the month 5–9pm

If politics is a little dry for young visitors, try taking them to this museum, which offers enough activities and exhibits to keep kids busy for a whole afternoon. The Puget Sound exhibit puts little ones in the captain's chair and brings sea life up close and personal; other interactive displays touch on topics such as forests, health, and 'arts and parts'.

Percival Landing Park Ⓒ

Tourists and locals mingle at the shops, restaurants, and cafés at cute **Percival Landing Park** (217 Thurston Avenue NW), a waterfront park and boardwalk. Next to the landing is Washington State's largest **Farmers' Market** (www.olympiafarmersmarket. com), a good place to buy local produce, crafts, and foods.

Sunrise Point at Hurricane Ridge in Olympic National Park.

Excursions

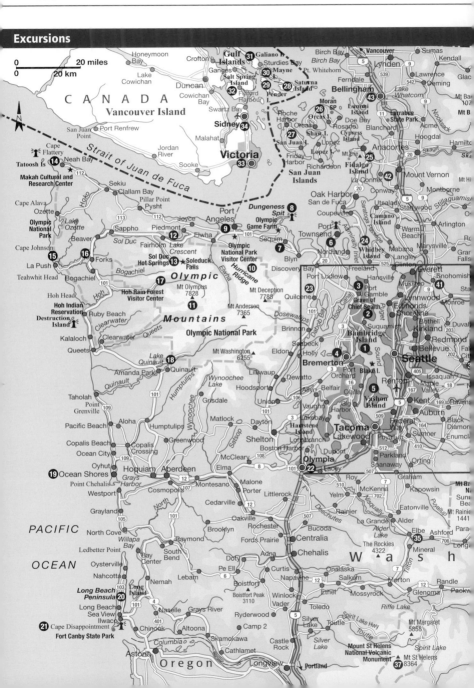

EXCURSIONS

One of the main reasons people live in Seattle is, ironically, the ease with which they can go somewhere else.

Escaping the urban bustle can be as easy as a 35-minute ferry trip to Bainbridge Island, or as bracing as several days' trek across the majestic Cascade Mountains. The jewels of Puget Sound are the San Juan Islands, the archipelago that gets more sunshine than the surrounding area, so in winter the weather is pleasant; in summer it's even better.

Jagged mountain peaks, temperate rain forests, Victorian towns, and remote, sandy islands: all are just a few hours from downtown Seattle. The middle of the Olympic Peninsula is Mount Olympus, towering 7,828ft (2,386 meters) over the surrounding mountains. The crown is 922,000-acre (373,000-hectare) Olympic National Park, with glacial rivers roaring down folds and crevices to empty into the Pacific Ocean, the Strait of Juan de Fuca, and Puget Sound itself.

The park encompasses one of the last wilderness forests on the US mainland. Rain and fog, coupled with a mild coastal climate, are essential for the temperate rain forest to thrive. Sitka spruce are dominant, and soaring trees draped in moss, shot through by hazy sunlight, make a lasting impression. One of the first expeditions across the mountains on foot took nearly six months, but now you can do it in four or five days.

Puget Sound is known for its wildlife, including orcas, bald eagles, and bears. Also in the area is the Olympic short-tailed weasel, found nowhere else in the world.

The ski slopes and hiking trails of the Cascades, the glacial Mount Rainier, Mount St Helens, and Mount Baker, plus more than 370 islands, with beaches, fishing, and water sports, all mean there's plenty to enjoy outside Seattle for either a day out, or a trip lasting several weeks.

ACROSS PUGET SOUND

Take a scenic ferry ride from downtown Seattle to
rural lanes, upscale amenities, and small towns.

A good ferry system, a few artfully placed bridges, and excellent roadways link Seattle to the nearby islands, peninsulas, and waterways that surround the city. Day trips can easily extend into longer excursions, with the assurance that all roads – and ferries – lead via a highly scenic route back to Seattle.

KITSAP PENINSULA

Some of the islands are developed and have good tourist amenities. Others give a glimpse of the wild without an expedition into the outback. The small, virtually uninhabited **Blake Island**, for example, accessible only by boat, has a park with 16 miles (26km) of trails and driftwood-strewn beaches. Deer and bald eagles are among the plentiful wildlife.

Blake Island is the location of **Tillicum Village**. Designed as a tourist attraction in the early 1960s, the village still attracts boats of visitors from downtown Seattle on organized excursions led by Argosy (www.argosycruises.com/argosy-cruises/tillicum-excursion). Visitors can see a Northwest Native American longhouse, lunch on salmon traditionally baked over alder fires, and watch a dance interpretation of local tribal myths and legends. Be aware that the show is more than a little stagey, but the setting is beautiful, especially at sunset.

Bainbridge Island

Nearby **Bainbridge Island** ❶ belongs jurisdictionally to rural Kitsap County (to which it is connected by Route 305), but culturally the increasingly upscale island, with its pricey homes and proliferating BMWs, is closer to Seattle, a pleasant 35-minute ferry ride away. The farmers, fishermen, and wealthy 'summer people' from the city who once populated the island are

Main Attractions
Winslow
Bloedel Reserve
Poulsbo
Port Gamble
Puget Sound Navy Museum

Map
Page 192

A cruise ship makes its way across Puget Sound

Commuter bus in Bainbridge.

A wintry view from the ferry.

being replaced by Seattle-commuting professionals or wealthy retirees.

At the end of the 19th century, little Bainbridge was home to the world's largest sawmill, at Port Blakely. Later, the economy turned to berry farming. Many of the farmers were Japanese immigrants – arriving in the 1880s as laborers for the sawmills and later becoming farmers – whose internment in government camps (some in California but most in Idaho) during World War II was vividly described in the 1995 best-selling novel *Snow Falling on Cedars*, written by Bainbridge resident David Guterson.

The big berry farms that once anchored the island's economy are gone, though there are still enough small farms left to justify a strawberry festival put on by the local Filipino-American community. Most of the pretty summer homes have been turned into year-round residences or bed-and-breakfast inns.

Winslow

Winslow is a tidy cluster of gift shops, cafés, and restaurants. At the Bainbridge Island Library, the **Japanese Haiku Garden**, part of the library's attractive grounds, commemorates the island's *issei* (first generation) Japanese-Americans. *Haiku*-inscribed plaques are scattered throughout the stone-and-bonsai garden: 'Ice and water/their differences resolved/are friends again', reads one poem, hinting at the World War II internment.

At the **Bainbridge Island Historical Museum** (tel: 206-842 2773; www.bainbridgehistory.org; daily 10am–4pm, free first Thu of the month), two photographs vividly underscore the impact of the internment on island life. The photographs show Bainbridge High School's 1942 and 1943 graduating classes. In the first picture, about one third of the faces are Japanese; the second shows a smaller, all-white class.

You can learn more about the internment of the Japanese population at the **Bainbridge Island Japanese American Exclusion Memorial**. Located on the site of the former Eagledale ferry dock, it honours the 272 Japanese men, women and children (the majority of them American

citizens) who on 30 March 1942 were rounded up by American soldiers and forcibly put on a ferry to Seattle where they were interned until the end of the war.

Around the island

Most descendants of the *issei* have moved away for opportunities on the mainland. One who remained was the late nursery-owner Junkoh Harui. He restored the nursery, **Bainbridge Gardens** (9415 Miller Road NE; tel: 206-842 5888), which his father started in the early 1900s from Japanese seeds, and then lost during the internment. The nursery sells an excellent selection of trees, shrubs, perennials, and bonsai, as well as garden statuary. It's a pleasant place for a stroll.

Take Route 305 north toward the Agate Pass Bridge to the Kitsap Peninsula. Before crossing the bridge you can visit wonderful **Bloedel Reserve** (tel: 206-842 7631; www.bloedel reserve.org; Tue–Sun 10am–4pm). This extraordinary 150-acre (60-hectare) preserve has woodland, meadows, a bird refuge, and outstanding world-renowned Japanese and Reflection Gardens. The leafy expanse makes a perfect wildlife habitat, so bring your binoculars to be on the lookout for eagles, osprey, and hummingbirds. This former summer retreat of a Seattle mayor's widow – you can also tour their preserved mansion – is a breathtaking daytrip from Seattle.

Suquamish

The Agate Pass Bridge onto the Kitsap Peninsula leads to **Suquamish**, where a right turn on Suquamish Way leads to the **grave of Chief Sealth ❷**, the tribal chief for whom Seattle is named. The tribal cemetery is peaceful and small, but as befits his importance, the leader is commemorated with a tall, white marker. Just up the highway, the renovated **Suquamish Museum** (6861 NE South Street; tel: 360-394

The Suquamish grave of Chief Sealth.

3499; www.suquamishmuseum.org; daily 10am–5pm) has historical photos and tribal artifacts. The 'Ancient Shore-Changing Tides' exhibit recounts the tribe's history using seven symbolic design elements.

Along Route 305 is **Poulsbo**, a Scandinavian fishing village turned tourist town. It was nicknamed 'Little Norway' for its setting on Liberty Bay, which is reminiscent of the Scandinavian fjords. This may have been the attraction for the Nordic families who emigrated here a century ago. Poulsbo is noted throughout the state for Poulsbo bread, baked fresh daily at Sluys Poulsbo Bakery (http://sluys poulsbobakery.com).

Port Gamble ❸

Heading northward toward the Olympic Peninsula is a worthwhile diversion. This takes you to **Port Gamble**, which, until a few years ago, was one of the last lumber towns to have a fully operational mill.

FACT

In June 2005, the Suquamish tribe received the deeds to small Old Man House Park. Chief Sealth had lived on the land, and its return by the Washington State Parks department helped to heal wounds. Old Man House Park is still managed by the department, but under tribal control.

Built by the Pope and Talbot lumber families, who arrived by clipper ship from Maine in the 1850s, the town's original trading center has been converted into a combination gift store, café, and museum. The tiny town, with refurbished Victorian clapboard houses, is a picture of a prim-and-pretty New England village – but one that is set against a dramatic Northwestern backdrop.

Bremerton ❹

South from Poulsbo is the seaport town of **Bremerton**. Founded in 1891 by William Bremer, a German immigrant, Bremerton is one of those towns in the West that for years was controlled by one family. Plotted by Bremer on land he had purchased, the town – today's downtown area – stayed in the hands of the Bremer family until the second of the two sons died in 1986. Neither son married – according to local lore, in accordance with their mother's wishes – and after the second son died, local Olympic College inherited most of Downtown.

To the outside world, Bremerton is known for the **Puget Sound Naval Shipyard**. The shipyard is still a large force in the local economy and culture, but gentrification has brought about a transformation in the town. The result is art galleries, specialty shops, and cafés, mixed in with a few reminders of older days, like tattoo parlors and gritty bars.

The former Woolworth department store has been converted into an indoor **antique market**, with dozens of vendors proffering a lively assortment of junk and treasure.

The **Harborside District** is a big, glossy development designed to lure corporations to the town, and with a conference center to attract the business trade. There's a marina, a boardwalk, fountains, and restaurants. The **Harborside Fountain Park**, constructed above the tunnel linking the ferry terminal with Highway 304, features five large fountains as well as wading pools.

For years Bremerton's biggest tourist attraction was the battleship USS *Missouri*, but Bremerton lost the most highly decorated ship of World War II to Honolulu in 1999. In its place now is an interesting footnote to the Vietnam War: the destroyer **USS Turner Joy** (300 Washington Beach Avenue; tel: 360-792 2457; www.uss turnerjoy.org; daily 10am–5pm, until 4pm in winter), which was one of the ships in the Tonkin Gulf incident that escalated the Vietnam War. Nearby is **Puget Sound Navy Museum** (251 1st Street; tel: 360-627 2270; www.pugetsoundnavymuseum. org; daily 10am–4pm, closed Tue Oct–Apr; free), which focuses on World War II, and on the shipyard's contribution.

VASHON ISLAND ❺

Southwest of Bremerton is a ferry link to **Vashon Island**, which is also accessible by ferry from Tacoma (Point Defiance terminal), from

An aircraft carrier in Bremerton.

the Kitsap Peninsula, and from West Seattle (Fauntleroy Terminal). Without a bridge connecting it to the mainland, Vashon remains the most rural and least developed of Puget Sound's nearby islands, and that's the way the residents like it.

The island's easygoing country attitude is symbolized by a famous landmark: the bike in the tree. It seems that, years ago, someone planted a bike in the fork of a tree and left it to rust. Today, the bike is completely engulfed by the tree; it's still in the woods, on Vashon Highway a few miles south of Downtown, but you may have to ask for directions locally.

Unfortunately, there isn't enough industry to support the island's 10,000 residents, so most commute to Seattle or Tacoma. But there are a few who manage to live on the island and work here, too. usually by running one of the small specialty shops. The main culinary draw these days is Sea Breeze Farm's fantastic onsite restaurant, La Boucherie (www.seabreezefarm. net). They say it best: 'We farm it, raise it, harvest it, clean it, process it, cook it and serve it.' Foodies from across the region are boarding ferries to get lunch to go or memorable dinners at this destination eatery.

Vashon is perfect for visitors who like their pleasures low-key. During the summer months, they can pick their own strawberries, rent a kayak, or go swimming. At other times of the year, the main leisure activities include hiking to Point Robinson Lighthouse or taking one of the horse-drawn hayrides.

In the 1960s and 1970s, Vashon was a counterculture retreat. 'There was only one cop on the island, so you could get away with a lot', one alumnus of the era reminisces. Today, intermingling with the locals is a lively community of artists, some of whose work is displayed in New York, San Francisco, and elsewhere,

Admiring the view from a harbor cruise.

not to mention the galleries scattered across the island.

Vashon Allied Arts, which is headquartered in the **Heron's Nest** (19600 Vashon Highway SW; tel: 206-463 5131; www.vashoncenterforthearts.org), presents a well-attended monthly show featuring local and regional artists.

MYSTERIOUS MYTHS

Myths are plentiful across the waters of Puget Sound and on the slopes of the Cascade Mountains. Sea serpents up to 100ft (30 meters) long with heads like horses and snouts like camels were reported in the Pacific Northwest waters long before the white man arrived. Centuries-old petroglyphs of these creatures adorn rock surfaces, while paintings and wood carvings depict them, too. The creatures were named 'Cadborosaurus' by a 1930s newspaperman after sightings in Cadboro Bay, Victoria.

Mountain tales of the elusive Bigfoot or Sasquatch are among the most popular and persistent in North American folk memory. A giant, hairy hominid who roams the forests has been recounted in stories and depicted on totem poles from northern California to British Columbia. Both native and white witnesses describe the creature as 6–11ft (1.8–3.4 meters) tall and weighing between 700 and 2,500 pounds (320–1,100 kg), walking erect or slightly stooped with long arms that swing back and forth. Its hair is black or brown. There is no solid evidence, however, to convince researchers of Bigfoot's existence.

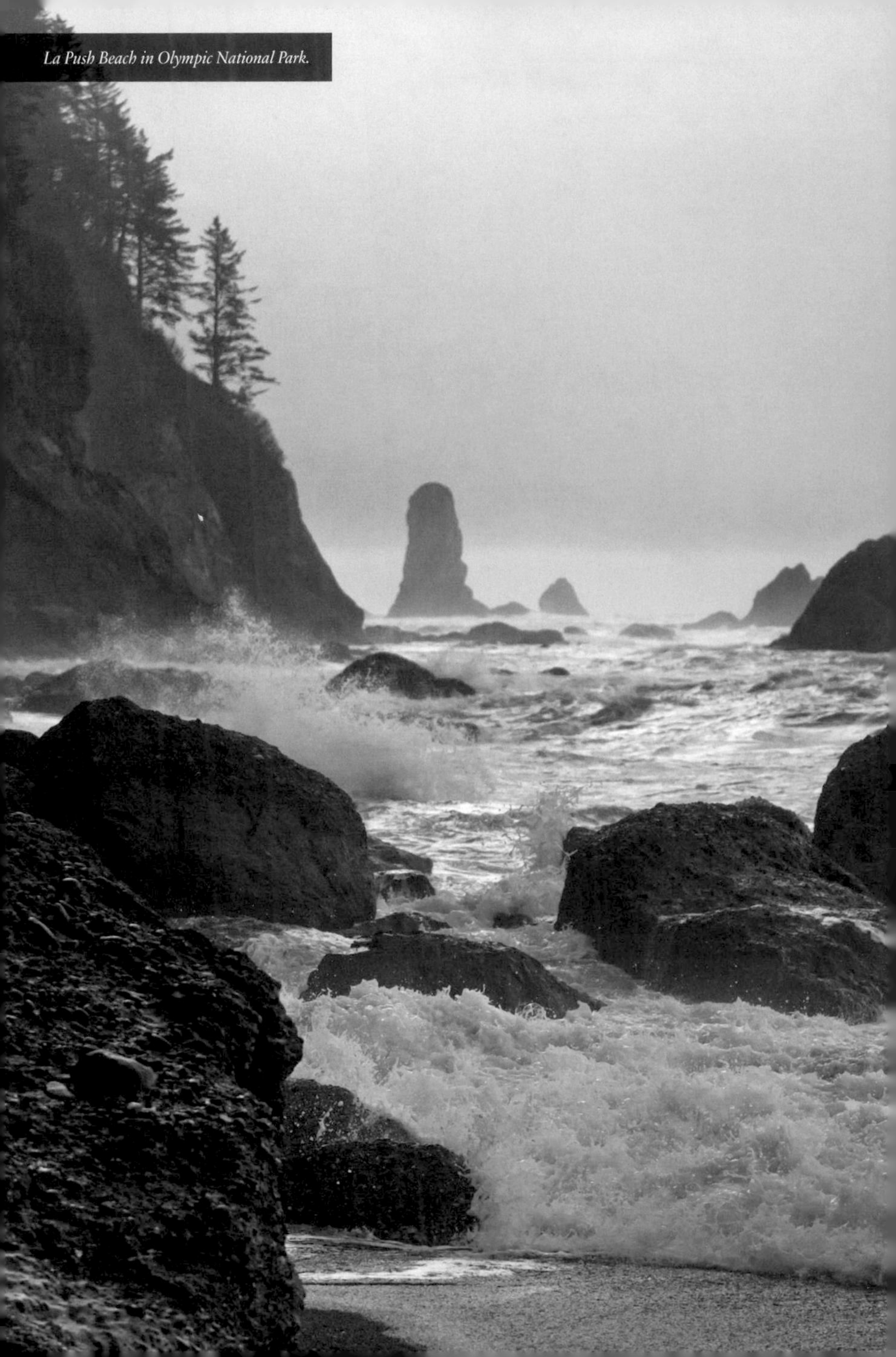

La Push Beach in Olympic National Park.

THE OLYMPIC PENINSULA

A rain forest, a Victorian town, a tribal reservation, and magnificent Mount Olympus urge travelers to 'go west' to this lovely peninsula.

Seattle

A
ll over Puget Sound, the peaks of the **Olympic Mountains** dominate the western skyline. Few regions can offer visitors such rugged coasts, prairies, and forests with views, above the timberline, of snowy, glacier-capped peaks.

To reach the peninsula from Seattle, take a ferry to Bremerton (see page 198) and head north 19 miles (30km) on State Route 3. Pass through Poulsbo (see page 197), Washington's Little Norway, and about 7 miles (11km) farther on State Route 3 is the **Hood Canal Bridge**. This floating bridge is a major gateway to the Olympic Peninsula, the only one over tidal waters and at 1.5 miles (2.5km) long, the third longest in the world.

A section swings aside for ships to pass, and Trident submarines from the base at Bangor may hold up traffic. Before crossing the bridge, you might want to take a short trip to historic Port Gamble just east of the bridge (see page 197).

Port Townsend ❻

Port Townsend is about 30 miles (50km) north of the bridge. The harbor here was discovered by Captain George Vancouver in 1792 while he surveyed the coast for the British Admiralty. In 1851 the city was

created, planned to be the main West Coast port. By the end of the century, the city was booming, but the dreams relied on a railroad connection to Tacoma, which never came.

Urban renewal and development passed it by, so Port Townsend has many lovely Victorian buildings, some of them now hotels or inns. **Water Street** has art galleries, antique and clothing stores, and restaurants in the old commercial center. Some of these back up onto the water, as they were built in the late 19th century

Main Attractions

Port Townsend
Dungeness Spit
Hurricane Ridge
Lake Crescent
Hoh Rain Forest
Kalaloch Beach
Lake Quinault

Map
Page 192

A Roosevelt elk in Olympic National Park.

The Historical District Courthouse, built in 1891, in Port Townsend.

to store goods from sailing vessels before they were transported onward. Many people use Port Townsend as a base to explore the surrounding area, returning each night to accommodations in a historic building and to dine in one of the town's excellent restaurants. The **Visitor Center** (tel: 360-385 2722; www.enjoypt.com) has maps and information.

Fort Worden

A rowing boat at Point Wilson lighthouse.

North of the city are the 434 acres (175 hectares) of historic Fort Worden, keystone of an 1880s network of forts, which guarded the entrance to Puget Sound until the end of World War II. The fort is now a state park, and the parade ground was featured in the movie *An Officer and a Gentleman*. The **Coast Artillery Museum** (tel: 360-385 0373; http://coastartillery.org; summer daily 11am–4pm; voluntary donation) illustrates the history of the fort.

Fine accommodations are available in restored officers' homes (tel: 360-344 4400), less luxurious lodging is in the barracks and the hostel. Campgrounds are also available.

Sharing the flat point with gun emplacements is the **Point Wilson Lighthouse**, built in 1913. The **Marine Science Center** (tel: 360-385 5582; www.ptmsc.org; summer Wed–Mon 11am–5pm, rest of year Fri–Sun noon–5pm) on the waterfront has exhibits and touch tanks of local marine life. It also sponsors marine-science activities and summer camps for kids.

Sequim ❼

From Port Townsend, 13 miles (21km) south on State Route 20 and then north and west another 13 miles on US 101, is the sunny town of **Sequim** (pronounced 'skwim'), in the Dungeness Valley.

The arid area was first homesteaded in 1854 and irrigated four decades later as Sequim became a farming community. Today it is known for its lavender farms. The **Museum and Arts Center** (tel: 360-683 8110;

http://sequimmuseum.com; Wed–Sat 11am–3pm; voluntary donation) has exhibits of farming, Salish (the local tribe) and pioneer life, and displays by local artists. Sequim's mild climate, in the rain shadow of the Olympic Mountains, attracts many retirees.

Head north 5 miles (8km) on Ward Road to the **Olympic Game Farm** (tel: 360-683 7621 or 1-800-778 4295; www.olygamefarm.com; daily spring and fall 9am–4pm, until 3pm in winter, until 5pm in summer), home to animals like bears, bison, elk, zebras, and lions. Over the years it has supplied animal 'actors' for movies and television. There's a selection of walking and driving tours.

Dungeness Spit ❽

Dungeness Spit is farther north. At 6 miles (8km) and growing, the spit is the longest sand hook (a sand spit growing out from the shore, then running parallel to it) in the United States. The Dungeness Recreation Area includes a 6-mile (8km) hike along the spit, and around the shore of the saltwater lagoon. Sturdy shoes make it easier to scramble over the driftwood. The lagoon is a national wildlife refuge for migrating waterfowl. At the end of the spit is the **New Dungeness Lighthouse**, built in 1857.

Port Angeles ❾

Follow US 101 west 17 miles (27km) to **Port Angeles**, the largest port city on the northern Olympic Peninsula. Port Angeles' huge harbor for Asian and Pacific ocean-going ships is formed by Ediz Hook, another long sand spit with a Coast Guard air station at its end. The car ferry *Coho* (tel: 360-457 4491; www.cohoferry.com) operates year-round to Victoria (see page 212) on Vancouver Island, in Canada's province of British Columbia.

Within a historic library, the **Museum at the Carnegie** (tel: 360-452 2662; www.clallamhistoricalsociety.com; Wed–Sat 1–4pm; voluntary donation) has displays on local history, fishing, genealogy, and Native American artifacts. There are spectacular views of both the Strait of Juan de Fuca and Vancouver Island to the north, and of the Olympic Mountains to the south.

Water Street, Port Townsend.

FORT WORDEN

If you're looking for a fun, quirky, artsy getaway from Seattle, consider joining the artists, musicians, writers, creative thinkers, and arts lovers who come together nearly every week at Fort Worden State Park, where the Centrum Foundation (http://centrum.org) hosts hundreds of concerts and residency workshops each year. Some of the highlights of the Centrum calendar include the Port Townsend Chamber Music Festival, the Port Townsend Acoustic Blues Festival, the Festival of American Fiddle Tunes, and Jazz Port Townsend. Literary-minded visitors might want to attend the two-week-long Port Townsend Writer's Workshop, with free nightly readings and lectures from authors such as Cheryl Strayed, Dorothy Allison, and Pam Houston.

Olympic National Park

The **Olympic National Park Visitor Center** (3002 Mt Angeles Road; tel: 360-565 3130; www.nps.gov/olym; open 24 hours a day, although some facilities are only open seasonally) in Port Angeles has maps and park information, and displays on the wildlife, plants, geology, and tribal culture of the Northwest coast.

To enter the park itself, follow Race Street in Port Angeles to the well-marked Hurricane Ridge Road, and then make the steep 17-mile (27km) ascent through dense forest to reach **Hurricane Ridge** ⓾, 5,200ft (1,600 meters) above sea level. From here are views of mountains, meadows with wildflowers, and forests.

To the southwest is glacier-capped **Mount Olympus** ⑪, at 7,828ft (2,386 meters), the highest peak in the Olympics. No roads lead to Mount Olympus, only hiking trails. In winter months, Hurricane Ridge is the only place in the Olympics for cross-country and downhill skiing.

A young buck grazing in the Olympic Mountains.

Lake Crescent ⑫

Return to US 101 and head west for 5 miles (8km) beyond Port Angeles; the road curves south around **Lake Crescent**, an immense cobalt-blue glacier lake surrounded by tall-timbered forest. Gorgeous **Lake Crescent Lodge** (tel: 888 896 3818), on the southern shore, is where President Franklin D. Roosevelt stayed in 1937 before he signed the act creating the 922,000-acre (373,000-hectare) Olympic National Park. Continue west along US 101 and turn south onto Sol Duc River Road to reach **Sol Duc Hot Springs** ⑬ (www.olympic nationalparks.com), where you can take a dip in the Olympic-sized pool or hot mineral pools, which are a pleasant 102–109°F (39–43°C). A short rain-forest hike leads to Sol Duc Falls and a less fancy geothermal spring, Olympic Hot Springs.

Neah Bay ⑭

Continue west on US 101 to **Sappho** and then north on State Route 113. At the intersection with SR 112, turn and head west 27 miles (43km) through Clallam Bay and Sekiu to **Neah Bay**, at the northwesterly tip of the peninsula. Alternatively, follow SR 112 from Port Angeles along the picturesque shore of the Strait of Juan de Fuca, bypassing Lake Crescent.

The remote village of Neah Bay is on the **Makah Indian Reservation**. The Makah, who call themselves Kwih-dich-chuh-ahtx – 'people who live by the rocks and seagulls' – have been here for hundreds of years. Majestic red cedars provided housing materials, tools, and sea-going canoes, in which they hunted migrating gray whales and seals.

The Makah still have the right by treaty to hunt whales, but commercial fishing is a mainstay. Sports fishing for salmon and halibut is an important industry for the Makah and a big attraction for thousands of anglers who visit annually; Neah Bay

is home port more for than 200 commercial and sports-fishing boats. The Makah welcome visitors to explore a hatchery, where salmon migrate up the fish ladders.

Makah Cultural and Research Center

This center (tel: 360-645 2711; http://makahmuseum.com; daily 10am–5pm) is a useful source of information, as well as a museum with Northwest Indian artifacts and a replica longhouse. the hub of Makah village life. Edward S. Curtis' photomurals are from more than 40,000 images of a 34-year photo-essay he began on the North American Indians in 1896.

Most of the 300 to 500 artifacts on display are from the archeological dig on the Ozette Indian Reservation or the coast, south of Neah Bay and the Makah lands. The village, buried by a mudslide more than 500 years ago, was sealed in clay soil, the contents of the houses closed off for posterity. The Ozette dig unearthed more than 55,000 artifacts and remains one of the most important archeological finds in North America.

Many beaches in the area are closed to non-Native Americans. At the Cultural and Research Center, maps of the reservation show open areas, and the car route and walking trail to **Cape Flattery**, on the northwestern tip of the Peninsula.

Cape Flattery

The boardwalk trail here threads through a forest to observation decks on the 60ft (18-meter) cliffs of the cape. Vistas are spectacular, with waves crashing on rocky shores and pristine beaches. In spring and late fall, migrating gray whales can sometimes be seen, as well as seals and birds.

A few hundred yards offshore is **Tatoosh Island**, home to seals. sea lions, and the **Cape Flattery Light**, first lit in 1857. The lighthouse overlooks the funnel-like entrance to the

Fort Worden State Park.

Strait of Juan de Fuca, a graveyard for the many ships wrecked on the Washington coast or Vancouver Island by storms, ocean currents. and fog.

South along the coast

South from the Makah Reservation is a national wildlife refuge: 57 miles (98km) of spectacular cliffs, sea stacks, and beaches. Just north of Forks is a turnoff – SR 110 – to the coast, leading to Rialto Beach and the Quileute village of La Push. **Rialto Beach** is a favorite spot for fashion photographers. **La Push** ⑮ has a jagged rock-lined beach, offshore sea stacks, and a justly famous 16-mile (26km) beach walk.

Century-old **Forks** ⑯, with a population of around 3,500, is on a broad prairie on the northwest of the peninsula and is the only sizable town. The **Forks Timber Museum** (tel: 360-374 9663; http://forkstimbermuseum.org; summer Mon–Sat 10am–5pm, Sun 11am–4pm, winter daily 11am–4pm) displays a pioneer kitchen, farm and logging equipment, vintage newspapers, and photos. The town is

FACT

Mount Olympus receives more than 17ft (5 meters) of precipitation each year and most of that falls as snow. Hurricane Ridge is covered with more than 10ft (3 meters) of snow for most of the winter.

Mountain goat on Hurricane Ridge.

beaches, from **Ruby Beach** and the **Hoh Indian Reservation** in the north to **Kalaloch** (pronounced 'clay-lock') **Beach** in the south. Part of Olympic National Park's coastal strip, the coast has a rugged and picturesque beauty. Waves crash against rocks and offshore islands, casting tree trunks up on the shore like toothpicks. A few miles offshore is reef-girdled **Destruction Island** and its lighthouse, built in 1890. On a foggy day, the mournful foghorn disturbs thousands of auklets – small sea birds – on the island.

The forest surrounding **Lake Quinault** ⓲ – at the southwest corner of Olympic National Park – is often called 'the other rain forest.' It's possible to drive a 25-mile (40km) loop around the glacial lake. **Lake Quinault Lodge** (tel: 360-288 2900), a huge, old-fashioned cedar hotel built in 1926 on the lake's southern shore, is a landmark. Winding trails lead from the lodge into the rain forest, including to **Big Acre**, a grove of huge, centuries-old trees.

a good base for hiking the rain forests and rugged coast. As the setting of Stephenie Meyers' *Twilight* book series, Forks draws loyal fans on the lookout for vampires.

The **Hoh Rain Forest Visitor Center** ⓱ (tel: 360 565 3130; www. nps.gov/olym/planyourvisit/visiting-the-hoh.htm) is south of Forks off US 101 and about 20 miles (30km) into the national park. There is a wealth of information here on the wildlife, flora, and history of the temperate rain forest. Moisture-laden air from the Pacific drenches the area with more than 150 inches (380cm) of rain annually – this is one of the wettest places in the US. Three loop trails (and a wheelchair-accessible mini-trail) lead into the rain forest, with its moss-draped trees, ferns, and a clear, glacial-fed river. Elk, deer, and other animals are often seen.

Farther south of the turnoff, US 101 swings west to the coast and follows cliffs overlooking beautiful

Ocean Shores

Head south to **Ocean Shores** ⓳, on a 6-mile (10km) -long peninsula, and enter through an imposing gateway. Originally homesteaded in the 1860s, Ocean Shores was only incorporated as a city in 1970, when investors, including singer Pat Boone, got the town under way. Ocean Shores is now a town of motels and vacation homes. **Grays Harbor** was discovered in 1792 by an American trader, Captain Robert Gray, who also discovered the Columbia River. The harbor is the only deep-water port on the outer Washington coast, and is a major terminal for Asia-bound lumber.

The tall ship *Lady Washington* (tel: 1-800-200 5239; www.historical seaport.org), a replica of Gray's ship, embarks on cruises from the Grays Harbor Historical Seaport, a working tall-ship dockyard.

Long Beach Peninsula

South on US 101 and along the east shore of **Willapa Bay** is one of the nicest stretches of beach in Washington. This is the lovely **Long Beach Peninsula** ㉓, fronted by a 28-mile (45km) shore. The lively town of **Long Beach** is a miniature Coney Island – the main street is filled with huge chainsaw art sculptures (a near-naked mermaid, the Louis and Clark duo, and more). Further north on the peninsula, the historic town of **Oysterville** had its heyday in California's 1850s Gold Rush, shipping oysters to San Francisco at the equivalent of $19 each in today's money.

Cape Disappointment

At the base of the Olympic Peninsula is one of the most spectacular spots on the Washington coast: **Cape Disappointment** ㉑, overlooking the treacherous mouth of the Columbia River, a graveyard for ships and sailors. This graveyard is **Fort Canby State Park**, home to two lighthouses. **Cape Disappointment Light**, one of the first on the West Coast, has warned sailors for over 150 years.

North Head Light was built later to guide ships coming from the north.

To complete the trip around the Olympic Peninsula, head east from Grays Harbor to the state capital at **Olympia** ㉒ (see page 188). A highway runs north along **Hood Canal**, known for oysters, through **Shelton** (Christmas trees and oysters) and Hoodsport. **Quilcene** ㉓, on Dabob Bay, has one of the world's largest oyster factories. Stop by for tangy oysters or clams to take home.

The home of Bella Swan – the fictional protagonist of the popular 'Twilight' series.

Cape Disappointment.

Glaciers on Mount Rainier.

ISLANDS AND MOUNTAINS

Watch orcas by the islands of the San Juan
archipelago, visit a Victorian town in Canada,
discover the magnificent Cascade Mountains, and
end up only a couple of hours away from Seattle.

Breathtaking trips into the
Northwest radiate from
Seattle in all directions. To
the north are the coastal islands
of the US and Canada, perfect for
sunsets and picnics. The Cascade
Mountains, with the volcanic show-
stoppers Mount Rainier, Mount St
Helens, and Mount Baker. are geographically to the east, but their
snowcapped glacial peaks can be
seen from everywhere.

ISLANDS OF THE NORTH

Whidbey Island ㉔ is the longest
contiguous island in the US. The
Keystone ferry travels from Port
Townsend on the Olympic Peninsula
to the rolling hills and rocky beaches
of Whidbey, a hideaway place for hikers and walkers. A ferry at Mukilteo,
45 minutes north of Seattle, also goes
to the island. The town of **Langley**
perches on a cliff over Saratoga
Passage, with water and mountain
views a backdrop to the century-
old shops, restaurants, art galleries,
and inns. **Coupeville** has Victorian
homes and shops, plus Fort Casey
Underwater Park (1280 Engle Road),
which is popular with kayakers and
bird-watchers as well as divers. **Oak
Harbor** is the largest town, with
Whidbey Naval Air Station nearby.

Whidbey island.

At the northern tip of the island,
narrow **Deception Pass** is spanned
by a 976ft (297-meter) -long, 180ft
(55-meter) -high steel bridge to
Fidalgo Island ㉕. The Deception
Pass State Park (http://parks.state.
wa.us/497) is a paradise for families,
hikers, birdwatchers and fishermen alike. Attractive, 19th-century
Anacortes is the ferry terminal for
the San Juan Islands and Vancouver
Island. Views from nearby Mount
Erie are well worth the drive to this
lovely spot.

Main Attractions

San Juan Islands
Victoria, British Columbia
Eutchart Gardens,
    Vancouver Island
Mount Rainier
Mount St Helens
Snoqualmie Falls
Chuckanut Drive
North Cascades National
    Park

Map

Page 192

Orca breaching in the San Juan Islands.

Kayaking in the San Juan Islands.

San Juan Islands

Of the 172 San Juans, only four – the islands of Shaw, Lopez, Orcas, and San Juan – have regular ferry service; the others can be reached by float-plane or chartered sailboat, via narrow channels and open water, passing on the way sandy beaches, shallow bays, sand spits, grassy estuaries, and forested slopes. In 2013, these beautiful islands were declared a national monument. Orcas (killer whales), seabirds, harbor seals, otters, and bald eagles can all be spotted. The flat rural terrain of Lopez, Shaw, and San Juan is great for bicycling.

Orcas Island ㉖ was named not for killer whales but for the Spanish patron of an explorer of the region in 1792. Bed-and-breakfast inns are all over the island, but the only traditional resort is **Rosario Resort & Spa** (tel: 360-376 2222; www.rosario resort.com), the handsome 1904 estate of shipbuilder and former Seattle mayor Robert Moran, for whom **Moran State Park** is named. A paved road and hiking trail winds up the mountain to a 50ft (15-meter) -high stone lookout tower. At the top is a 360-degree view of the islands and, on a clear day, Mount Baker 50 miles (80km) east in the Cascade Range.

On **San Juan Island** ㉗, the ferry docks at **Friday Harbor**, a highly attractive village of restaurants, hotels, and shops. The **Whale Museum** (62 1st Street N; tel: 360-378 4710 ext. 30; www.whalemuseum.org; daily 10am–4pm) explains whale behavior and sounds, and has skeletons of an adult orca and a baby gray whale. Also on display are photos of the region's resident orcas, whose distinctive markings enable researchers to follow individuals in each 'pod'; in 2006, Puget Sound was designated a critical habitat for orcas. The museum organizes whale-watching tours in season (mid-April through October).

Relics of a dispute between Great Britain and the US between 1859 and 1872 are in the **San Juan Island Historical Museum** (www.sjmuseum. org). A replica of a 19th-century barn on the museum's grounds is currently being converted into the interactive **San Juan Island Museum of History and Industry** (completion date late 2017), telling the story of the island's fishing, farming, logging, lime quarrying, and processing industries. Located in a sleek modern building, the **San Juan Islands Museum of Art** (http://sjima.org) offers rotating exhibitions of painting, drawing, sculpture and photography.

Charming **Roche Harbor**, once the richest deposit of limestone west of the Mississippi, is at the island's north end. At the harbor's edge is the delightful 1880s **Hotel de Haro** (tel: 800-451 8910; www.rocheharbor.com).

Canada's Gulf Islands

The southern Gulf Islands – Salt Spring, Galiano, Mayne, the Penders, and Saturna – are near Victoria and mainland British Columbia.

Saturna Island ㉘, the most southerly, is large in area but tiny in population – about 350. The ferry from Swartz Bay on Vancouver Island docks at Lyall Harbour. The island is a rural hideaway with wildlife, quiet roads, scenic walks, and accessible beaches. Rent a boat for fishing or a kayak to tour the shoreline. **Winter Cove Marine Park** (http://gulfislands nationalpark.com) has an excellent harbor, a boat launch, picnic areas, walking trails, and a tidal marsh with wildlife. A stiff hike leads to Mount

Warburton Pike for a panoramic view of the Gulf and San Juan islands.

The **Pender Islands** ㉙ are two islands connected by a wooden bridge. The ferry from Vancouver Island docks at Otter Bay on North Pender. Explore the islands by car, bicycle, scooter, or on foot to discover hidden coves and beaches. Bedwell Harbour on South Pender has a large resort with a full range of facilities.

Mayne Island ㉚ was the center of commercial and social life in the Gulf Islands during the Fraser River/Cariboo Gold Rush in the 1850s. Would-be miners rested at **Miners Bay** before rowing across the Strait of Georgia. Miners Bay now has shops, eateries, and a museum in the old jail. The island has lovely hiking trails to peaks, and beaches with sandstone caves.

Skinny **Galiano Island** ㉛ lies just east of the larger Salt Spring Island. It is reached from the west through Active Pass, an S-shaped passage with Mayne Island on the south. Seabirds, eagles, herons, and – sometimes – orcas can be seen, though these mighty predators are threatened by shrinking salmon stocks.

TIP

The Gulf Islands and Victoria fall under Canadian territory, so US and other foreign visitors need to take a passport.

Bald eagle with lunch.

Wildflowers and migrating birds draw naturalists in the spring. Kayakers and other boaters enjoy the protected west coast, while the waters of Active Pass and Porlier Pass at the north end attract scuba divers and fishermen.

Salt Spring Island ㉜ has 14 salt springs, ranging in size from a few feet to 100ft (30 meters) in diameter. It is the largest of the Gulf Islands, with a population of a little over 10,000, mostly in the flatter northern part of the island. **Ganges** is the only town. Salt Spring is home to many artists, and there is a summer-long arts-and-crafts fair. Cyclists enjoy flat roads, and hikers find trails on the level, up mountain slopes, or along beaches. Freshwater lakes are lovely for swimming and fishing.

The south is punctuated by two mountain ranges separated by a valley. The ferry from Swartz Bay docks at Fulford Harbour at the south end of the valley, but ferries from mainland British Columbia and the other Gulf Islands dock at Long Harbour, on the east coast. Yet another ferry connects Vesuvius Bay, in the northwest, to Crofton, north of Victoria.

Vancouver Island

On the south tip of **Vancouver Island** is **Victoria ㉝**, the capital of British Columbia. Victoria's center of activity is the **Inner Harbour**, where float planes, pleasure and fishing boats, and tiny harbor ferries scurry like water bugs among larger ferries. The harbor is dominated by two buildings. The first is the **BC Government Parliament Buildings** (tel: 250-387 3046; free daily tours in summer). It was designed in 1898 by 25-year-old English architect Francis Rattenbury, who made a fortune in British Columbia's Gold Rush. An imposing mix of European styles, Parliament is especially impressive at night when illuminated by thousands of light bulbs.

Building began on the **Empress Hotel** (tel: 250-384 8111; www.fairmont.com/empress-victoria), the harbor's other structure, in 1904 on what had been muddy James Bay. The Empress sits on 2,855 pilings of Douglas fir, which extend 50ft (15 meters) down through the mud of the bay. Ever since this French château-style hotel opened in 1908, it has played

Victoria's illuminated BC Government Parliament Buildings.

host to royalty, ghosts (allegedly), intrigue, and movie stars. Few people come to Victoria without partaking of traditional afternoon tea at the Empress Hotel, where appropriate dress is appreciated. Renovations (completed in 2017) have upgraded the spa, lobby, health club, and 229 guest rooms.

Victoria's history

A good way to learn about the province is to visit the excellent **Royal British Columbia Museum** (675 Belleville Street; tel: 250-356 7226 or +1888-447 7977; www.royalbcmuseum. bc.ca; daily 10am–5pm), which has exhibits that document the culture of the original native inhabitants and early life in Victoria, and an IMAX theater. The Native American exhibit centers on a replica of a Northwest longhouse, with canoes and tribal clothes. Adjacent to the museum is **Thunderbird Park**, where First Nation carvers produce totem poles and gifts for sale. Replicas and real totems are scattered around the green lawns, and in front of a couple of historic buildings.

Head north on Victoria's main boulevard, **Government Street**, with its many stores, most in 19th-century

Victoria's harbor front.

buildings, and be pulled into shops selling chocolate, Scottish woolens, or Irish linens. At the corner of Fort Street is the four-story **Bay Centre**, a huge indoor mall looking out of place in a 19th-century environment. Turn right on Fort Street for the section known as Antique Row.

Opposite the north end of the Bay Centre, a pedestrian walkway leads west to **Bastion Square**, the former site of Fort Victoria (no longer in evidence). If time allows, explore the **Maritime Museum of British Columbia** (28 Bastion Square; tel: 250-385 4222; http://mmbc.bc.ca; summer daily 10am–5pm, winter Tue–Sat 10am–4pm) in the old Law Courts building where Matthew Begbie, the 'hanging judge', worked. Begbie was the first judge in British Columbia, and rode on horseback to mining camps to dispense justice from a tent.

Head up Government Street to Wharf and Store streets and the waterfront. This is **Old Town**, where fine 19th-century buildings survived the 'urban renewal' after World War II. **Market Square**, once a produce market, has been rejuvenated with shops and restaurants.

Totem poles.

CITY OF FLOWERS

Victoria is known as the City of Flowers – flowers in gardens, window boxes, road dividers, and, in summer, hanging from the blue lampposts Downtown. The world-famous Butchart Gardens north of Victoria are the floral masterpiece. It rains just enough to keep plants and lawns green, and a warm offshore current moderates the temperatures. Visitors are drawn to this classy little town from around the world. The Hudson's Bay Company built a trading fort on the site of modern-day Victoria in 1843, and the city retains a pleasing English ambience with tea rooms, double-decker buses, horse-drawn carriages, and, of course, flowers.

Totem poles

Northwest First Nations (Canadian Native Americans) are carvers by tradition, and the totem pole is one of the more notable of their crafts, with the practice ranging from the Puget Sound area north to Alaska.

The natives of British Columbia and Alaska, however, were the first to carve them. The history of these works is surprisingly brief, for it wasn't until the mid-1700s, when European explorers first encountered these remote people, that the unique sculptures began to appear. Although the local tribes were already expert carvers of canoes, tools, longhouses, and furniture, they lacked the iron tools necessary to fell a massive tree in one piece and carve its length.

First Nations totem pole in Stanley Park, Vancouver, Canada.

With the iron axes for which they traded, the coastal tribes could now take advantage of the trees that grew so tall and straight in their wet climate. Initially, the poles were made to stand against the front of a home, with figures facing out and a door cut through the base, so all would enter the house through the pole. In these cases, the totem pole functioned as a family crest, recounting genealogies, stories, or legends that in some way identified the owner.

Poles served the function of recording the lore of the clan, much like a book. The top figure on the pole identified the owner's clan, and the succeeding characters (read from top to bottom) tell their stories. There is a story behind almost every image on a pole. If a legendary animal – Raven, the trickster, for example – had the power to transform into, say, a person, then the carver would depict Raven with both wings and limbs or with a human face and a raven's beak.

Potlatches and government bans

Toward the end of the 1800s, the poles stood free on the beach or in the village outside the carvers' homes. Some villages were virtual forests of hundreds of poles. The family that carved the pole held a potlatch (ceremony) with feasting, games, and gift-giving. These gatherings were costly and required a great deal of preparation and participation. The custom frustrated white men trying to 'civilize' the tribes, especially local missionaries, who solved the problem by chopping down the poles. Employers, too, complained that their Native American workers were unreliable when a pole was being carved or a potlatch planned. Eventually, both the Canadian and United States' governments banned potlatches, and pole carving nearly died out. (The ban was finally lifted in the 1950s.)

Learning to read – and appreciate – totem poles is like learning to read a language. The poles speak of history, mythology, social structure, and spirituality. They serve many purposes, for both individual and community, and continue to be carved by descendants of the original carvers.

The Butchart Gardens in Victoria.

Farther along Government Street is Fisgard Street and the 'Gate of Harmonious Interest', a red-tiled arch emblazoned with Chinese art, supported by two red columns. Stone lions guard each side. This is the entrance to Victoria's **Chinatown**, once the largest on the North American West Coast but now only a fragment of the original. Look out for **Fan Tan Alley**. Only 5ft (1.5 meters) wide in places, it is one of the narrowest roads in Canada.

The Johnson Street Bridge (Blue Bridge) leads to the town of **Esquimalt**, home of Canada's Pacific Fleet. Britain used the deep-water anchorage as early as 1837, and it's been in use ever since.

Beyond Esquimalt is the community of **Colwood** and Royal Roads University, a former military college. **Fort Rodd Hill and Fisgard Lighthouse National Historic Sites** (tel: 250-478 5849; www.pc.gc.ca/en/lhn-nhs/bc/fortroddhill/visit; canteen, batteries and lighthouse mid-Oct–Feb Sat–Sun 10am–4.30pm, Mar–mid-May Wed–Sun 10am–5.30pm, mid-May–mid-Oct daily 10am–5.30pm, grounds and washrooms open daily throughout the year) was a coastal defense complex, used between 1895 and 1956. Visitors can explore underground magazines and barracks. Fisgard Lighthouse, on the shoreline of the fort, was built in 1860, the first in British Columbia.

Coastal views

For spectacular coastal views, drive west past the motels and hotels on Belleville Street, and follow the waterfront past the Canadian Coast Guard base and the docks for cruise ships at Ogden Point. This is Dallas Road, the beginning of **Marine Drive**, a marked scenic route. Between Dallas and the shore are walks along the cliffs and beaches on the Strait of Juan de Fuca.

On the left is **Beacon Hill Park**, with flowers and a lookout with a view of the Strait and the Olympic

Colorful flower baskets in Victoria.

Mount Rainier dominates the skyline from Seattle.

Naturalists are drawn to the Pacific Northwest for its marvelous marine life.

Mountains. Beyond, the road becomes **Beach Drive**, lined by the fairways and greens of the oceanfront Victoria Golf Club. This is **Oak Bay**, said to be 'behind the tweed curtain' because of its many British residents. About 20 miles (30km) north of Victoria is **Sidney** ㉞, site of Victoria's international airport and a ferry connection to the San Juans. The **British Columbia Aviation Museum** (1910 Norseman Road, North Saanich; tel: 250-655 3300; www.bcam.net; daily May–Sept 10am–4pm, Oct–Apr 11am–3pm) is by the airport, and it has several historic aircraft.

Butchart Gardens (800 Benvenuto Avenue, Brentwood Bay; tel: 250-652 4422; www.butchartgardens.com; daily from 9am, closing times vary) showcases 55 acres (22 hectares) of flowers in the Rose Garden, Japanese Garden, and the Show Greenhouse. Conceived by Jennie Butchart, the wife of a cement tycoon, in order to fill the gap created by her husband's exhausted limestone quarry, the gardens blossomed into the Sunken Gardens. By

the 1920s more than 50,000 people came each year to see her creation.

Not far from Butchart are the pretty **Butterfly Gardens** (1461 Benvenuto Avenue, Brentwood Bay; tel: 250-652 3822; www.butterflygardens. com; Mar–Sept daily 10am–4pm, until 3pm in winter), an indoor tropical garden with numerous species of free-flying butterflies and birds.

THE CASCADE MOUNTAINS

All over Puget Sound, views are dominated by the majestic Cascade Mountains (see page 220), and their lure is constant. From the Tacoma area south of Seattle, follow the Nisqually River south to the tiny town of **Elbe** ㉟, the only train town this side of Strasberg, Pennsylvania. Dine or even stay the night in a railroad caboose at the **Hobo Inn** (tel: 888-773 4637; www.rrdiner.com), or hop aboard the steam-powered **Mount Rainier Scenic Railroad** (tel: 888-783 2611; http://mtrainierrailroad. com) as it chugs into the mountain forests on short excursions (mainly during the summer months). Behind the depot is the 'tiniest church in the world', at least at one time, according to *Ripley's Believe It or Not*.

Mount Rainier ❸❹

First named Tahoma – 'The Mountain That Was God' – by Native Americans, **Mount Rainier** was renamed in 1792 by English explorer Captain George Vancouver. Visible for more than 100 miles (160km) in all directions, thousands of feet above the other peaks of the Cascades, Rainier is the fifth-highest summit in the contiguous United States and an active volcano.

A single road loops the mountain, through much of the 378-sq-mile (980-sq-km) **Mount Rainier National Park** (www.nps.gov/mora/index.htm). The park is open all year, but in winter months passes at Cayuse and Chinook are closed.

Mount Rainier's history dates back more than 75,000 years when volcanism drove the peak to its 16,000ft (5,000-meter) height. Erosion by glaciers stripped nearly 2,000ft (600 meters) off its top, and the summit is now 14,410ft (4,392 meters) above sea level. Rainier has the largest glacier system – 26 glaciers – in the lower 48 states. The last major eruption was around 1,000 years ago, with the most recent eruption some 150 years ago.

There are four entrances to the park. At **Longmire**, just inside the southwestern border near the Nisqually entrance, the modestly priced **National Park Inn** (tel: 360-569 2275; http://mtrainierguestservices.com/accommodations/national-park-inn) is the only lodge open all year; the rustic inn has a wildlife museum and stuffed animals on display. Longmire is also the only place in the park to buy gas. Follow the road to where a short hike leads into the **Grove of the Patriarchs**, the tallest trees in the park.

Paradise is the most popular destination and has paved parking, the **Henry M. Jackson Memorial Visitors' Center**, a gift shop, and a cafeteria. There are spectacular views of **Narada Falls** and **Nisqually Glacier**, as well as of Mount Rainier. The fabulous **Paradise Inn** (tel: 360-569 2275; http://mtrainierguestservices.com/accommodations/paradise-inn), built in 1917, is an excellent base from which to explore the park.

Head east, then north at the Stevens Canyon entrance in the park's southeast corner, to the 4,675ft (1,425-meter) -high **Cayuse Pass**. Just beyond the pass is the White River entrance. Turn left to drive up to the **Sunrise Visitors' Center** (at 6,400ft/1,950 meters; closed in winter), a breathtaking entry to lush wildflower meadows. The Emmons Glacier, the largest in the conterminous US, is visible from a trail by the visitors' center.

North of the White River entrance is **Crystal Mountain**, with some of the best winter skiing in the state of Washington. In summer, riders in chairlifts get to catch glimpses of Mount Rainier, while tennis, horseback riding, and easy park access all entice tourists during the months when skiing is not possible.

Snoqualmie Falls.

Snowshoeing in Snoqualmie National Forest.

salishlodge.com), made famous by the cult *Twin Peaks* TV series and known locally for huge Paul Bunyan-size country brunches. Much of the TV series was shot in the small town of **North Bend**, on Interstate 90, and Twedes Cafe still serves cherry pies. Long a stopping point for Snoqualmie Pass skiers, the city also draws shoppers to its outlet mall, the **Factory Stores at North Bend** (461 South Fork Avenue SW; tel: 425-888 4106; www.premiumoutlets.com/outlet/north-bend).

Another 25 miles (40km) farther is 3,022ft (921-meter) **Snoqualmie Pass**, with trailheads into the mountains and three easily accessible winter ski areas near the summit.

Continuing east on US 2 is a route along the Skykomish River through the **Mount Baker-Snoqualmie National Forest**, toward the jagged peaks of the Cascade Range. The road is breathtaking in the fall, when the leaves of the vine maple trees turn scarlet. At **Wallace Falls State Park** (http://parks.state.wa.us/289/Wallace-Falls), a 7-mile (11km) round-trip trail leads to the 365ft (111-meter) cascade and a view of **Mount Index**, nearly 6,000ft (1,800 meters) high.

Kayaking, fishing, and river-rafting are popular along the Skykomish, and trailheads lead off the route. Stop at the US Forest Service Ranger Station in **Skykomish** ❷ itself for maps and information. In winter, the downhill and cross-country ski slopes are at the 4,061ft (1,237-meter) **Stevens Pass** ❹, 25 miles (40km) past Skykomish.

Mount St Helens ❸

Only two hours south of Elbe is **Mount St Helens**, the active volcano that erupted in May of 1980. The area is designated as the **Mount St Helens National Volcanic Monument** (tel: 360-449 7800; www.fs.usda.gov/recarea/giffordpinchot/recarea/?recid=34143). Five visitors' centers dot the Spirit Lake Highway, all supplying information on the eruption. Nonprofit private organization Mount St Helens Institute (www.mshinstitute.org) organizes guided excursions, climbs and field seminars throughout the year. It operates under a special-use permit from the Gifford Pinchot National Forest.

EAST OF SEATTLE

There are many wonderful excursions into the countryside from Seattle, some just a couple of hours' drive away. For instance, east of Issaquah (see page 169) is **Snoqualmie Falls** ❸, a sensational 268ft (82-meter) avalanche of water, far higher than Niagara Falls.

Perched above the falls is **Salish Lodge & Spa** (tel: 800-272 5474; www.

NORTH OF SEATTLE

From Everett (see page 177), head east to arrive at one of Washington's oldest communities. **Snohomish** ❶ was founded in 1859. The town is an antique center of the Northwest, and its downtown historic district is a pleasant place to stroll around. Six miles (10km) east is Highway 203, which joins up with **Snoqualmie**.

Climb aboard the **Snoqualmie Valley Railroad** for a scenic tour after visiting the **Northwest Railway Museum** (38625 SE King Street, Snoqualmie; tel: 425-888 3030; www.trainmuseum. org; daily 10am–5pm).

Back on Interstate 5, head north to Mount Vernon, and then west for the busy tourist town of **La Conner** ㊷. In the 1970s, local entrepreneurs filled their tiny shops with art galleries, antique stores, and restaurants. The best-known town in the **Skagit Valley**, La Conner's claim to fame is tulips. Visitors in busloads come each April to attend the Skagit Valley Tulip Festival.

Chuckanut Drive, a historic part of the old Pacific Highway, goes through the valley and along the coast. It's one of the state's most scenic drives, an alternative to the interstate. The train from Seattle to Vancouver does the same.

The roadway curves north about 25 miles (40km) and follows the water up to **Bellingham** ㊸, a fun college town where a good number of top-notch restaurants serve regional oysters and seafood.

North Cascades parks

From La Conner, SR 20 shoots east into the Cascade Range, which divides the eastern and western parts of the state of Washington. The mountains are 700 miles (1,100km) in length, and extend from northern California, where they join the Sierra Nevada Range, to the Fraser River just south of Vancouver, in British Columbia.

The entire mountain range is a jigsaw puzzle of different national parks, national forests, and wilderness areas. Five hundred miles (800km) of scenic highway loop through **North Cascades National Park** ㊹ (www. nps.gov/noca/index.htm), traversing snow-covered mountains, rushing rivers, and pretty towns.

Prominent on the skyline directly west is **Mount Baker** ㊺ at 10,778ft (3,285 meters), one of several volcanic mountains.

On the southern end is **Glacier Peak Wilderness**, the heart of the North Cascades, named after 10,541ft (3,213-meter) **Glacier Peak** ㊻. Its glaciers end in ice-blue lakes, and meadows blanket small corners between broken rock spires.

Hiking in the rugged backcountry terrain around the North Cascades.

A VOLCANIC LANDSCAPE

The city of Seattle sits within the 'Ring of Fire,' the Pacific horse-shoe of volcanoes that have the potential to erupt at any time.

Daybreak at Tipsoo Lake.

Local tribal mythology tells the story of a pair of warriors, Wyeast and Pahto, who fought each other for the love of a beautiful maiden.

Their monumental battle involved earth-quakes and firing vol-leys of rock and flames across the Columbia River. To settle the dispute, the gods trans-formed the warriors into mountains along the Cascade Chain: Wyeast became Mount Hood and Pahto became Mount Rainier.

Seattle sits on the Pacific Rim, where 850 active volcanoes in mountain ranges on all sides of the Pacific Ocean form a 'Ring of Fire'. This includes the Cascade Range, a 700-mile (1,130km) chain of mountains that runs north–south through the state of Washington. The most recent major vol-canic eruption in the Cascades occurred in May 1980, when Mount St Helens gave a powerful demonstration of the natural forces that created much of the Northwest landscape.

The view from the summit of Mount St Helens.

Ryan Lake, a small lake near Mount St Helens, covered in ice and snow.

Mount St Helens, in the background, still steams on 5 May 1981, one year after its powerful eruption. New growth has already begun, bringing new life to the area around the mountain in the southern Cascades of Washington state.

MOUNT ST HELENS ERUPTION

On 18 May, 1980, skies darkened as Mount St Helens, in southwestern Washington state, literally blew its top. The explosion took a cubic mile off the summit, reducing the mountain's elevation from 9,677ft (2,950 meters) to 8,364ft (2,550 meters). The eruption of ash and molten lava transfigured the hillsides and sent a gray cloud across the state. Repercussions were said to have been felt as far away as Europe.

The volcano had shown signs of activity well before the blast, and although the region had been evacuated, the death toll reached as many as 60, as lava and mudslides flattened 230 sq miles (595 sq km) of forest. There was extensive damage to wildlife, and the ash-covered slopes and fallen trees serve as modern reminders of the day. 7,000 big game animals died (deer, elk, and bear), although many small animals survived because they were below ground level or the water surface. The mountain continued to shudder with minor eruptions into the 21st century.

Sunrise on Mount Rainier, the tallest mountain in Washington, rising a majestic 14,410ft (4,367 metres) above sea level.

Mount St Helens began erupting on 16 March 1980, and continued until the magnitude 5.1 eruption at 8.32am on 18 May. It was the most destructive ever recorded in the United States.

Bicycle storage on a Seattle bus.

TRAVEL TIPS

SEATTLE

TRANSPORTATION

GETTING THERE AND GETTING AROUND

By air

Seattle-Tacoma International Airport, known as **Sea-Tac**, is 13 miles (20km) south of Seattle. It is served by many major carriers (see below).

For information on the airport, its services, parking, or security, call the Sea-Tac International information line, tel: 1-800-544 1965 or 206 787 5388, or visit www.portseattle.org.

Access to Sea-Tac is via Interstate 5 (take exit 154 from south I-5 or exit 152 from north I-5), or via Highway 99/509 and 518. Stop-and-go traffic on I-5 is not uncommon, especially during rush hours, so the alternative route on the highway is often much quicker.

At the airport

Many services are available at Sea-Tac to ease the transition from air to ground; some are especially helpful to foreigners, as this can be a confusing airport, especially if arriving jet-lagged after a long flight. For passengers arriving on international flights, once you clear customs, you place your bags back on a conveyer belt, then ride the subway to the main terminal where you collect your luggage at the baggage claim carousels.

Aside from restaurants, restrooms, gift shops, and resortwear clothing stores, three Travelex **currency exchange booths** are scattered throughout the airport. Two are in the main terminal; the third booth is in the north satellite (open daily 9.30am–9pm). Tel: 206-248 4995 for more information.

Free Wi-fi is available throughout the airport.

A **children's area** with an enclosed carpeted play area, a crib, and a nursing room with rocking chairs, provides relief for parents and kid-sized travelers.

A **meditation room/chapel** is available on the mezzanine level that has a Sunday-only inter-

INTERNATIONAL AIRLINES

Major airlines flying into and out of Seattle include:

Air Canada
Tel: 1-888-247 2262
www.aircanada.com
Air France
Tel: 1-800-237 2747
www.airfrance.com
Alaska Airlines
Tel: 1-800-252 7522
www.alaskaair.com
All Nippon Airways
Tel: 1-800-235 9262
www.ana.co.jp
American Airlines
Tel: 1-800-433 7300
www.aa.com
British Airways
Tel: 1-800-247 9297
www.britishairways.com
Delta/KLM
Tel: 1-800-241 4141
www.delta.com

Hawaiian Airlines
Tel: 1-800-367 5320
www.hawaiianairlines.com
JetBlue Airways
Tel: 1-800-538 2583
www.jetblue.com
Korean Air
Tel: 1-800-438 5000
www.koreanair.com
Lufthansa
Tel: 1-800-645 3880
www.lufthansa.com
Southwest Airlines
Tel: 1-800-435 9792
www.southwest.com
United Airlines
Tel: 1-800-864 8331
www.united.com
Virgin America
Tel: 1-877-359 8474
www.virginamerica.com
Virgin Atlantic
Tel: 1-800 862 8621
www.virginatlantic.com

denominational service. For the chaplain, tel: 206-433 5505.

In the inspection booths at Customs and Immigration, and at the **Airport Information Booth**, right outside the exit from the B gates (pre-security, south of the Central Security Checkpoint), are Language Phone Lines that connect travelers and inspectors to interpreters for more than 150 different languages.

The **Lost and Found** is located on the mezzanine level in the main terminal. It is open Mon–Fri 8am–5pm, tel: 206-787 5312.

Last but not least, **Ken's Baggage and Frozen Food Storage**, on the baggage level, between carousels 12 and 13, will take care of odds and ends for travelers, such as baggage storage, stroller and car-seat rentals, dry-cleaning services, UPS and Federal Express package services, as well as notary public, ticket- and key-holding services and more. Hours: daily 5.30am–12.30am. Tel: 206-433 5333.

By bus

Transcontinental bus lines providing services throughout Seattle and the United States include the following:
Greyhound
811 Stewart Street (at 8th Avenue)
Tel: 1-800-231 2222
www.greyhound.com
The ubiquitous Greyhound bus service offers the most comprehensive choice of scheduled routes from Seattle and across the North American continent.
Green Tortoise
Tel: 1-800-867 8647
www.greentortoise.com
This famous service is an alternative (in both senses of the word) form of bus travel connecting Seattle to San Francisco and Portland. Easy chairs replace bus seats, music plays in the background, and stops are scheduled for soaking in hot springs and having a campfire cookout.
Quick Shuttle
Tel: 1-800-665 2122

CITY = FROM SEATTLE = DRIVING TIME

This is a list of estimated times and distances to several cities within a day or two's journey, driving a car under safe road conditions.
Spokane, WA = 280 miles (450km) = 5 hours approx.

San Francisco, CA = 850 miles (1,370km) = 15 hours approx.
Portland, OR = 175 miles (280km) = 3 hours approx.
Vancouver, BC = 140 miles (225km) = 3 hours approx.

www.quickcoach.com
This company operates 5–8 daily express runs between Vancouver BC and downtown Seattle and the airport.

By rail

Amtrak is the USA's national rail network. It can be found in Seattle at 3rd Avenue and S Jackson Street, tel: 1-800-USA-RAIL www.amtrak.com.

The train is a convenient way of getting to the other Pacific Rim cities of Portland, San Francisco, and Vancouver in Canada's British Columbia. The distances are not far, and the train times flexible and frequent.

Amtrak connects Seattle with the east coast via the 'Empire Builder' from Chicago. It connects with the south via the 'Coast Starlight' from Los Angeles. The 'Coast Starlight' is the most popular route with beautiful coastal scenery and stops in Tacoma, Olympia, Vancouver (Washington), and Portland (Oregon) along the way. Amtrak's 'Cascades' run also connects Vancouver (British Columbia, Canada) and Seattle. In the summer months early reservations for this popular trip are essential.

By road

Major land routes into Seattle are Interstate 5, known as 'I-5', which stretches from the Canadian to the Mexican borders; and Interstate 90, or 'I-90', which leaves downtown Seattle and travels eastward toward the cities of Chicago and Boston.

Federal and state highways are

generally well maintained and policed, with refreshment areas and service stations at regular intervals. There are no highway fees payable in or around Seattle, but there is a toll to cross the 5-20 bridge and to cross the Tacoma Narrows Bridge.

Leave a lot of time for getting into the city, however. Traffic in Seattle itself and its outlying areas has increased dramatically in the last few years. So though you may make good time getting to the city limits it doesn't mean you're there yet.

GETTING AROUND

To and from the airport

Shuttle buses and taxis can be found in the airport parking garage. Cross Skybridge 3 or 4 to the garage, then go down to the third floor. The check-in kiosks are at the curb.

All limos and taxis serving the airport must be licensed. With normal traffic, the trip to

It's easy to get around in downtown Seattle.

→	🚈	Link Light Rail
	🚌	Tunnel Buses
↖	♿	Elevator to Link Light Rail to SeaTac/Airport & Bus Bays C & D
		2nd/3rd Ave & University St

Downtown should take no more than 25 minutes ($45–55 plus tip). Since 2016, rideshare companies such as Lyft, Uber and Wingz have been allowed to operate in the airport area.

Bus or van companies that link the airport with metropolitan Seattle or Bellevue include: **Metro Transit**, tel: 206-553 3000; http://kingcounty.gov/depts/transportation/metro.aspx. Buses link the airport with various points throughout the region (but not downtown Seattle) and provide the least expensive method of transportation. The bus stops are located on International Boulevard (State Highway 99) and South 176th Street by the Link Light Rail Station. At the time of writing, a single ticket for two zones (City of Seattle and King County) cost $2.50 (off peak) and $3.25 (peak). A good option for those who want to travel around the city on different means of transport is the ORCA regional card ($8 for one day of unlimited travel). For details, see the Metro Transit website. **Shuttle Express**, tel: 1+425 981 7000; https://shuttleexpress.com. Provides door-to-door van service to and from the airport 24 hours daily throughout the metropolitan Seattle area. **Quick Shuttle**, tel: 1-800-665 2122; www.quickcoach.com.

The Monorail at Seattle Center.

Operates fast bus connections between the airport, downtown Seattle (Best Western Executive Inn, 200 Taylor Avenue N) and Vancouver (Holiday Inn, 1110 Howe Street) 4–8 times daily. Trips between the two cities take four hours. Some buses stop at the Seattle Waterfront (Piers 66 and 91) for cruise ship terminals. **Seattle Limo Service**, tel: 206-2297288, a well-established and reliable service, available by reservation only.

The **Sound Transit Light Rail Link** (tel: 888-889 6368; www.soundtransit.org) is the most economical way to reach Downtown, with trains departing every 6–15 minutes for the 39-minute journey. Trains run 5am–1am Mon–Sat and until midnight on Sun. The ticket costs about $3. Once Downtown, passengers can transfer to a wide range of buses.

Orientation

Seattle has many one-way streets and steep hills Downtown (which is generally considered to lie between Denny Way to the north and Yesler to the south, and bordered to the west by Elliott Bay and to the east by I-5.) The city is very walkable; jaywalking, though, is illegal, and most Seattleites wait for the light to change before crossing the street.

Public transportation

Buses

Metro Transit buses have both peak- and non-peak-hour fares. Monthly passes are available. Buses operate from around 5am to around 2am on most routes daily. You pay your fare on boarding, online, at vending machines, or through the mobile app (found along with detailed information at http://kingcounty.gov/depts/transportation/metro.aspx).

You may either pay the exact fare in cash, or buy an ORCA (One Regional Card for All) card, which acts as a debit card for each journey you make; you tap the smart card against a sensor to record the fare. ORCAs are valid on Metro buses, Sound Transit trains and light rail, Seattle Streetcars, and Washington State Ferries.

Light Rail

The **Sound Transit Light Rail Link** that connects Downtown (via the Downtown Seattle Transit Tunnel) with Sea-Tac Airport stops at various places in South Seattle, including SoDo, Beacon Hill, Columbia City, and Rainier Beach. Sound Transit also runs commuter trains between Tacoma, Seattle, and Everett.

Monorail

The **Monorail**, which was built for the 1962 World's Fair, runs every 10 minutes between Seattle Center and Fourth and Pine streets to Westlake Center. The ride is just under 1 mile (1.5km) and takes only two minutes. It's clean and spacious, with large windows. More information at www.seattlemonorail.com.

Streetcars

The **Seattle Streetcar South Lake Union Line** connects Downtown (a block from Westlake Center) with Eastlake through the growing South Lake Union

TRANSPORTATION

neighborhood. The **First Hill Streetcar** (10 stops) links the International District with Capitol Hill. A new line that will link the South Lake Union neighborhood and the First Hill Streetcar lines (called the Center City Connector) is in the pipeline, due to be completed by 2020.

By ferry

The **Washington State Ferry** system, the largest in the country, covers the Puget Sound area, linking Seattle (at Pier 52) with the Olympic Peninsula via Bremerton and Bainbridge Island. State ferries also depart from West Seatt e to Vashon Island and Southworth and from Edmonds, 7 miles (11km) north of Seattle, to Kingston on the Kitsap Peninsula. It also goes from Anacortes, 90 miles (145km) northwest of Seattle, through the San Juan Islands to Victoria, on Canada's Vancouver Island. For information: tel: 206-464 6400 or 1-888-808 7977 (www.wsdot. wa.gov/ferries). Passengers to Canada should carry a passport.

Passenger-only water taxis operated by the county run during rush hours from Pier 50 in downtown Seattle to West Seattle and Vashon Island. For schedules and information: 206-684 1551 or www.kingcounty.gov/depts/ transportation/water-taxi.aspx.

Clipper Navigation operates a passenger-only ferry, the *Victoria Clipper*, between Seattle and Victoria, BC (year-round) and Seattle and the San Juan Islands (seasona). Reservations required. Tel: 206-448 5000 (www.clippervacations.com).

The **Black Ball Ferry** the *M.V. Coho*, departs from Port Angeles on the Olympic Peninsula to Victoria, BC, four t mes a day in summer and twice daily the rest of the year. Ferries carry cars. Tel: 360-457 4491 (www.cohoferry.com).

Victoria–San Juan Cruises, Bellingham Cruise Terminal, Bellingham, operates passenger ferries to San Juan and Orcas

islands and Victoria, May to September; also day cruises. Tel: 1-800-443 4552 (www.whales.com).

Taxis

There are **taxi** stands at major hotels, bus depots, train stations, and the airport. Taxi fares are regulated. There is an initia hire charge, with each additional mile (1.5km) then costing a flat rate.

Taxi companies

Farwest Taxi Tel: 206-622 1717; www.farwesttaxi.net
Orange Cab Tel: 206-522 8800; www.orangecab.net
Yellow Cab Tel: 206-622 6500; www.seattleyellowcab.com

Cycling

Despite its many steep hills, cycling is popular in Seattle for both transportation and recreation. The Seattle Bicycle Master Plan is aiming to make Seattle the best US community for cycling by 2030. Over 200 miles (322km) of roadways have bicycle-lane designations added to them to support cycling while making city transportation more socially sustainable. Helmets are required in Seattle and King County. A map of bicycling routes is available from the **City of Seattle's Bicycle and Pedestrian Program** (tel: 206-684 7583; www.seattle.gov/ transportation/bikeprogram.htm).

Driving

Car rental tips

A wide selection of rental cars is available. Rental offices are located at the airport and Downtown. Generally, a major credit card is required to rent a

Alamo Tel: +1 800 992 9823
Avis Tel: 206 448 1700
Budget Tel: 206 682 8989
Dollar Rent-A-Car Tel: 206

381 1323
Enterprise Tel: 206 382 1051
Hertz Tel: 206 903 6260
National Tel: +1 888 445 5664

car and the driver must be at least 25 years old and possess a valid driver's license. Local rental companies sometimes offer less expensive rates. Be sure to check insurance provisions before signing any paperwork.

Road tips

Avoid driving during the rush hours of 7–9am and 4–6pm. Although extra express lanes operate on parts of I-5 and I-90 to help alleviate the backup, it is a time-consuming and sometimes frustrating experience.

A right turn is permitted, after stopping, at a red light unless street signs indicate otherwise

Parking laws in Seattle require that when facing downhill, the front wheels are turned into the curb and when facing uphill, front wheels are turned outward. Doing so will decrease the likelihood of the car rolling downhill. Also be sure to set the emergency brake.

Street signs, usually on corners, will indicate what type of parking is permitted for that side of the street. However, red-painted curbs mean no parking is allowed and yellow curbs indicate a loading area for trucks or buses only.

There are p enty of traffic police around (except when you need them) who earn their living by passing out fines and having cars towed away. Picking up a towed car is not only inconvenient, but costly ($200–600, depending on where the car was parked).

Pedestrians always have the right of way (although they should still be careful crossing the street, both for safety and because jaywalking may result in a traffic-violation ticket). Although legal, except on freeways, picking up hitchhikers or hitchhiking is potentially dangerous.

A – Z

AN ALPHABETICAL SUMMARY OF PRACTICAL INFORMATION

A

Accommodations

The highest concentration of hotels is Downtown, though they are on the luxurious side. More economical choices can be found in the surrounding areas of Pioneer Square and the International District, Capitol Hill, or South Lake Union. All of these areas are within easy reach of the main sights, and are easily accessible by public transportation. However, many folks will tell you that although Pioneer Square and the International District are fun to visit by day, they usually aren't the best spots for lodging. If you want to get away from the tourist areas, you may prefer to stay in another Seattle neighbor-hood in a Victorian B&B or smaller hotel, to get a different feel of the city. It's from these cozy B&Bs that you can wander to local coffeehouses with the morning newspaper, and rub elbows with the locals to really get a sense of the city. There are a number of chain hotels that offer good value for money near Sea-Tac Airport, but you trade location for price, since the airport is 13 miles south of Seattle.

Addresses

In Seattle, avenues run north–south, while streets run east–west. Streets and avenues can be designated with numbers or names. When trying to locate an address, be sure to note whether the address includes directionals (north, south, east, or west). For example, E Madison Street or Queen Anne Avenue N will indicate the location in the east or north part of town.

Admission charges

Fees to most attractions range from $10 to over $35, with reduced fees for children and seniors. On the first Thursday of the month, many museums have extended evening hours and offer free admission.

Most festivals at the Seattle Center are free, except for Bumbershoot, which charges a hefty admission price (more for the Platinum and Gold passes). The Seattle City Pass card allows you to visit five of the most popular Seattle attractions for $79 ($59 for kids); it's available at www.citypass.com/seattle.

B

Budgeting for your trip

It is best to research your trip in advance and look for internet discounts for hotels and attractions. Keep in mind the 9.6 percent sales tax added to all purchases.

When dining out, a glass of house wine costs around $6–9, and a beer $4–6. To get more bang for your buck, take advantage of the happy hour offerings at many restaurants and bars. An entrée at a budget restaurant will be about $10–15, at a moderate restaurant $20–25, and at an expensive restaurant $35 and more.

Accommodations will set you back $100 or less for a budget option, $100–200 for a moderate hotel, and $200 plus for room in a deluxe hotel.

A taxi to and from the airport is in the region of $45–55 plus tip. At the time of writing, a single bus fare within Seattle was $2.75 during peak times, and $2.50 during off-peak.

C

Climate

The temperature in western Washington (west of the Cascade Mountains) is usually mild. Daytime temperatures range from 70–79°F (21–26°C) in summer and 41–48°F (4.5–9°C) in winter.

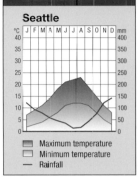

CLIMATE CHART

Seattle

- Maximum temperature
- Minimum temperature
- — Rainfall

From October through April, Seattle gets 80 percent of its annual quota of rain. In summer, Seattle is frequently covered by some form of marine mist or fog in the morning that dissipates by the afternoon. Seattleites, on average, receive the sun's light and warmth uninterrupted for the whole day only about 55 times a year.

Snow tends to stay in the mountains, which keeps skiers and almost everyone else happy, but because of quirky weather patterns you can sometimes find yourself in a hail shower on one side of town while the other side of the city experiences clear skies and a rainbow.

What to wear

A raincoat or umbrella are mandatory from October through April, and a warm coat, hat, and gloves are recommended for November through February. In spring and fall it's advisable to dress in layers, due to the frequently changing conditions. Sandals, shorts, skirts, and light clothing are appropriate for summer, though do bring a light jacket. Seattle is a casual place, and jeans are acceptable at most places.

When to visit

Late May to September brings the best weather, least rain – and the most visitors. July and August are the warmest and busiest months.

For winter sports enthusiasts, the nearby mountains usually offer decent skiing, snowboarding, and snowshoeing from December through March, and the sights are far less crowded (though rain is definitely a factor).

Crime and safety

The streets of Seattle and most adjoining neighborhoods and islands are relatively safe during the day. However, as with most large cities, at night caution is advised. It is best not to walk alone at night on deserted city streets. Lock your car and never leave luggage, electronics, or other valuables in view.

Never leave money, valuables, or jewelry in your hotel room, even for a short time. Instead, take advantage of the hotel's safety deposit service or in-room safe. Carry only the cash you need; most visitors find it convenient to use credit cards, which are widely accepted.

Customs regulations

An individual over the age of 21 is allowed to bring one bottle of liquor free of tax and 200 cigarettes duty free into the USA. Any currency exceeding $10,000 or a foreign equivalent must be declared upon arrival/departure

Visitors and non-US residents are normally entitled to a personal exemption of $100 on all goods being brought into the US that will remain in the US; in most cases returning US residents are entitled to an $800 personal exemption on goods acquired while abroad. All goods must be declared.

D

Disabled travelers

Disabled travelers can obtain information about discounts, transportation, assistive technology, community resources, and more from the

city's Human Services website (www.agingkingcounty.org/about-us/advisory-council) or by calling 206-684-0660.

By law all new public buildings are wheelchair accessible. The majority of Seattle's hotels and restaurants are wheelchair accessible, though some of the older buildings may not be; call ahead to confirm. Metro buses are equipped with a wheelchair lift; Sound Transit's light rail link trains are fully wheelchair accessible; and the Seattle Streetcar features wheelchair ramps that deploy on the press of a button. You can find more information at http://wheelchairjimmy.com.

E

Embassies/consulates

The following embassies or consulates can be contacted in an emergency. For information on those of other countries, contact your embassy or consulate before leaving home:

Australia
575 Market Street, Suite 1800, San Francisco, CA 94105
Tel: 415-644 3520

Canada
1501 4th Avenue Suite 600, Seattle, WA 98101
Tel: 206-443 1777

Ireland
100 Pine Street, Suite 3350, San Francisco, CA 94111
Tel: 415-392 4214

Mexico
2132 3rd Avenue, Seattle, WA 98121
Tel: 206-448 3526

New Zealand
2425 Olympic Blvd, #600E, Santa Monica, CA 90404

ELECTRICITY

The United States uses 110 volts. Electrical adaptors are readily available in electronics stores, luggage stores, and at many airport stores.

Tel: 310-566 6555
South Africa
6300 Wilshire Boulevard, Los
Angeles, CA 90048
Tel: 323-651 0902
UK
1 Sansome Street, Suite 850,
San Francisco, CA 94104
Tel: 415-617 1300

Festivals and events

The Seattle Convention and
Visitors' Bureau maintains an
up-to-date calendar of events at
www.visitseattle.org/things-to-do/
events/festivals.

January
Chinese New Year
www.cidbia.org
Based on the lunar calendar, this
festival is held sometime in
January or February in the
International District. Festivities
include a parade with dragons,
dancers, great food, and fireworks.

February
Chilly Hilly Bike Ride
www.cascade.org
Held on Bainbridge Island (third
Sunday in February). Hop aboard
the early morning ferry for this
33-mile (53km) ride sponsored by
the Cascade Bicycle Club.
**Northwest Flower and Garden
Show**
www.gardenshow.com
Tel: 253-756 2121
On almost 5 acres (2 hectares) of
the Washington State Convention
and Trade Center, landscape
architects, nurseries, and
gardeners try their best to outdo
each other at over 300 booths.
Admission charge.

March
**Dine Around Seattle (March
and November)**
www.dinearoundseattle.org
For a great opportunity to try out
some of the city's best
restaurants, three-course prix-fixe
meals are offered throughout the

EMERGENCIES

For police, fire or medical
emergencies, dial **911**.
Coast guard emergencies
Tel: 206-217 6000 or the 911
emergency operator
Crisis clinic
Tel: 206-461 3210

month on Sundays through
Thursdays; menus cost $22, $33
or $44.
Irish Week Festival, includes a
film festival, dancing, a parade
(see below), and events such as
the St Patrick's Day Dash, an easy
3.5-mile (6km) run or walk from
lower Queen Anne to Safeco Field.
www.irishclub.org
St Patrick's Day Parade
www.irishclub.org
Tel: 206-412 2960
The parade travels from City Hall
(600 4th Avenue) to Westlake
Center (1601 5th Avenue),
featuring bagpipes, Irish dancers,
marching bands, and the laying of
the green stripe down 4th Avenue.
Whirligig
Seattle Center
www.seattlecenter.com
Tel: 206-684 7200
The Seattle Center hosts this
indoor carnival with bouncing and
inflatable rides for kids from about
mid-March to mid-April. Free
entertainment; small fee for rides.

April
**Daffodil Festival and Grand
Floral Parade**
Tacoma
http://thedaffodilfestival.org
Tel: 253-826 7765
One of the largest floral parades, it
travels through Tacoma, Puyallup,
Sumner, and Orting in one day,
making creative use of the
daffodils grown around Puyallup.
Skagit Valley Tulip Festival
Tel: 360-428 5959
Held on 1,500 acres (600
hectares) of colorful tulip fields,
this spectacular scene is like a
slice of Holland, but with the
backdrop of majestic mountains.
Bicycle and bus tours are popular.

May
Northwest Folklife Festival
Seattle Center
www.nwfolklife.org
Tel: 206-684 7300
Music, dancing, ethnic food, and
crafts over Memorial Day
weekend from more than 100
countries. Many people unpack
their instruments and join some
of the many jam sessions that
spring up all around the Center's
lawns.
Opening Day of Boating Season
www.seattleyachtclub.org
Tel: 206-325 1000
Held first Saturday in May.
Yachting clubs bring out a parade
of boats from Lake Union to Lake
Washington, stopping traffic on
the bridges. Also features a
rowing regatta.
**Seattle International Film
Festival (SIFF)**
www.siff.net
Tel: 206-464 5830
This three-week long, huge film
festival screens more than 400
local, national, and international
independent films at venues
throughout the city.
University Street Fair
University Way
www.udistrictstreetfair.org
Tel: 206-547 4417
Held the third weekend in May, the
fair features over 350 artists'
booths and food stalls in a
10-block area. Mimes, clowns,
street entertainment, and
children's events draw the crowds.

June
Festival Sundiata
Seattle Center
www.festivalsundiata.org
Tel: 1-866-505 6006
Held during Black Music month,
this two-day celebration includes
African-American and African
food, music, dancing, and cultural
events.
**Fremont Solstice Parade and
Street Fair**
www.fremontfair.org
Tel: 206-547 7440
A well-known neighborhood fair,
featuring live music, local crafts,
jugglers and mimes, along with a

zany street parade on the Saturday closest to the summer solstice.

Seattle PrideFest
www.seattlepride.org
Tel: 206-322 9561
Usually at end of June. The Northwest's largest Lesbian/ Gay/Bisexual/Transgender (LGBT) Pride Parade is a lively celebration through Downtown, with creative costumes, music, and dancing. Other activities include block parties, feasts, and Pride Idol events on Capitol Hill.

July

Bellevue Arts Museum Artsfair
510 Bellevue Way, Bellevue
www.bellevuearts.org/bam-artsfair
Tel: 425-519 0770
Sponsored by the Bellevue Arts Museum, the Artsfair features exhibits and booths throughout Bellevue Square shopping center and the Museum, including artists-at-work demonstrations, concerts at the fountain outside Macy's, and entertainment for kids.

Bite of Seattle
Seattle Center
www.biteofseattle.com
Tel: 425-295 3262
A taste-tester's delight in mid-July, with over 60 local restaurants participating.

Seafair Summer at Lake Union
Gas Works Park
www.seafair.com/events/2017/seafair-summer-4th
Tel: 206-728 0123
Independence Day fireworks event, with picnics, entertainment, and a spectacular fireworks display from Lake Union after dark.

Fourth of July Parades
Downtown, Bothell, Issaquah, Bainbridge Island and other neighborhoods; check newspapers for listings.

Lake Union Wooden Boat Festival
1010 Valley Street, south end of Lake Union
www.cwb.org
Tel: 206-382 2628
Features rowing, sailing and boat-building competitions, workshops, food, crafts, and

water taxis from the Center for Wooden Boats.

Seafair
www.seafair.com
Tel: 206-728 0123
Seattle's largest **summer festival** is a series of events, parades, and celebrations that take place over a 2.5-week period (usually the third weekend in July to first week in August) in different parts of the city. Highlights include: the milk carton derby races at Green Lake, the Blue Angels Air Show (aerobatic flights with dynamic maneuvers that take your breath away), Hydroplane Races on Lake Washington, Chinatown Seafair Parade, a Dragon Fest in Hing Hay Park, the Torchlight Parade, and a grand, nighttime parade through Downtown.

Seattle International Beerfest
www.seattlebeerfest.com
Tel: 206-486 2089
Three days of music, food, and beer tasting from national and international breweries. Held at the Seattle Center.

Summer Celebration
www.mercergov.org
The downtown Mercer Island area overflows with display booths of local artists. Sponsored by the Mercer Island Visual Arts League.

August

King County Fair
http://cityofenumclaw.net
Enumclaw Exposition Center, Enumclaw.
Begins third Wednesday in July and continues for five days of music, rodeos, logger competitions, crafts, and food in celebration of the county's agricultural heritage. The oldest county fair west of the Mississippi.

Evergreen State Fair
Monroe
www.evergreenfair.org
Tel 360-805 6700
Held third week in August–Labor Day weekend. A country fair with big-name country stars, plus rodeos, logging competitions, carnival rides, and a chili cook-off.

Hempfest
www.hempfest.org

Tel: 206-364 4367
Elliott Bay Park, Myrtle Edwards Park, and Olympic Sculpture Park. The nation's leading cannabis policy reform event. Live music acts, food, and vendors.

Seattle Tennis Club Washington State Open
www.seattletennisclub.org
Tel: 206-324 3200
During first week in August (order tickets well in advance).

Snoqualmie Railroad Days
Snoqualmie
www.trainmuseum.org
Tel: 425-888 3030
Steam trains from the late-19th century. A 10-mi e (16km) ride from the Snoqualmie depot takes visitors up to the historic depot and quaint town of North Bend.

Summer Village Festivals
Camlann Medieval Village, 10320 Kelly Road NE, Carnation
www.camlann.org
Tel: 425-788 8624
Camlann recreates the everyday experiences of a 14th-century rural village in Somerset, England. It hosts lots of medieval festivities every weekend from May through September.

September

Bumbershoot
Seattle Center
Tel: 206-673 5060
www.bumbershoot.org
Music and arts festival over the Labor Day weekend, featuring big names and local acts. The entry fee entitles guests to attend hundreds of concerts in all styles throughout the complex.

Festa Italiana
Seattle Center
www.festaseattle.com
Tel: 206-282 0627
Around the end of September; Italian arts, dancing, and, of course, food to celebrate the roots of Italian Americans.

Fremont Oktoberfest
Under the Aurora Bridge, Fremont
www.fremontoktoberfest.com
Tel: 206-633 0422
Sample from more than 80 brews at this three-day street fair

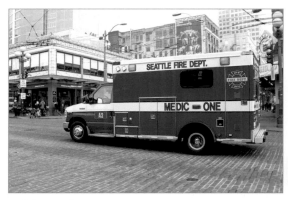

Firefighters on call.

with craft vendors, a kids' area, music, etc.

Greek Festival
St Demetrios Church, 2100 Boyer Avenue E
www.seattlegreekfestival.com
Tel: 206-631 2500
Held in late September at this Byzantine church, with folk dancing, arts and crafts, and Greek cuisine.

Puyallup Fair
www.thefair.com
Tel: 253-841 5045
Western Washington's largest state fair, about 35 miles (55km) south of Seattle. A 17-day-long extravaganza with fairground rides, food, chainsaw pumpkin carving, animals, rodeos, and fun for the entire family.

October

Halloween
Parades, festivities, and pranks at nightclubs and bars. Many shopping centers offer free candy for children in costumes.

Issaquah Salmon Days Festival
Main Street, Issaquah
www.salmondays.org
Tel: 425-392 0661
The street is closed to traffic and open to arts and crafts booths with artists from all over the Northwest. Street entertainment, mimes, clowns, and musicians are here, as well as the salmon jumping up to the hatchery. Big salmon cookout.

November

Seattle Marathon
www.seattlemarathon.org
Tel: 206-729 3660
Starts east of the MoPOP and loops through Downtown and along Lake Washington, ending at the Memorial Stadium.

December

Christmas ships
www.argosycruises.com
Tel: 1-888-623 1445
Illuminated and decorated boats parade around Lake Union and Lake Washington, making stops at public parks while choral groups entertain. Check newspapers or the website for updated schedules.

Christmas tree-lighting and caroling
Leavenworth
www.leavenworth.org
Tel: 509-548 5807
A picturesque Bavarian-style town in the Cascade Mountains is the setting for traditional Christmas activities.

Community Hanukkah Celebration: Hanukkah Under the Stars
http://sjcc.org
Stroum Jewish Community Center, 3801 E Mercer Way, Mercer Island
Tel: 206-232 7115
Arts and crafts, live music, children's games, and candle-lighting.

Jingle Bell Run/Walk for Arthritis
www.seattlejinglebellrun.org
Tel: 206-547 2707
A 5km (3-mile) run and walk; festive costumes and jingle bells welcome.

New Year's at the Needle
www.spaceneedle.com
Tel: 206-905 2100
The 605ft (184-meter) landmark offers a traditional fireworks show, and parties on the restaurant and observation deck levels.

Gay and lesbian travel

Seattle has one of the largest gay communities in the United States, with much of it concentrated in the Capitol Hill neighborhood, where there are bars, clubs, and businesses that cater to the LGBT community. Seattleites are generally open-minded and accepting of different lifestyles. More information and LGBT resources can be found at www.visitseattle.org/things-to-do/lgbtq.

Gay City
517 E Pike Street; tel: 206-323 5428 (resource and referral line), 206-860 6969 (general number); www.gaycity.org; Mon–Fri 11am–8pm, Sat 11am–5pm. A valuable resource offering advocacy, legal and spiritual support, and many other types of support.

H

Health and medical care

Health care & insurance

The medical care in Seattle is excellent, but as throughout the US, it is prohibitively expensive if a long hospital stay is required. To avoid unwelcome bills, it is vital that you have adequate health insurance before traveling to the US. Check with your current insurance provider that you are covered, and bring your health and travel insurance documents with you.

TRANSPORTATION

Most hospitals have a 24-hour emergency-room service. Here are some major hospitals in the Seattle area that can provide emergency care:

In Seattle
Children's Hospital and Medical Center
4800 Sand Point Way NE
Tel: 206-987 2000
Harborview Medical Center
325 9th Avenue (corner of Jefferson Street)
Tel: 206-744 3000
Swedish Medical Center, First Hill
747 Broadway
Tel: 206-386 6000
Swedish Medical Center, Ballard
5300 Tallman Avenue NW
Tel: 206-782 2700
Swedish Medical Center, Cherry Hill
500 17th Avenue
Tel: 206-320 2000
University of Washington Medical Center
1959 NE Pacific Street
Tel: 206-598 3300
Virginia Mason Hospital
1100 9th Avenue
Tel: 206-223 6600

In Bellevue
Overlake Hospital Medical Center
1035 116th Avenue NE, Bellevue
Tel: 425-688 5000

In Kirkland
Evergreen Hospital Medical Center
12040 NE 128th Street, Kirkland
Tel: 425-899 2560

Referrals
King County Medical Society
Tel: 206-621 9393 (physician referral)
Seattle–King County Dental Society
Tel: 206-443 7607 (dentist referral)

Pharmacies

Certain drugs can only be prescribed by a doctor and purchased at a pharmacy. Bring any regular medication with you and a copy of your prescription if you will need a refill.

24-hour pharmacies
Bartell Drugs
600 First Avenue N
Tel: 206-284 1354
Walgreens
5409 15th Avenue NW
Tel: 206-781 0056

I

Internet

Seattle is one of the most wired cities in the world, and it's very easy to find internet access. Most hotels offer Wi-fi free or for a fee; often, there is free access in the lobby. The majority of Seattle coffee shops have free Wi-fi; you may need to ask the barista for the password. Several public spaces offer free Wi-fi, including libraries, parks in Columbia City, the University District, and Downtown. Select Community Transit and Metro buses also have Wi-fi, as do many of the ferries that ply back and forth across Puget Sound. All branches of the Seattle Public Library offer free Wi-fi; you can use one of their computer terminals free or for a small fee.

L

Lost property

If valuables are lost or stolen, report them to the local police department. A description of the items will be filed, and if they turn up, the police will return them as soon as possible.

M

Maps

The **Seattle Convention and Visitors' Bureau** (Washington State Convention Center, 800 Convention Place; te l: 866-732 2695) offers free maps to tourists. If these maps are insufficient for a particular destination, the American Automobile Association, better known as the 'Triple A', can offer advice on planning trips, the best routes to take, and detailed maps, for a fee.
AAA, 4734 42nd Avenue SW; tel: 206-937 8222; www.aaa.com.

The *Thomas Guides* contain detailed street maps in a book format. They are available in most bookstores. **Metsker Maps** has plenty of maps and guides.

Media

Print

Seattle's last-standing daily newspaper is *The Seattle Times*, though the *Seattle Post-Intelligencer* continues an online presence at www.seattlepi.com. The *Times* Friday tabloid section is a useful guide to weekend events. However, the most complete guides to the week's recreation and entertainment, including visual arts, theater, music, and film, are found in the two fabulous free weeklies, the *Seattle Weekly* (www.seattleweekly.com) and *The Stranger* (www.thestranger.com), available from bars, coffee shops, and other locations throughout the city. Also included is dining and shopping information. The *Puget Sound Business Journal* is published weekly.

Foreign-language newspapers include the *North American Post* (www.napost.com), a Japanese daily, the *Northwest Asian Weekly* (http://nwasianweekly.com), and *El Hispanic News* (weekly; www.elhispannews.com).
Public libraries offer reading rooms stacked with periodicals and, often a good selection of foreign newspapers and magazines.

Newsstands that sell foreign publications include:
Bulldog News
4208 University Way NE
Tel: 206-632 6397
www.bulldognews.com

A – Z

First & Pike News
93 Pike Place (in Pike Place Market)
Tel: 206-624 0140
http://firstandpikenews.tumblr.com

Television and radio

Excluding cable television, seven major stations serve the Seattle area. The public broadcast station is KCTS. It does not air commercials, but supports itself through public donations and grants.

There are numerous radio stations in the city to cater to all tastes.

Money

Credit/debit cards are the easiest ways to bring money to Seattle, and cards are accepted at most places. ATMs are widely available, so you can withdraw money in Seattle directly from your bank back home (usually for a fee; check with your bank before you travel).

Currency & credit cards

Foreign currency exchange is available at Sea-Tac Airport, major Seattle banks, and at some major Downtown hotels. Daily newspapers print exchange rates for most major currencies.

Having a credit card can be valuable for emergencies and transactions such as renting a car. Visa and American Express are widely accepted throughout the United States. In case of a lost or stolen card, use their toll-free numbers to report the incident immediately:
Visa Tel: 1-800-847-2911
American Express Tel: 1-800-528 4800.

O

Opening hours

Most businesses in central and greater Seattle are generally open from 9am–5pm Monday–Friday

and are closed or have shorter hours on Saturday, Sunday, and public holidays.

Banks are usually open from 9am–6pm Monday–Friday, with many in Downtown also opening on Saturday mornings. Most banks, government agencies such as the post office, and some other businesses close on public holidays.

P

Postal services

The United States Postal Service is easy to use. The main post office in Downtown is at 301 Union Street, Seattle, WA 98101; tel: +1 800 275 8777; Mon–Fri 8.30am–5.30pm. Travelers uncertain of their address in a particular town may have mail addressed in their name, sent care of General Delivery at the main post office of that town. Mail will be held there for you to pick up (be sure to bring current picture identification).

You can buy stamps, envelopes, packing materials, and even wrapping paper at post office branches. Be sure to include a five-digit zip code for all addresses within the US. For overseas packages, a customs declaration form needs to be filled out. Overnight delivery service and Express Mail is also provided by the post office and some private companies.

Stamps may also be purchased from vending machines, which can often be found in hotels, stores, airports, and bus and train stations.

Dark blue mailboxes are located on many street corners, or you can post your letters at the post office itself.

Public holidays

New Year's Day January 1
Martin Luther King's Birthday 3rd Monday in January

President's Day 3rd Monday in February
Memorial Day last Monday in May
Independence Day July 4
Labor Day 1st Monday in September
Columbus Day 2nd Monday in October
Veteran's Day November 11
Thanksgiving 4th Thursday in November
Christmas December 25

R

Religious services

Many different faiths are represented in Seattle, including Christian, Jewish, Muslim, Hindu, and Buddhist. To find a place of worship contact:
Church Council of Greater Seattle
4 Nickerson, Suite 300; tel: 206-525 1213; www.churchcouncil.org
Jewish Federation Of Greater Seattle
2031 Third Avenue; tel: 206-443 5400; www.jewishinseattle.org
Islamic Educational Center Of Seattle
23204 55th Avenue W; tel: 425-243 4327; www.iecseattle.org
Seattle Buddhist Center
12056 15th Avenue NE, Unit C-2; tel: 801-872 8332; www.seattle buddhistcenter.org
Hindu Temple and Cultural Center
3818 212th St SE, Bothell; tel: 425-483 7115; www.htccwa.org

S

Smoking

Seattle has one of the toughest no-smoking laws in the nation. It is prohibited in all public places, workspaces, bars, and restaurants. Smokers must be at least 25ft (7.6 meters) away from doors, windows, and vents when smoking. The vast majority of Seattle hotels are 100 percent non-smoking.

T

Tax

In Seattle, a 9.6 percent sales tax is added to all purchases, with an additional 17.2 percent rental car tax, 15.6 percent hotel tax, and 0.5 percent restaurant tax on top of the sales tax. Be sure to check if prices quoted, for example when reserving accommodations, include all taxes or not.

Telephones

There are several area codes in the Puget Sound region: Seattle (206), the Eastside and northern suburbs (425), Tacoma and southern suburbs (253), and outlying areas (360). Calling long-distance between area codes requires a '1' to be dialed before the area code and phone number. To call Seattle from abroad, dial your country's exit code, then the US country code (1), followed by the area code and phone number.

For assistance in long-distance dialing, first dial zero and an operator will assist you. Phone numbers that are preceded by 1-800, 1-866, 1-877, and 1-888 are free of charge only when dialed from within the US.

To place an international call, dial 011 followed by the country code, city code, and telephone number. Some useful country codes are Australia (61), Ireland (353), New Zealand (64), South Africa (27), and the UK (44).

Public payphones are a rare sight nowadays, but you can find them in airports, bus and train stations, and in the public libraries. Local calls cost 50 cents; most payphones accept quarters, dimes, and nickels.

Visitors from abroad should check with their cell-phone service provider as to what rates will be charged for using the phone in the US. In the US, GSM operates on the primary mobile communication bands 850 MHz and 1900 MHz. Most phones today are multi-band phones that can be used in the US with local roaming. Visitors can a so purchase a pre-paid cell phone in the US that you top up as needed.

Time zone

Seattle is within the Pacific Standard Time Zone, which is two hours behind Chicago, three hours behind New York City and seven (during daylight saving time) or eight hours behind GMT. Daylight Saving Time begins at 2am on the second Sunday of March and ends at 2am on the first Sunday of November.

Tipping

Tips are intended to show appreciation for good service and should reflect the quality of service rendered. The accepted rate is 15–20 percent of the bill in restaurants for waiting staff (10 percent for bar staff), 10–15 percent for taxi drivers and hairstylists. Porters and bellhops generally warrant $1 per bag; valets $1 to $2. However, with the new, higher minimum wage, some restaurants have begun raising prices and scrapping tips.

Tourist information

A wealth of information on attractions, activities, accommodations, and restaurants is available from the **Seattle Convention and Visitors Bureau** in the Washington State Convention Center (One Convention Place, 701 Pike Street; tel: 206-461 5840; www.visitseattle.org; Mon–Fri and summer weekends 9am–5pm).

The bureau also operates an **information center** at the southwest corner of 1st Avenue and Pike Street at the Pike Place Market (daily 10am–6pm).

Washington State Tourism can provide information on the entire state; you can request a travel planner to help you plan your trip. Tel: 1-800-544 1800; www.experiencewa.com.

V

Visas and passports

To enter the US you must have a valid passport. Currently most nationals of 38 countries (including Australia, Ireland, New Zealand, and the UK) can enter the US on the Visa Waiver Program, for stays of 90 days or less. Note that the Department of Homeland Security requires those participating in the Visa Waiver Program to fill in the automated Electronic System for Travel Authorization (ESTA) before traveling; this can be done online any time in advance of your trip up until 72 hours before you depart. Visit https://esta.cbp.dhs.gov/esta. Always check the latest regulations before traveling.

Check with the US embassy in your home country to see if you require a visa; visas must be obtained prior to traveling to the US. All Canadian or US citizens traveling to their neighboring country need valid passports, whether by car, train, boat, or plane. For more information, go to http://travel.state.gov.

WEIGHTS AND MEASURES

The US uses the imperial system of weights and measures.	1 quart = 0.9464 liters
	1 ounce = 28.3 grams
1 inch = 2.54 centimeters	1 pound = 453.5 grams
1 foot = 0.3048 meters	1 yard = 0.9144 meters
1 mile = 1.609 kilometers	

FURTHER READING

NON-FICTION

The Battle in Seattle: The Story Behind and Beyond the WTO Demonstrations, by Janet Thomas. Analysis of the events surrounding the violent clashes that took place in Seattle in 1999.

The Best Party of Our Lives, by Sarah Galvin. Twenty-three masterful essays tell the stories of gay and lesbian couples who got married shortly after same-sex marriage was legalized.

Business @ the Speed of Thought, by Bill Gates. Microsoft CEO Bill Gates makes the case that businesses must make use of technology to succeed.

Eccentric Seattle: Pillars and Pariahs Who Made the City Not Such a Boring Place After All, by J. Kingston Pierce. A good read to get to know the characters of the early days, and how their influence is still felt in Seattle.

The Great Northwest Nature Factbook: A Guide to the Region's Remarkable Animals, Plants and Natural Features, by Ann Saling.

Journals, by Kurt Cobain. The lead singer of Nirvana in his own words.

Native Peoples of the Northwest: A Traveler's Guide to Land, Art and Culture, by Jan Halliday. Highly informative guide to places of interest related to Native Americans of the Pacific Northwest and their culture, arts, and history.

Native Seattle Histories from the Crossing-Over Place, by Coll Thrush. A fascinating history of Seattle's native people whose identity and culture the city for too long failed to recognize.

Of Men and Mountains: The Classic Memoir of Wilderness

Adventure, by William O. Douglas. Inspirational book revealing a love and deep knowledge of the Cascade Mountains.

Pour Your Heart into It: How Starbucks Built a Company One Cup at a Time, by Howard Schultz and Dori Jones Yang. The chronicle of the Seattle-based coffee empire, written by the CEO.

Redhook: Beer Pioneer, by Peter J. Krebs. The struggles and triumphs of a fledgling brewery that became a star in the Northwest's craft-brewing industry.

Seattle and the Demons of Ambition, by Fred Moody. The former managing editor of the *Seattle Weekly* provides an interesting perspective on Seattle in the 1990s.

Seattle Cityscape #2, by Victor Steinbrueck. Evocative sketches of the city by talented architect and civic activist.

Shaping Seattle Architecture: A Historical Guide to the Architects, by Jeffrey Karl Ochsner, editor. Engaging words and pictures about the city's diverse architectural styles.

Skid Road: An Informal Portrait of Seattle, by Murray Morgan. Morgan paints a great narrative of Seattle's history and its wild characters.

Wet and Wired: A Pop Culture Encyclopedia of the Pacific Northwest, by Randy Hodges and Steve McLellan. A humorous take on the arts, food, music, and attractions of the Northwest.

FICTION

Fifty Shades of Grey trilogy, by EL James. These wildly popular S&M-tinged erotic novels are based in Seattle.

Hannah West in the Belltown Towers, by Linda Johns. A mystery, with a sleuthing 12-year-old protagonist in a Seattle high-rise.

Longtime Gone, by J.A. Jance. Heart-stopping suspense and local flavor in this thriller revolving around a Seattle investigator.

Snow Falling on Cedars, by David Guterson. A riveting tale set on a fictional island based on Bainbridge Island in the Puget Sound.

Ten Little Indians, by Sherman Alexie. Wise, funny and touching stories about modern Native Americans by this Seattle resident and Native American.

Twilight series, by Stephenie Meyer. The best-selling vampire romance series set in the small logging town of Forks, Washington.

Waxwings, by Jonathan Raban. British expat Raban's novel, set in his adopted hometown of Seattle, follows the story of two immigrants and their struggles in a foreign land.

When She Flew, by Jennie Shortridge. Local author weaves a compelling tale based on a true story.

While the City Slept: A Love Lost to Violence and a Young Man's Descent into Madness, by Eli Sanders. The Pulitzer-winning author weaves a powerful narrative about a horrific crime that left a scar on the city's psyche and one young man's path to murder.

OTHER INSIGHT GUIDES

Insight Guides publishes numerous other guides covering the United States, from *Alaska* to *Florida*, and *New England* to *California*. Insight City Guides include *Boston*, *Las Vegas*, *New York*, and *San Francisco*.

SEATTLE STREET ATLAS

The key map shows the area of Seattle covered by the atlas
section. An index of street names and places of interest
shown on the maps can be found on the following pages. For
each entry there is a page number and grid reference.

Map Legend

Freeway with Junction	✈✈ Airport	Freeway	🚌 Bus Station
Freeway (under construction)	✝✝ Church (ruins)	Divided Highway	❶ Tourist Information
Divided Highway	✝ Monastery	Main Roads	✉ Post Office
Main Road	🏰 Castle (ruins)		✝ Cathedral/Church
Secondary Road	∴ Archeological Site	Minor Roads	☾ Mosque
Minor Road	∩ Cave		✡ Synagogue
Track	★ Place of Interest	Footpath	🛈 Statue/Monument
International Boundary	🏠 Mansion/Stately Home	Railway	Ⓛ Central Link light rail
Province/State Boundary	❋ Viewpoint	Pedestrian Area	Ⓢ South Lake Union Streetcar Line
National Park/Reserve		Important Building	Ⓜ Monorail

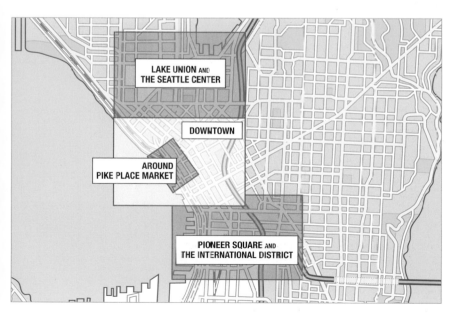

LAKE UNION AND
THE SEATTLE CENTER

DOWNTOWN

AROUND
PIKE PLACE MARKET

PIONEER SQUARE AND
THE INTERNATIONAL DISTRICT

Map Labels

A

B

Prospect Street

Queen Anne Avenue N

Warren Avenue N

1st Avenue N

Ward Street

2nd Avenue N

3rd Avenue N

Ward Street

Ward Street

Ward Pl.

5th Avenue N

6th Avenue N

Ward Street

Aurora Avenue North

1

Aloha Street

Aloha Street

4th Avenue N

5th Avenue N

Taylor Avenue N

6th Avenue N

99

Valley Street

Valley Street

Warren Avenue N

2nd Avenue N

Nob Hill Avenue N

3rd Avenue N

Valley Street

COUNTERBALANCE PARK

Roy Street

Queen Anne Avenue North

St Paul's ✝

Marketplace at Queen Anne

Roy Street

Roy Street

2

Mercer Street

Mercer Street

Queen Anne Avenue N

Uptown Cinemas

Seattle Repertory Theatre

Intiman Theatre

Exhibition Hall

Phelps Center

Marion Oliver McCaw Hall

Mercer Arena

KCTS-TV Studios

The Bill and Melinda Gates Foundation

Republican Street

1st Avenue N

Northwest Rooms

International Fountain

Memorial Stadium

5th Avenue N

The Bill and Melinda Gates Foundation Visitor Center

99

Harrison Street

Ticket office

KeyArena

Seattle Center

Seattle Center House

Monorail Terminal

Museum of Pop Culture (MoPOP)

Broad Street

6th Avenue N

KIN Studi (NBC)

Seattle Center Pavilion

Fisher Pavilion

Children's Museum
Center House Theatre

Ⓜ

Seattle Center

Thomas Street

3

Thomas Street

Children's Theatre

Chihulu Garden and Glass

Queen Anne Avenue North

1st Avenue N

Warren Avenue N

2nd Avenue N

Space Needle

Sculpture Gardens

West John Street

Boeing and Eames IMAX Theaters

Pacific Science Center

Ⓜ

John Street

4th Avenue N

KOMO-Studios (ABC)

Taylor Avenue N

6th Avenue N

Aurora Avenue North

Denny Way

Denny Way

Denny Way

1st Avenue

2nd Avenue

Broad Street

KIRO-Studios (CBS)

3rd Avenue

Clay Street

TILIKUM PLACE

Vine St

5th Avenue N

Wall St.

Battery Street

Bay Street

Eagle

Western Avenue

Cedar Street

Vine Street

4th Avenue

3rd Avenue

Battery Street

5th Avenue

Bell S

4

Elliott Avenue

Olympic Sculpture Park

Ⓜ

Pavilion

1st Avenue

2nd Avenue

Wall Avenue

A

B

Lake Union

Yale Street
Landing

8th Avenue N

Westlake Avenue N

Aloha Street

Prospect St

Fairview Avenue North

9th Avenue N

LAKE
UNION
PARK

Museum of
History and
Industry

Ⓜ

Chandler's
Cove

Ⓢ

Ward
Street

Fairview &
Campus
Drive

Yale Avenue N

Eastlake Avenue E

Center for
Wooden Boats

Ⓜ

Aloha Street

Valley St

8th Avenue N

Valley Street

Ⓢ

Lake Union
Park

LAKE UNION

Valley Street

Shurgard
Building

Minor Avenue North

Roy Street

Broad Street

Roy Street

Mercer Street

Fairview Avenue

North

9th Avenue

Westlake
& Mercer

Ⓢ

Terry &
Mercer

Ⓢ

Boren Avenue N

Mercer Street

Pontius Avenue N

Yale Avenue N

Minor Avenue N

Interstate 5 Expressway

Republican Street

8th Avenue N

9th Avenue N

Republican Street

Republican Street

5

Harrison Street

Westlake Avenue N

Westlake
& Thomas

Ⓢ

Terry &
Thomas

Ⓢ

Harrison Street

Harrison Street

CASCADE
PLAYGROUND

Pontius Avenue N

Yale Avenue N

Minor Avenue N

Thomas Street

8th Avenue N

9th Avenue N

Thomas Street

Thomas Street

Seattle Times
Building

John Street

John Street

Boren Avenue N

Fairview Avenue North

John Street

DENNY
PARK

DENNY
PLAYFIELD

Westlake
& Denny

Ⓢ

Terry Avenue N

Eastlake Avenue E

Melrose Avenue E

Denny Way

Denny Way

Denny Way

Westlake
& 9th

Ⓢ

Bell Street

8th Avenue

7th Avenue

Westlake Avenue N

9th Avenue

Lenora St

Terry Avenue

Lenora St

Stewart
Street

Minor
Avenue

Boren
Avenue

Yale Avenue

Howell Street

Library

✉

Virginia

9th Av

8th Avenue

Street

Terry Avenue

Street

Blanchard Street

King Cat
Theatre

0   100   200 yds

0   100   200 n

N
↑

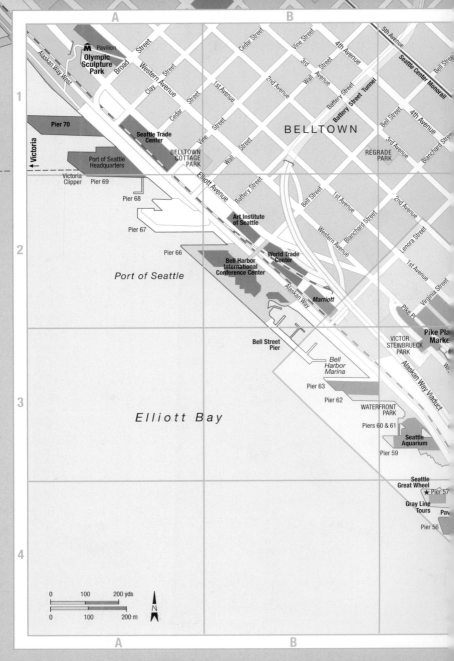

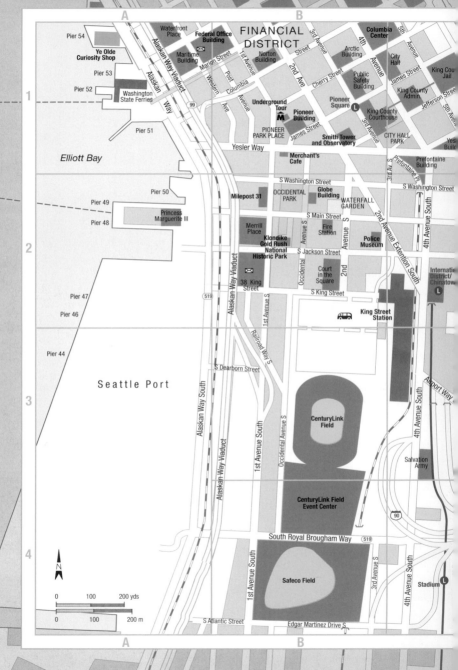

A

B

Pier 54

Ye Olde
Curiosity Shop

Pier 53

Pier 52

Washington
State Ferries

Waterfront
Place

Maritime
Building

Federal Office
Building

**FINANCIAL
DISTRICT**

Columbia
Center

Marion Street

Norton
Building

Arctic
Building

City
Hall

King Cou
Jail

Cherry Street

Public
Safety
Building

King County
Admin.

King Cou
Stree

Alaskan Way Viaduct

Alaskan
Way

99

Post
Avenue

Columbia
Avenue

1st Avenue

2nd Ave

3rd Avenue

4th
Avenue

5th

James Street

5th Avenue

Jefferson Street

Pier 51

**Underground
Tour**
M

Pioneer
Building

Pioneer
Square **L**

King County
Courthouse

Yes
Buildi

PIONEER
PARK PLACE

James Street

**Smith Tower
and Observatory**

CITY HALL
PARK

Elliott Bay

Yesler Way

Merchant's
Cafe

Prefontaine
Building

S Washington Street

S Washington Street

Pier 50

Pier 49

Pier 48

Princess
Marguerite III

Milepost 31

OCCIDENTAL
PARK

Globe
Building

WATERFALL
GARDEN

2nd Avenue South

Alaskan Way Viaduct

Merrill
Place

**Klondike
Gold Rush
National
Historic Park**

S Main Street

Fire
Station

Avenue S

Occidental

Avenue S

2nd

**Police
Museum**

4th Avenue South

Internatio
District/
Chinatow **L**

S Jackson Street

38 King
Street

Court
in the
Square

2nd Avenue Extention South

Pier 47

Pier 46

519

S King Street

**King Street
Station**

Pier 44

Seattle Port

Railroad Way S

S Dearborn Street

Airport Way

Alaskan Way South

1st Avenue South

Alaskan Way Viaduct

Occidental Avenue S

**CenturyLink
Field**

4th Avenue South

Salvation
Army

90

**CenturyLink Field
Event Center**

South Royal Brougham Way

519

N

0   100   200 yds

0   100   200 m

1st Avenue South

Safeco Field

3rd Avenue S

4th Avenue South

Stadium **L**

S Atlantic Street

Edgar Martinez Drive S

A

B

1

2

3

4

Jefferson St
9th Avenue
Terrace Street
Terry Avenue
Broadway
E Alder Street
10th Avenue
11th Av
14th Avenue

FIRST HILL
PARK

9th Av
Alder Street
Spruce Street
E Spruce Street

E Fir Street

8th Avenue
9th Avenue
10th Avenue
10th Avenue S
Boren Avenue S
12th Avenue
13th Avenue
15th Avenue

1

Yesler Way
Yesler Way
Yesler Way
East Yesler Way

Nippon Kan
Theatre

6th Ave
6th Avenue

KOBE
TERRACE
PARK

S Main Street
S Washington Street
LITTLE
SAIGON

Orient
Center

Boren Avenue S
12th Avenue

YESLER
TERRACE
PLAYFIELD

15th Avenue S
14th Avenue S
S Washington St

WESTERIA
PLAZA

2

S Jackson Street
S Main Street
Asian
Plaza
Viet Wah
Jackson
Square
S Main Street

S Jackson Street
HING
HAY
PARK
Theater
Off Jackson
S King
Street
Wing Luke
Museum
M
S Jackson Street
Ding How
Shopping Center
S Jackson Street

Rainier Avenue S
S Jackson
Place

6th Avenue S
Maynard Alley
Maynard Avenue
7th Avenue S
Canton Alley
8th
9th Avenue S
10th Avenue S
S King Street
12th Avenue S
S King Street

S Weller Street
S Weller Street
S Weller Street

maya
se Street

INTERNATIONAL
CHILDRENS PARK

International
District
Village

INTERNATIONAL
DISTRICT

S Lane Street
S Lane Street

3

n Dearborn Street
South Dearborn Street

Harbor
Light
Center

S Charles
St

Maynard Avenue
7th Avenue S
8th Avenue S
9th Avenue S

Poplar Place S

6th Avenue S

S Plummer
St

90

Golf Drive

S Royal Brougham Way

Airport Way South

DR RIZAL
PARK

12th Avenue S
13th Avenue S
14th Avenue S

Sturgus Avenue S

Golf Drive

4

205

S Judkins Street

16th Avenue S

D
E

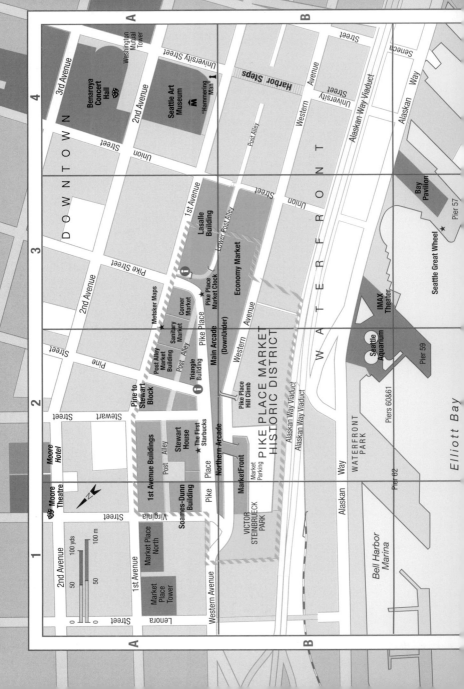

A

B

4

3rd Avenue

Washington
Mutual
Tower

Benaroya
Concert
Hall

University Street

2nd Avenue

Seattle Art
Museum

"Hammering
Man"

Street

Street

Harbor Steps

Avenue

University
Street

Seneca

Union

Street

Alaskan Way Viaduct

Alaskan Way

D O W N T O W N

Post Alley

Western

Union

W A T E R F R O N T

Bay
Pavilion

Pier 57

Seattle Great Wheel

3

1st Avenue

Lasalle
Building

Lower Post Alley

Avenue

Street

IMAX
Theater

Metsker Maps

Pike Place
Market Clock

Economy Market

Corner
Market

2

2nd Avenue

Pike Street

Sanitary
Market

Post Alley

Pike Place

Western

Avenue

Pine

Street

Post Alley
Market
Building

Triangle
Building

Main Arcade
(DownUnder)

Pike Place
Hill Climb

Seattle
Aquarium

Pier 59

Piers 60&61

Alaskan Way Viaduct

Stewart

Street

Pine to
Stewart
Block

The First
Starbucks

Stewart
House

Northern Arcade

Post Alley

Alaskan Way Viaduct

PIKE PLACE MARKET
HISTORIC DISTRICT

Moore
Hotel

1st Avenue Buildings

MarketFront

Pike
Place

Market
Parking

WATERFRONT
PARK

Pier 62

Alaskan

Way

1

Moore Theatre

Soames-Dunn
Building

Virginia
Street

VICTOR
STEINBRUECK
PARK

Western Avenue

Bell Harbor
Marina

Elliott Bay

2nd Avenue

Market Place
North

1st Avenue

Market
Place
Tower

Lenora
Street

0   50   100 yds
0   50   100 m

A

B

STREET INDEX

ART AND PHOTO CREDITS

Alamy 150, 166, 166/167, 168, 171
AWL Images 96/97T
Ben Benschneider/SAM 42
Bigstock 4/5, 25, 110B, 112, 137, 152, 173BR, 175, 198, 209, 218
Bruce Bernstein Collection/ Courtesy of the Princeton University Library 32/33
Corbis 54/55T, 220/221, 220/221
Dreamstime 8ML, 12/13, 40, 68, 71, 91B, 92/93T, 104B, 126T, 147, 154/155, 158, 159, 160B, 160/161, 162, 164/165B, 168/169, 170, 174, 176, 180, 183, 184, 186, 188, 190/191, 200, 201, 202T, 202B, 203, 205, 206/207B, 214/215T, 216B
Elaine Thompson/AP/REX/ Shutterstock 78/79
FLPA 172BL, 172/173T
Fotolia 187, 204, 208, 212
Getty Images 16/17, 28/29T, 58, 58/59, 92, 117T, 125B
Gregg M. Erickson 220BL
Historical Society of Seattle and King County/Museum of History and Industry 31, 35R, 39R
iStockphoto 6/7T, 11, 29B, 50, 69, 70, 72L, 72R, 72/73, 114/115, 116T 148, 148/149T, 149B,

172/173B, 173TR, 176/177, 178, 179, 185, 206, 207T, 210T, 210B, 211, 213T, 214, 215B 217, 218/219, 220MR, 220ML, 236
Kirkland Arts Center 162/163
Lara Swimmer/SAM 6CB
Library of Congress 26B, 26/27, 54MR, 54ML, 55TC
Loren Javier 55BR
MoPOP Museum 120B
Nathaniel Gonzales/APA Publication 6ML, 6ML, 6/7T 7TR, 7MR, 8M, 10M, 18/19B 20, 21, 22, 24TL, 24BL, 44/45T, 45B, 52, 56, 60T, 80/81B, 64B, 64T, 64/65, 74/75. 76/77. 81T, 85, 86, 87B, 88, 88/89B, 89T, 94, 95B, 96T, 97TR, 99, 100/101B, 101T, 104/105B, 106B, 106/107, 113, 114T, 114B, 120/121B, 121BR, 120/121T, 121TC, 122, 123, 124/125T, 130/131B, 132/133, 142, 144, 216T, 228, 7MC, 7MR, 8BR, 9B, 8/9T, 24TR, 49 50/51, 52/53T, 53B, 106T, 108, 108/109E, 109T, 116B, 117B, 118T, 118B, 119, 126B, 127T, 127B, 128/129, 130T, 135, 138B, 138T, 139, 140B, 140T, 140/141T, 141B, 172MR, 181, 182B, 182T, 194, 195, 196T, 196B, 199, 226, 1, 6/7M, 23T. 66/67, 102/103. 104T,

110T, 213B, 225L, 232
National Anthropological Archives 30
Photoshot 40/41
R.F. Zallinger/Museum of History and Industry 34
REX/Shutterstock 80
Seattle Art Musuem 26T
Seattle Municipal Archives 90, 151
Seattle Parks 95T
Shutterstock 10/11T, 22/23B, 48, 145, 178
SuperStock 197
The Jim Henson Company. 120T
Tim Thompson/Apa Publications 6/7B, 10TL, 14/15, 18, 19T, 47, 57, 61, 62, 63, 65B 66T, 84, 86/87T, 90/91T, 93B, 96B, 96/97M, 97B, 98, 102T, 102B, 105T, 111, 132, 134, 143, 146, 152/153, 172MR, 222, 224
TopFoto 32T, 34/35, 36, 36/37T, 37B, 38, 39, 43 54B, 54/55M, 220BR
Underground Tours 32B
United States Geological Survey 28
Vetala Hawkins/Filmateria Digital for Microsoft 164, 165T
Whisper of the heart 160T
World Economic Forum 44

Cover Credits

Front cover: City view *SuperStock*
Back cover: Downtown at night *Dreamstime*
Front flap: (from top) Public Market *iStock*; Museum of Glass

Dreamstime; Bumbershoot *Dreamstime*; Sailing on Lake Washington *Dreamstime*
Back flap: Ferry Boat in Puget Sound *Dreamstime*

INDEX

INSIGHT ● GUIDES
OFF THE SHELF

Since 1970, **INSIGHT GUIDES** has provided a unique perspective on the world's best travel destinations by using specially commissioned photography and illuminating text written by local authors.

Whether you're planning a city break, a walking tour or the journey of a lifetime, our superb range of guidebooks and phrasebooks will inspire you to discover more about your chosen destination.

INSIGHT GUIDES

offer a unique combination of stunning photos, absorbing narrative and detailed maps, providing all the inspiration and information you need.

PHRASEBOOKS & DICTIONARIES

help users to feel at home, when away. Pocket-sized with a free app to download, they go where you do.

CITY GUIDES

pack hundreds of great photos into a smaller format with detailed practical information, so you can navigate the world's top cities with confidence.

EXPLORE GUIDES

feature easy-to-follow walks and itineraries in the world's most exciting destinations, with our choice of the best places to eat and drink along the way.

POCKET GUIDES

combine concise information on where to go and what to do in a handy compact format, ideal on the ground. Includes a full-colour, fold-out map.

EXPERIENCE GUIDES

feature offbeat perspectives and secret gems for experienced travellers, with a collection of over 100 ideas for a memorable stay in a city.

www.insightguides.com

INSIGHT ⊙ GUIDES
SEATTLE

Editor: Helen Fanthorpe
Authors: Heidi Johansen, Cedar Burnett, and Maciej Zglinicki
Head of Production: Rebeka Davies
Update Production: Apa Digital
Pictures: Tom Smyth
Cartography: original cartography Berndtson & Berndtson, updated by Carte

Distribution
UK, Ireland and Europe
Apa Publications (UK) Ltd
sales@insightguides.com

United States and Canada
Ingram Publisher Services
ips@ingramcontent.com

Australia and New Zealand
Woodslane
info@woodslane.com.au

Southeast Asia
Apa Publications (SN) Pte
singaporeoffice@insightguides.com

Hong Kong, Taiwan and China
Apa Publications (HK) Ltd
hongkongoffice@insightguides.com

Worldwide
Apa Publications (UK) Ltd
sales@insightguides.com

Special Sales, Content Licensing and CoPublishing
Insight Guides can be purchased in bulk quantities at discounted prices. We can create special editions, personalised jackets and corporate imprints tailored to your needs. sales@insightguides.com; www.insightguides.biz

Printing
CTPS-China

ABOUT THIS BOOK

What makes an Insight Guide different? Since our first book pioneered the use of creative full-color photography in travel guides in 1970, we have aimed to provide not only reliable information but also the key to a real understanding of a destination and its people.

Now, when the internet can supply inexhaustible (but not always reliable) facts, our books marry text and pictures to provide that more elusive quality: knowledge. To achieve this, they rely on the authority of locally based writers and photographers.

This new edition of *City Guide Seattle* was edited by **Helen Fanthorpe** and updated by **Maciej Zglinicki**. The book builds on the success of earlier editions, the last of which was thoroughly overhauled by **Heidi Johansen**, an editor and writer living in Seattle, who loves exploring the dining scene in the Emerald City, as well as the quick escapes to incredible outdoor excursions – especially the Olympic Peninsula. Heidi was assisted by **Cedar Burnett**, a fellow Seattle-based writer and journalist.

The text of writers who contributed to previous editions include **Helen Townsend**, an experienced Seattle-based writer and editor who has contributed to dozens of guidebooks, including several on Seattle and the Pacific Northwest region; freelance editor **Anna Chan**, who wrote the original chapter on the Space Needle and Seattle Center; foodie **Matthew Amster-Burton**, who penned the Salmon and Simple Ingredients essay; girl-about-town **Allison Lind** who wrote the chapter on Music, Culture and the Arts; and newspaper editor **Steve Wainwright** who wrote the piece entitled Seattle and Seattleites.

The book was indexed by **Penny Phenix**.

SEND US YOUR THOUGHTS

We do our best to ensure the information in our books is as accurate and up-to-date as possible. The books are updated on a regular basis using local contacts, who painstakingly add, amend, and correct as required. However, some details (such as telephone numbers and opening times) are liable to change, and we are ultimately reliant on our readers to put us in the picture.

We welcome your feedback, especially your experience of using the book 'on the road'. Maybe we recommended a hotel that you liked (or another that you didn't), or you came across a great bar or new attraction that we missed.

We will acknowledge all contributions, and we'll offer an Insight Guide to the best letters received.

Please write to us at:
Insight Guides
PO Box 7910, London SE1 1WE
Or email us at:
hello@insightguides.com